HISTORY BY NUMBERS

HISTORY BY NUMBERS

An introduction to quantitative approaches

PAT HUDSON
Professor of History, Cardiff University, UK

A member of the Hodder Headline Group
LONDON
Co-published in the United States of America by
Oxford University Press Inc., New York

First published in Great Britain in 2000 by
Arnold, a member of the Hodder Headline Group,
338 Euston Road, London NW1 3BH

http://www.arnoldpublishers.com

Co-published in the United States of America by
Oxford University Press Inc.,
198 Madison Avenue, New York, NY10016

British Library Cataloguing in Publication Data
A catalogue record for this book is available from the British Library

Library of Congress Cataloging-in-Publication Data
A catalog record for this book is available from the Library of Congress

ISBN 0 340 66322 7 (hb)
ISBN 0 340 61468 4 (pb)

1 2 3 4 5 6 7 8 9 10

Production Editor: Rada Radojicic
Production Controller: Martin Kerans
Cover Design: Terry Griffiths

Typeset in 10/12pt Sabon by Phoenix Photosetting, Chatham, Kent
Printed and bound in Great Britain by MPG Books, Bodmin, Cornwall

What do you think about this book? Or any other Arnold title?
Please send your comments to feedback.arnold@hodder.co.uk

If you are hunting rabbits in tiger country, you must still keep your eye peeled for tigers, but when you are hunting tigers you can ignore the rabbits.

H. Stern, quoted by David Hurst Thomas, *Refiguring anthropology: first principles of probability and statistics* (Illinois, 1986), p. 64

Contents

List of figures

List of tables

Preface

Numbers have the power to mesmerise and to control, to create order where none exists and to destroy an order or pattern by superimposing arbitrary divisions or categories. Numbers are not neutral: they are framed and defined by their creators, distorted and redefined by those responsible for their collection and reconstituted and reordered by those who select, display, use and analyse them for their own purposes. Numbers are a powerful tool in the hands of those who decide to gather them and to use them. In history, numbers play a key role in setting up debates and arguments and in creating periodisations and chronologies. Numbers are so central in history and in social science that they cannot be left to be gathered, manipulated and analysed by a restricted group of specially numerate academics. Too often the bulk of readers and writers sit back and leave the numbers to someone else but this is a dangerous and self-limiting practice. All those interested in studying society, past or present, need to take charge of quantitative data: to command it rather than to be the slave of a seeming authority of numbers emerging from documents or the writings of a small body of numerically inclined researchers.

Over the past four decades quantitative research has extended into all branches of history. This has mirrored a general extension of mathematics and statistics as the language of enquiry in the social sciences and in public debate over economic and social issues. Increasingly sophisticated statistical techniques have been applied to historical research in many fields: studies of crime, social protest, slavery, literacy, the composition and functioning of households, voting patterns, class structures, industrial output, population change, to name just a few. Findings in quantitative economic, social and political history are often presented in a highly technical manner, inaccessible to those with little specialist training or knowledge. Conclusions may appear interesting or provocative but the reader is often faced with the necessity of taking the research and analysis behind many historical arguments entirely on trust and without criticism. Fault also lies with historians themselves. Even with simple quantitative expositions, many historians are content with 'flicking through numerical matter as if it is not only distasteful but an unnecessary distraction from real historical analysis.'[1] The mystification frequently created by techniques and presentation in quantitative work, together with the abrogation of responsibility on the part of academics and students in confronting and questioning this mystification, limits intellectual debate and both the wider appreciation and the criticism of quantitative analyses.

Many historians and most students of history do not wish to take findings on trust but are unable easily to challenge the authority of figures because some training in 'history by numbers' is essential to enter into a dialogue with those engaged in quantitative research. Students recognise this both with respect to their studies and in relation to the broader and longer term requirements for a basic numeracy in order to participate fully in most professions and in active citizenship. But most textbooks which seek to introduce scholars to quantification and statistical analysis in the social sciences and specifically in history tend to be too technical and inaccessible for most historians.[2] They tend to throw people in at the deep end and spend little or no time explaining basic methods or how quantitative initiatives and ideas started and evolved: an obvious point of entry for a history scholar.

Historians do not generally desire to become trained statisticians but they frequently do wish to clarify and evaluate quantitative evidence and arguments which they have encountered in their reading. Some will also wish to be able to do some quantitative processing themselves for essay or dissertation work, especially if this involves the use of raw data from primary sources. At minimum they recognise the need to understand those techniques of data display and analysis most commonly found in history, in wider social science and in public life. Not to understand these basic procedures is to be disenfranchised from significant areas of scholarly argument and debate and from a full participation in modern society. The level of analysis and the technical nature of examples given in most existing undergraduate statistics texts are such as to alienate history students from even the most basic quantification and encourage them either to ignore quantitative evidence altogether or not to question it at all. This is a shame because some of the most important elements of quantitative history are very simple and straightforward. They often involve only a common-sense reorganisation and display of data. As with all historical evidence, these data may be fragmentary, distorted or biased, and historical skills will be required to evaluate and to analyse them. The statistical skills most commonly in use are a great deal easier to acquire than the essential historical skills but they are not perceived as such. The association of quantitative history with dull and difficult abstract techniques more than with the 'normal' processing, evaluation and assessment of historical evidence promotes an unhealthy bifurcation in history and its research methods between quantitative and qualitative approaches, despite the fact that each shares many of the same methodological difficulties and potentialities. Instead of a wise integration of the two, the relationship between quantitative and qualitative history has too often been acrimonious.

This volume aims to attract historians, at all stages of their training, to some basic techniques of quantitative history, not as a separate, marginal or suspect activity, nor as a be-all and end-all of being a historian but as an essential tool and a necessary skill for everyone interested in the past. It is an essential tool to be integrated with others and used where appropriate and it is a necessary skill for critical engagement with other historians. We stress the ways in which quantification is compatible with and complementary to other approaches. The volume aims to equip economic, social, political and cultural historians, who have little or no background training in quantification, with the insights and skills necessary fully to understand a range of approaches which they are likely to encounter on degree courses in their fields, and in literatures they may need to read for project and research work. This also involves some emphasis upon evaluating quantitative evidence found in, or derived from, primary sources. The book, however, starts with an overview of the advantages and disadvantages of quantitative history and a consideration of the origins, nature and development of quantitative approaches to social and historical enquiry. Historians know best that an understanding of the past can be a vital guide to engagement in the present. The nature and place of quantification, the controversies which surround it and the need to engage with it are largely explained by looking at its history.

Now is a good time to ensure that historians have a book of this kind to guide them, but this is not because the popularity of quantitative history continues to accelerate. On the contrary, the use of statistical analysis in history has levelled off or has been arrested during the past decade by a growing preference for descriptive, narrative and prose-based approaches and methods. Quantitative history is frequently accused of attempting to be more precise and free of subjectivity than the nature of historical evidence and the processes of historical research can possibly allow. These sorts of criticisms are not new, as we shall see, but they grow in volume, and the need to address them grows more urgent. Furthermore, even if quantitative history is not a major methodological growth point, the use of computer-aided analysis continues to expand across a range of subjects, time periods and types of data analysis. Computer-aided research of various kinds has become central in history, witnessed by the spread of undergraduate courses and by the incorporation of computing into postgraduate training. As most sorts of computer use involves numerical analysis in some shape or form (to be explained in Chapter 9), historians vitally need to understand the quantitative thinking and the methods behind it. Too often undergraduate history and computing courses treat quantitative techniques as if they were simply a matter of inputting some data and applying the correct chain of software commands. This neglects the reasoning and logic behind quantitative methods and the need to be alive to the pitfalls and weaknesses both of the techniques and of the data. Computers have recently made the application of quantitative techniques so easy and accessible that procedures are often carried out with little understanidng of their basis, their potential pitfalls or of the problems of the source materials which are manipulated. Perhaps at this point, more than ever before, a straightforward discussion of basic techniques, their advantages and their problems, in the context of historical sources and historical enquiry, is much needed.

Throughout the volume no prior knowledge of statistics or of quantitative skills will be assumed and techniques will be presented in a straightforward, accessible manner, illustrated with a variety of historical examples. A short glossary is provided to assist those struggling with an entirely new 'language' but all technical terms are fully explained in the text as they are encountered. The role of computers in speeding up and extending the scope of quantitative enquiry is acknowledged and quantitative techniques are in all cases explained in relation to the role which computer software might usefully play in their application.

This book started life as a course of lectures and classes for students at the University of Liverpool in the late 1980s and the 1990s. My thanks go to the cohorts of economic and social history undergraduates and graduates who endured my teaching, often with a more successful outcome (and perhaps more enjoyment?) than most feared and expected. If this volume proves useful to students of the future it will be partly a result of the constructive criticisms and feedback provided by their lively predecessors at Liverpool. Colleagues struggling to teach quantitative methods to historians in other institutions have also been a source of encouragement. They have stressed the need for a short and accessible volume which would appeal to all types of student, even those with an aversion to numbers. Such colleagues have given freely their advice, sending me details of their courses and relaying their experiences. I must particularly mention Sue Bowden, Ron Weir, Nick Crafts and Bob Millward. Nearer at hand, my colleagues in the Department of Economic and Social History at Liverpool were also a great help: encouraging me, reading drafts, being critical. In this respect I must especially thank Bernard Foley, Mike Power, Rory Miller, Henry Finch and William Ashworth. In recent months new friends at Cardiff, Royal Holloway and Bristol have been generous in reading drafts, providing critical feedback and in helping to get the figures right. Thanks particularly to Roger Middleton, Emmett Sullivan, Caitlin Buck, Geoff Boden and Karen Adler. For the title I am equally in debt to Peter Greenaway and John Tosh. I much admire the work of both.

It was hard to leave Liverpool after more than 20 years, leaving behind such good friends and colleagues. To them, and to the generations of students whom we taught, this volume is dedicated with love, appreciation and fond memories.

Pat Hudson
November 1999

Notes

1 Roger Middleton, *The British economy since 1945: engaging with the debate* (London, 2000), Appendix III.
2 One exception amongst social science text books is Frances Clegg, *Simple statistics: a course book for social sciences* (Cambridge, 1988). Because this has nothing on computing it has not dated much and the cartoons are a hoot. The more recent Open University volume *Calculating and computing for social science and arts students* (Buckingham, 1994) by Robert Soloman and Christopher Winch is also pitched at an intelligible level (perhaps too simple in its computer instruction, which is in any case now dated). Of the bewildering variety of recent and slightly more involved social science statistics texts the best appears to be A. Aron and E. N. Aron, *Statistics for the behavioural and social sciences* (London, 1997). Catherine Marsh, *Exploring data: an introduction to data analysis for social scientists* (Cambridge, 1988 and reprints) remains the best social science text and incorporates much discussion of British data. There were two simple introductions to quantitative methods for historians in Britain in the 1970s: Michael Drake's excellent short text prepared for the Open University D301 course, *The quantitative analysis of historical data* (Milton Keynes, 1974) and Roderick Floud, *An introduction to quantitative methods for historians* (London, 1973, second edn 1979). Both were out of print by the mid-1980s, and by that time the latter was particularly dated with its chapter on electronic calculators and mainframe punch-card computers! The structure of Floud's volume and the level at which it was pitched were, however, very appropriate for the history students whom I taught at Liverpool and, for this reason, I have adopted similar chapter divisions and roughly the same coverage of techniques. The alternative texts introducing quantitative methods to historians in the 1990s have been rather more advanced US publications of varying quality, the best being L. Haskins and K. Jeffrey, *Understanding quantitative history* (Cambridge, MA, 1991).

Acknowledgements

The author and publishers would like to thank the following for permission to use copyright material in this book:
  Blackwell Publishers for Figures 3.6, 3.8 and 3.14 and Tables 3.2, 4.1, 4.7, 5.7, 5.10, 7.3 and 7.4 © Economic History Society; Cambridge University Press for Figures 3.1, 3.12, 3.13, 3.15, 4.3, 5.1 and 6.5 and Tables 4.2, 4.5, 4.6, 4.8 and 7.5; Roderick Floud for Figure 5.4 and Tables 5.5, 5.6 and 6.8; Evan Mawdsley and Thomas Munck for Figure 3.4(b); The MIT Press for Figure 3.5.
  To the best of our knowledge all copyright holders of material reproduced in this book have been contacted. Any rights not acknowledged here will be noted in subsequent printings if notice is given to the publisher.

PART

I

QUANTITATIVE HISTORY

|1|

The prospects and the pitfalls
of history by numbers

*The secret language of statistics, so appealing in a fact minded culture,
is employed to sensationalize, inflate, confuse, and oversimplify.
Statistical methods and statistical terms are necessary in reporting the
mass data of social and economic trends, business conditions,
'opinion' polls, the census. But without writers who use the words
with honesty and understanding and readers who know what they
mean, the result can only be semantic nonsense.*[1]

This chapter considers the growth in popularity of quantitative history since
the 1960s against the background of debate, reaction and controversy
which has surrounded it. The various ways in which quantitative
approaches and techniques can be of real value in historical work are
discussed but the many pitfalls and difficulties involved in assembling and
analysing historical data are also emphasised.[2] The chapter concludes by
arguing that quantitative methods and numbers do pose problems for historians but so too do historical approaches based on texts and words. Many
of the problems are similar or identical in each case.

1.1 The growth of history by numbers

Quantification has long been a hallmark of much economic history and is
the foundation of most historical demography. Since the 1960s and 1970s,
however, it has spread into many other kinds of history. One major factor
encouraging this development has been a shift in the nature of history, especially since the Second World War. Change from history based almost exclusively upon the lives of great men, elites and diplomacy to histories of the
mass of the population, economic growth and social change made numerical analysis almost unavoidable. Linked to this general change, the influence of the Annales School of French historians, since its foundation in the

1920s, has further precipitated a statistical approach to understanding the past. The aim of the Annales School was to write ecologically-based *histoires totales* of local and regional societies and communities over several centuries which required the gathering and use of long-run series of prices, output figures, population data, wages. This is often referred to as *histoire serielle* as it is based on the movement of long-run series of vital variables. François Furet maintained that the integration of the subordinate classes into general history could be accomplished only through 'number and anonymity', by means of demography and sociology, 'the quantitative study of past societies.'[3] Emmanuel Le Roy Ladurie's study of the *Peasants of Languedoc* was written very much from this perspective. His series of population, food prices and outputs covering the sixteenth and seventeenth centuries reflected the fluctuating fortunes of the rural labour force in the region, enabling him to observe the 'immense respiration' of the social structure.[4] The Annales approach had a more limited impact in Britain than on the continent but the emergence and growing influence of economic history as a separate academic discipline in this country spawned similar attempts by historians to chart the long-term movement of economic variables, particularly prices and wages. The period from the 1900s to the 1950s saw classic British studies of money wages and of prices and moves to synthesise major population, output and trade figures: those of Bowley, Wood, Phelps-Brown and Hopkins, Mitchell and Deane to name only the more important examples.[5]

The growing popularity of the social sciences, especially in Britain and the United States since the 1960s, has further encouraged the wider use of quantitative analysis in history. The close relationship between economic history and economics, for example, has encouraged quantitative techniques. In the United States in particular economic history was heavily influenced by econometric analysis, which was taking a strong hold over economics at this time. Econometrics involves the mathematical modelling of economic systems. By the 1960s attempts to understand the functioning of the economy or of business firms or sectors within it by means of econometric tools were finding their way into many branches of historical research, notably into analysis of the wisdom of technological choices made in the past.[6] Many economic historians were converted to the idea that econometric techniques were revolutionising the subject and injecting new certainties into historical debates. Those wedded to the claims of the so-called 'new economic history' argued that definitive answers to many questions would now be possible and, at the extreme, it was anticipated that these new quantitative tools of analysis would reveal general laws of human behaviour which it had not been possible to research before. A similar fever was gripping sociology in the late 1950s and 1960s. Great stress was placed upon empirical research in which mass survey data, large-scale interviewing and questionnaires were used. Sociologists were pioneering the development of statistical techniques, such as sampling theory and significance testing, to handle large bodies of social data. Social and political historians were particularly influenced by this trend and a 'new political history' (largely concerned with voting patterns) and a 'new urban history' (mostly studies based on sampling from census data) emerged to match the new methods of sociological investigation and the 'new economic history'.

At the time, Lawrence Stone complained that historians were becoming 'statistical junkies', and there was increasingly less contact and sympathy between those who were and those who were not immersed in the quantitative endeavour.[7] Some branches of economic history became generally more quantitative and some crept closer to formal economics in method and approach and became less concerned with social, cultural and institutional matters, than with stylised facts and implicit assumptions about motivation and behaviour. This inhibited any close alliance or integration of economic with social and cultural history, a characteristic which has dogged the development of both ever since, despite many attempts at rapprochement.[8] As early as 1963 the President of the American Historical Association, with characteristic unconcern for gender sensibilities, warned colleagues about 'worship at the shrine of that Bitch-goddess QUANTIFICATION'.[9] By the 1970s and 1980s statistical approaches and their critics were reaching their height. Judt likened quantitative historians to 'clowns in regal purple', suggesting that they had succumbed to a 'delirium of statistical series'. What interested him was 'not so much that historians cannot count but that they proclaim the need to do so'![10] At the same time, Liam Hudson remarked that 'most social scientists who rely on punched cards and computers seem in practice to abandon their powers of reasoning'. Computers in history were seen, by some, to be causing an 'atrophy of the critical faculties'.[11]

The computer revolution

In the 1960s and 1970s the computer revolution had begun in earnest, giving a major impetus to the spread of quantification in the social sciences and in history. Early computer use was both time-consuming and expensive. The need to employ an army of semi-skilled workers to feed in data on punched cards, to have access to expensive and slow mainframe machines and to employ specialists or to learn complex programming and computer languages limited the use of computers amongst historians. Their major initial impact in history was in econometric history (where projects often shared the resources and expertise of economists working on allied subjects and often in the same departments) and in some branches of social history, which similarly drew on the experiences and skills accumulated in sociological studies. Despite their limited use, by the early 1970s the potential for computers to extend quantification both within and beyond reasonable bounds in historical analysis was becoming recognised. Cobb, for example, warned of the degree to which the computer encouraged spurious and *ad hoc* manipulation of data merely to confirm already well-understood phenomena. He warned of 'historians in white coats' clinically involved with the manipulation of cold numerical data but detached from the heat of real historical research and historical sources.[12]

From the mid-1970s, computers rapidly became cheaper and more accessible with the microchip revolution and the innovation of personal computers (PCs) and portable machines. More user-friendly software was also being developed. There was now no need to learn programming or a computer language. Instead, a range of software packages became available, including several specifically designed for use by social scientists and some for use by historians. PCs became more affordable, with larger memories enabling easy storage, retrieval and reordering of information as well as statistical manipulation. This encouraged many historians, who had previously been hostile to computer use in their subject, to become zealous converts. This new wave of computer-aided research, using PCs and portables, often involved quantitative methods. Software and hardware developments made many large-scale quantitative studies feasible, in financial and practical terms, for the first time.[13]

By the 1980s and 1990s, quantitative history was well established in many areas of research. In some fields of history the quantitative approach became dominant but in others it made little impact and continued to be derided. This polarisation is at first glance surprising and requires explanation particularly because it has been endorsed by a growing indifference to quantification in the 1990s. The latter indifference has occurred alongside the increasing popularity of a cultural history which generally concentrates upon analysing the sense of actions or symbols through detailed description of events or of texts and has little apparent need for quantification. We will see in Chapter 2 that much criticism of quantification in history is rooted in an opposition to the 'scientific' or positivistic approaches to history with which quantification is usually, but not always rightly, associated and which the new cultural history largely eschews. In the rest of this chapter we assess both the potentialities and the difficulties of quantification in history. This helps us further to understand both the popularity of quantification within the historical profession and the widespread misgivings which it has generated.

1.2 Advantages of quantitative history

From the elite to the masses

Many historians are attracted to broad statistical and numerical analysis because quantitative evidence is usually less elitist and more representative than are qualitative data. It is perhaps surprising, given the greater opportunities which quantification presents for writing histories of the mass of the population, that so many historians of popular culture and society feel so negative about it. Personal papers and official records leave the historian with more information on elites than on the working classes, on adult males than on women and children, on settled natives rather than on migrant or ethnic minorities and on political and social activists rather than on the more passive majority of the population. Greater quantification can help to make best use of the documentation from the past particularly where that documentation deals with large numbers and with ordinary people.

For example, early statements that people married late in pre-industrial England were originally based on just a few pieces of evidence drawn from diaries and contemporary commentary of middle-class and upper-class elites. Only a broad-based quantitative study linking baptism and marriage data from a range of different parishes was able to provide reliable figures on gender-specific marriage ages and deviations from the average across society as a whole. This was a very important step in understanding the rise of fertility in the eighteenth century and in extending our knowledge from the small, mostly elite, section of the population whose lives are recorded in literary and official sources to a wider and more representative group.[14] Similarly, in business history much of our knowledge about capitalisation and about entrepreneurial success or failure used to be based upon studies of a few large firms whose records had survived and were easily available but whose experiences were certainly atypical of the bulk of smaller or less successful firms. In the past two decades major quantitative studies of British business have appeared which have drawn upon insurance records, rate books, government surveys and bankruptcy figures. These are able to analyse the characteristics of a much wider variety of firms, including those which were small or short-lived.[15] Once large data sets, which cover a range of experience, become recognised as a way of gaining a more representative and more accurate picture of general experiences, numerical analysis becomes essential. Quantification in this context is thus likely to be associated with more representative and more accurate analysis than studies which are not willing to examine the characteristics of large numbers of cases. Such quantification can provide detail of patterns of experience of death, employment, trade, marriage, etc. between different social groups, regions and cities. The more qualitative approaches of social and cultural history which investigate what it was like for people living these experiences on the ground can then be placed properly in context.

Descriptive statistics

The need to be both accurate and representative is facilitated by the clear display of data. Often, after only a little simple processing (into percentages or into an index, matrix or a histogram, pie chart or graph, all more fully explained in Chapter 3), data can be presented in a way which enhances our understanding of change or of particular circumstances in the past. A great deal of information can be relayed in summary form in this way. Where isolated figures are merely quoted in a prose argument with phrases such as 'larger than' or 'smaller than' or 'rapidly growing' or 'steeply declining' one is left in doubt about the range of available data, the representative nature of figures chosen for quotation and thus the validity of arguments surrounding the evidence. A table or figure representing the character of the data is very useful indeed. Elementary processing of figures to yield simple measures of average (or typical) experience and to give some idea of the range of variation in measurements over time or space is also valuable. The pitfalls as well as the benefits of numerical summary measures and display techniques (often called 'descriptive statistics') are more fully investigated in Chapter 3. Whatever the criticisms of quantitative approaches to history, no historian should be unable to understand or to undertake statistical work of this kind. Providing one remains aware of the distortions which can be created by poor use of descriptive statistics, the ability to display data and to summarise their character accurately and concisely should be as essential a part of the armoury of a historian as the ability to read and to summarise a text.

Inferential statistics

Many historians and many more social scientists go well beyond simple descriptive statistics in their use of quantitative methods. Descriptive statistics are concerned with summarising and describing a body of numerical information without implying that the observed patterns tell us anything beyond the information which is directly available. Inferential statistics, on the other hand, attempt in various ways to take the statistical knowledge which is given and to use it to infer information or to generalise about other times, places or populations. This involves further processing, manipulating, extrapolating, modelling and testing of the data. Inferential statistics can be a powerful analytical tool if used with care but as the explanatory potential of statistical techniques increase so also do their pitfalls and dangers.

The foundation of inferential statistics is probability theory. Probability theory is important in quantitative analysis in all branches of study but particularly in those where it is impossible to repeat experiments hundreds of times in order to test the reliability of a hypothesis. In a subject like history (as with other social sciences) if we wish to test a hypothesis such as 'the incidence of crime is closely related to unemployment levels' we would have to rely upon the data of crime and unemployment rates which we have and which may well be limited. We are not able to experiment by adjusting levels of unemployment in order to see what happens to crime. The available data might well show that crime figures go up and down in cycles which appear to shadow those of the unemployment rate but we will need to know if these patterns are very much more significant than patterns which might have occurred entirely by chance. Statistical measures of chance or probability are used to assess this. These measures of the significance of statistical findings can then be used as a possible indication of real or historical significance. Inferential statistics can similarly assist in the extrapolation (or extension) of data beyond the figures available and in measuring the probability that sample results will reflect wider characteristics in a population.

Time-series and causal analysis

As much historical research adopts a chronological perspective, it is not surprising that one of the most common sets of quantitative methods used in the study of history is time-series analysis. Time-series analysis is the study of movement of measures such as wages, prices, exports, crime or wheat yields over time. Measures which change over the course of observation are known as variables. As we shall see in Chapter 5, time-series analysis involves the reconstruction and investigation of movements of a variable, or several variables, over time and usually comprises a mix of descriptive and inferential statistics. The construction of time-series graphs, for example, enables one to see clearly the chronology of the rise and fall of outputs, prices, wages, strikes, murders, thefts, or whatever, revealing seasonal or other periodic fluctuations alongside longer-term trends and tendencies. From such graphs, and associated calculations, growth rates and rates of acceleration of growth and decline can be measured. Time-series analysis frequently requires the construction of indices. This involves converting original units into percentage measures, a simple process which is fully discussed in Chapter 5.

Indices enable movements in several variables to be more clearly compared one with another even where their original units of measurement were different, for example they may be used for comparing wheat yields in bushels per acre with wheat prices per bushel expressed in shillings. With the help of indices such variables as money wages can also be adjusted to take account of changes in prices to give a real wage series (a measure of the purchasing power of wages). Indices also enable one to calculate the overall movement of a number of separate variables in weighted combination (via a composite index). This is especially useful in calculating the movement of average wages from information on the wage movements of a spectrum of specific occupational groups or in calculating the overall output trends of the economy from evidence of the output of various separate sectors.

Time-series and indices also allow the historian to consider how the movement of one variable over time may be related to another or to a whole series of others: for example how prices over time might relate to the movement of wages, or how the incidence of riots may be related to levels of unemployment or changes in living standards (see Chapter 5). Techniques of statistical inference which are used to identify, isolate and measure the degree of association between two or more variables (whether they are in a time-series or not) are very commonly used in quantitative social science and history. Examples include the relationship between party affiliation and voting behaviour, between type of crime and sentence length, between occupation and household structure and between wages and prices. Statistical techniques of correlation and regression can neither suggest nor prove that a relationship, let alone a causal relationship, exists between two or more variables but they can add support to a well-grounded hypothesis about causal connections and can indicate the strength or weakness of a possible relationship. These techniques, which are based upon probability measures, are discussed in Chapter 6.

Sampling

A further area of statistical analysis important in history is in the use of samples. Samples are generally used where there is too much data: where use of all the data available would be impractical, too costly or too time-consuming. Study of a small sample can yield accurate information about the population as a whole. For his oral history *The Edwardians* (1977), for example, Paul Thompson deliberately chose a representative sample of interviewees by region, class, occupation and sex.[16] Similarly, Michael Anderson's study of household composition and change from the 1851 Census aimed to get a representative 2 per cent sample by utilising the Census enumerators' books of 1 in every 15 registration districts.[17]

Sampling theory alerts us to the dangers of choosing a sample which may not reflect the character of the wider population, instructs us in best practice regarding the selection of samples and enables us to predict the extent to which our sample results may be out of line compared with analysis of the whole population. Sampling theory, together with basic historical skills and judgement, also alerts the historian to the biases inherent in 'samples' of data which just happen to have been recorded or to have survived. Surviving samples are the sort which historians often encounter and it is important to be able to judge whether the characteristics of such samples are likely to reflect wider experience. The analysis of sample results is again based upon inferential statistics and upon what we can draw from measures of probability (or chance) that a sample result will mirror wider characteristics or changes. These points are explored in Chapter 7.

Large-scale studies

Any investigation which involves consideration of sizeable amounts of data will potentially be aided by quantitative methods and approaches. This is particularly the case with data reflecting the movement of variables over long time periods and/or with research which questions the causes or the impact of certain changes or characteristics where these are measurable.

One such field of historical enquiry which has felt the impact of quantification in recent years and which has expanded its role as a major branch of the discipline is demographic history. Under the influence of the Annales School, and of the growth of urban sociology, especially in the United States, groups of historians in most European countries and in Japan and North America have established major research projects which consider the movement of vital demographic variables (births, marriages and deaths). These studies are based on large samples and aim to reflect national movements, over long time-periods. In Britain the work of the Cambridge Group for the History of Population and Social Structure has been important in this research. The aggregative analysis of parish register data has demonstrated that a decline in the age of marriage and a rise in the rate of marriage were more important causal variables than changes in mortality in accounting for early modern population growth in England. More intricate research on parish register data at the local level, involving the reconstitution of families by linking the evidence of vital events, provides the statistical evidence for detailed demographic analysis of family size and structure, age of marriage and remarriage, population movements and age-specific mortality and even enables calculation of the possible incidence of family limitation and breastfeeding.[18] Demographic analysis has also developed using data in the study of household compositions, migration, occupations and health, whilst the history of medicine (incidence and causes of ill health and death, impact of hospitals and medical developments) has seen a major growth in the past decade using a mixture of statistical, biological and cultural historical approaches.[19] These fields have all benefitted from the fact that early statisticians, reformers and civil servants were preoccupied with collecting figures relating to population, health and mortality.

Mathematical modelling

Quantitative history was promoted by the popularity of mathematical modelling and the statistical testing of such models which became popular in the 1960s and 1970s. Such modelling and testing remains an important branch within economic history in particular. In the past decade improved estimates of the long-term movement of many important national-level economic variables have been assembled: crop yields, rents, incomes, industrial outputs, gross national product, exports, imports, capital formation. These variables have been integrated into formal models of the functioning of the economy and have generated studies of the causes of movement in national income and output, living standards, wages and prices, industrial capital formation, factor productivity and so on.[20]

Modelling the behaviour of individual sectors or firms within the economy has also been prominent. The application of mathematical and statistical models of the behaviour of economic variables is called 'econometrics', and where these are applied to the past the term 'econometric history' is used.[21] The idea of some of these studies is to allow historians to assess the economic effect of a given policy or innovation by measuring it against the economic impact of what would have happened if the policy or innovation had not been implemented. In practice this involves measuring the outputs and costs in a real economy against their counterparts in a counterfactual (or hypothetical) case where a particular policy or innovation is absent. This approach has been applied to many issues. The most popular application has been to the impact of railway development in various countries but it has also been important in studies of American slavery, enclosure in Britain and of late nineteenth-century economic policies in the United States. These applications and more recent developments in econometric history are critically discussed in Chapter 8.

Quantification as a common language

It can be argued that numbers, graphs and formulae should be regarded first and foremost as strategies of communication.[22] They are designed to convey information or results in a standardised form which can be understood across distances of culture and class where face-to-face trust and confidence are difficult if not impossible to establish by other means. The language of quantification has been thrashed out over the past century or so as a highly structured and rule-bound discourse which has enabled it to be applied with little variation across the globe. The rules for collecting and manipulating numbers are widely shared and can be used to coordinate activities, to share research results and to agree policies. The growing use of quantification across many disciplines, including history, has thus been part of the globalisation of research and of academic discourse more generally. This is a great strength of quantification but it is also the 'Achilles heel' in the eyes of its detractors. 'Precision' and ease of communication are often gained at the expense of rigid categories, unquestioned assumptions, loss of rich detail and insufficient attention to vagaries in the quality and realiability of the 'raw' data. This brings us to the limitations of quantification.

1.3 Limitations of quantitative history

All approaches to historical study have their limitations and require the historian to be aware of them. The most severe limitations of quantitative history are those it shares with all methods which use data from primary sources. Historical statistics, their display and manipulation are similar to prose-based evidence, narrative or rhetorical argument: they are only ever as valid or as reliable as the sources on the one hand and as the individual historian on the other.

Reliability of data

A common pitfall in statistical research is that statistical methods are brought to bear upon data which are not sufficiently robust. Figures may be partial or incomplete, wittingly or unwittingly distorted. Even where the degree of measurement error in an original source is limited, distortions can become magnified in statistical manipulation and this may then become crucial if the statistical analysis is the sole basis of a historical argument.

One must always bear in mind that the figures which pass down to us from the past were collected and assembled for purposes very different from those of the historian. Just as a historian using parliamentary papers, for example, must be aware of their general bias in favour of establishment and elite views of social problems, poverty, trade unions, strikes, commercial or agricultural depressions, so also historians using statistical sources from parliamentary papers or any other source should be aware of those who collected them, the purposes which the statistics were geared to serve and the omissions and distortions which this will inevitably introduce. Official values of exports and imports in the eighteenth and early nineteenth century, for example, were not altered to take account of price changes or innovations, and unofficial trade, such as smuggling, escaped record entirely. Thus the figures for the value of English international trade which the historian has to deal with before 1798 for exports and before 1854 for imports and re-exports can provide only a very rough idea of the growth of quantity of trade (not of its value). They are of limited use for modern balance-of-payments assessments or as a measure of the value of output of particular industries.[23]

Similarly, figures for unemployment for all periods are usually wildly inaccurate and distorted. This results from changing official definitions of unemployment, for example whether married women or students are included. They are also inaccurate because large numbers of people who are looking for work do not register as unemployed (especially those not eligible for benefits). The most significant bias in unemployment data is the omission of the bulk of unemployment of women and juveniles. Women's employment has traditionally been regarded as supplemental to household income. The unemployment of women is therefore seen as less important than that of adult males and it is less frequently registered and recorded. It was assumed that women and children would be reabsorbed into domestic subsistence activity during depressions in the nineteenth century. The shifting nature of education, movement of the school leaving age and the changing treatment of student 'vacations' has resulted in poor measures of juvenile unemployment over the nineteenth and twentieth centuries, exacerbated by the short-term nature of training and apprenticeship initiatives. Restrictions on the benefit eligibility of unemployed women and 'students' in the twentieth century has created the situation where many fail to register as unemployed (or employed) because there is no incentive to do so. They are thus omitted from official figures, and historians must make allowances for this.

Demographic evidence is also misleading largely because, as with many sources, the figures provided are not those most appropriate to the historian's needs. These have to be derived from what *is* recorded or known. Parish registers (the main source in England before the introduction of Civil Registration in 1837) generally record evidence only of the parish populations who were of Anglican faith. Dissenters kept separate registers which have a poor survival record, and non-Christians are missing from both Anglican and nonconformist documents. The numbers of those unrecorded often need to be estimated and added, a difficult task when nonconformity varied so widely across parishes and over time. In addition, parish registers provide baptism dates rather than birth dates. The latter are more interesting and useful to the historian and the demographer but can only be inferred by using an estimated birth–baptism interval, which is a source of major potential error especially when trying to estimate birth spacing or prenuptial conception rates.

Census enumerators' books for Britain and elsewhere are a commonly used historical source but have many pitfalls. Although reasonably accurate for male occupations, for example, they are hopelessly inaccurate in recording female work. Female occupational data were not regarded as a priority by those who designed the census nor by enumerators charged with collecting the evidence or giving advice to householders. Many women were also unwilling to reveal details of paid work because of social stigma.[24] Low-status, casual and intermittent employment was often not regarded as 'work' anyway. What should be regarded as 'work' was not well stipulated by the design of the census or the training of enumerators. In some of the late nineteenth-century censuses women working full time in their family business were specifically not to be recorded as working.[25] These sorts of issues surrounding women's work dog most sources purporting to record such employment.

Taxation data have similar problems especially when used as a source to estimate population levels in the pre-census era. Records of hearth tax, window tax, land tax, poor rates all refer to households and can only be used to estimate populations if a multiplier is used. Gregory King estimated that the population of England and Wales in 1695 was 5.2 million on the basis of a multiplier of 4.5 of the numbers of households listed in hearth-tax schedules. For three centuries nobody knew whether this multiplier had resulted in a reasonably accurate population estimate until Wrigley and Schofield's broader quantitative work confirmed that King probably got it about right.[26] It is frequently necessary for the historian to use proxy variables: baptisms rather than births, male employment and unemployment figures as an indication of the employment structure of the economy as a whole, the ability to sign a register instead of real literacy levels. Sometimes historians use proxies which may be some way away from the variable which is really under consideration; for example, records of Easter communicants or weights of candles burnt have been used as indices of the 'de-Christianisation' of modern Italy and France, respectively.[27]

Coleman writes that numbers seem

> so central and seductive to the analytical mind, that if needed statistics are not to be found then the search for proxies gets underway. It is well regularly to recall that most of the commonly used historical statistics, at least before the mid nineteenth century, are in effect proxies. Numbers of manors held are made to act as surrogates for wealth; wage rates do duty for earnings; rents for profits. The heights of soldiers or marines are brought in to inform us about the standard of living.[28]

This is a major problem with much quantitative work: decisions have to be made about the degree of reliability of proxy figures. 'Guesstimated' adjustments must often also be made to allow for omissions and distortions in the original data. Such adjustments are sometimes largely responsible for a major thesis such as in the work of Wrigley and Schofield on the timing of the late eighteenth-century baby boom.[29]

All quantitative data should be subjected to historians' judgements concerning their reliability and accuracy, particularly where allowances have to be made to convert proxy variables to those required for the historian's purpose. Questions should always be asked. Who assembled the data and for what purpose? How were questionnaires or interview questions phrased and how may this have distorted the responses? How was the information sorted and reordered at the time and what factors may have biased the survival as well as the recording of evidence? How accurate is quantitative evidence from the past, how attuned is it to the historian's needs and how representative are those pieces of evidence and series of figures which have survived as an indication of wider trends and circumstances? There is also an important problem which often occurs with statistical measurements, past or present: the process of measurement itself often causes shifts in behaviour which bias the results. If managers are told that their profit levels are to be the subject of measurement, there will be a strong incentive to optimise profitability by creative accounting in case this measurement is a prelude to new payment structures, bonuses or security of employment:

> In economic and social affairs quantitative predictions and manage-ment by numbers often create inducements for business people, medical patients, tax payers and criminals (among others) to alter their behaviour in a way that undermines the numbers. That is, though the world described by social as well as natural scientists is partly a world of their own construction, they cannot make it however they choose.[30]

In the same way, interviewees are likely to behave differently (and give different answers) in the dynamics of different interview situations, espe-cially where the class, gender or ethnic character of the interviewer differs from that of the subject. The problem of distortion caused by the collection of data is not unique to quantitative work, and closeness to the source carries no guarantee of greater precision.[31]

Whether figures are sufficiently reliable depends upon the purposes for which they are required by the historian. If the figures are to be subjected to detailed statistical analysis or if they are to form the foundation of a thesis, they will need to be more reliable than if they are to be quoted simply as a supplement to an argument. Data from the past, whether quantitative or qualitative, will always be unreliable or unrepresentative to some degree. Whether a researcher accepts the degree of error which this injects into the analysis must depend on well-informed and well-reasoned historical judge-ment: it is certainly never an objective or 'statistical' decision.

Statistical categories and comparability of data

Statistical categories are initially devised by those who collect the data. These are usually private individuals, voluntary bodies or the state. They choose which figures to collect, and what categories to employ, to suit their own purposes. Quantification has always been part of a strategy of indi-vidual improvement or advancement, social reform or state intervention, so its categories are never simply descriptive. The discrete classifications into which varied and continuous information is often forced frequently distorts the data in the interests of a larger purpose or project. This may be done consciously but is usually a problem even where efforts are made to avoid the distortion caused by the selection and classification of data. The big problem is how do we fit a rich and continuous variety of individuals into a manageable number of discrete categories for the purpose of analysis? Where in any standard occupational classification should we fit a part-time but essentially retired taxidermist who is also a ski instructor and helps out in an Oxfam shop? Reality is uncomfortably complex whereas statistical categories are necessarily gross simplifications. Sometimes the categories themselves should be questioned because they have been developed in such a way as systematically to minimise or exclude or to maximise a particular group in the population, for example, ethnic or religious minorities. Historians need to be particularly aware of these issues not just as a guide to their own subjective bias but because they are also at the mercy of categories created by their predecessors and often have limited opportunity to rework or to adjust them. Categories are powerful because they often become entrenched and unquestioned even when they are misleading. If they are created by the state and are regarded as 'official' they are too often seen as unquestionable and representing real entities: they become 'reified'. Once a category of official statistics or classification such as 'skilled white-collar workers' gets fixed in the mind and once it is used by commerce or the state as an object of policy it can become a self-fulfilling entity as people themselves come to identify with the category.

Reliability and wisdom of classification criteria and thoughtful production of categories are important but so also is comparability, especially for studies which compare the same variables across nations, regions, localities, institutions or over time. A series of figures is only accurate over time or across space if it continues to measure exactly the same thing. The longer the period covered and/or the more diverse the geographical or cultural area the less likely are series (whether wills, occupations, exports, sexual harassment cases or whatever) to be directly comparable. In coding death certificates two researchers in 1978 admitted that 'comparable statistics cannot be obtained if everyone does what he or she thinks is correct'.[32] Following rules may be necessary to achieve comparability of a series but it is often done at the expense of the richness of the evidence. The problem can become particularly serious where long-run or diverse statistical series are being used and with proxy variables. Crime figures are especially difficult to compare across time and space because of legal changes, different definitions of crime in different regions or countries, different responsibilities of the courts as well as different levels of policing and detection.

Only a minor change in the basis of collection, measurement or assessment makes comparisons of statistical series very difficult. In the British census, for example, major changes occurred in occupational definitions and in the design of schedules from one census to another during the nineteenth and twentieth centuries as the census evolved to become a more efficient tool of social and economic management. Similarly, in studies of living standards, changes in the composition of the workforce make difficult the estimation of average money wages. Average real wage estimates (i.e. estimates of the purchasing power of wages) are a further headache because it is necessary to take account of changes in consumption patterns over time (creating shifts in the cost of living). In studies of the movement of industrial output, changes in the sectoral composition of the economy, in the industrial mix and in the quality and types of outputs make the estimation of output growth problematic. In assessing the reliability and comparability of quantitative historical data the skill of the historian is paramount. Assessment is likely to be based on familiarity with the institutional and administrative origin of the sources and with the historical context: one requires knowledge of the likely missing and non-surviving data, of how data were collected and for what purpose, of how documents were conceived and of how all these varied across time and space.

Choice of technique: use and misuse

Historians' skills are also those most important in the choice of which statistical techniques to use and in decisions about how to use them. It is easy to get carried away in using statistical techniques and manipulation when the data themselves are insufficiently representative or reliable to withstand such processing. Another common pitfall in the historians' use of statistics is manipulation of data which creates results or impressions that are misleading or false. At its simplest, this can occur, for example, in the choice of unit of measurement on the axes of a graph which can either magnify or reduce the appearance of trends and variations in the data. Choices about the display or analysis of data in distinct subperiods also have to be very carefully made as these can create misleading impressions of chronological change and indicate false discontinuities and turning points in data. For example, the timing and degree of discontinuity in English output and national income series for the eighteenth and nineteenth centuries depend very much on which subperiods are chosen for comparison.[33] A number of other techniques are commonly used carelessly and in such a way as to create erroneous impressions or results; these include moving averages, correlation and regression analysis and sampling (more will be said about these in later chapters).[34]

Historians should always be on the lookout for deliberate as well as accidental misuse of techniques. This often occurs when statistics are placed in the service of some ideologically inspired thesis, such as biological determinism. In his book *The mismeasure of man* Stephen J. Gould demonstrates the extent to which attempts to measure and predict human intelligence from late nineteenth-century craniometry (skull measurement) to sophisticated intelligence quotient (IQ) investigations have been dangerous reflections of personal motives and of racial, class and gender prejudices.[35]

Analysis of results

Finally, the skills of the historian are required in analysing the statistical results obtained from the manipulation of data, as they do not speak for themselves. Sampling and then estimating the reliability and significance of sample results can be a minefield, as we shall see: measures which appear significant in a statistical sense may require a different assessment once the reliability of the original sources and the needs of a particular historical argument are borne in mind. In analysing the relationship between the movements of two variables over time a statistical result may suggest a close relationship and imply the possibility of a causal connection. But the statistical result may be quite accidental or spurious, and only the historian can decide. There must be a good historical justification in seeking a statistical test for the existence of a relationship between two or more variables in the first place. We would be justified, for example, in suggesting that the price of cotton cloth on sale in Manchester would decline rapidly with the increasing supplies deriving from the spread of mechanisation. We might wish to explore the possible strength of the connection between the movement of price and output figures in the industry. Similarly, we might wish to investigate the links between income levels and the ownership of different consumer durables in the 1950s and 1960s. But a close statistical correlation or association between the movement of variables, however well founded our expectations of this may be, does not prove any sort of causality; it merely indicates that the historian's initial hypothesis may be justified and that it may be worth pursuing that avenue of enquiry. Statistical significance and historical significance are entirely separate phenomena. The same is true of the difference between statistical and real significance in all other fields of study in both the natural and the social sciences. The historian and the reader must decide whether statistical results have any use or relevance to our understanding of the past. Statistics may point to the plausibility of possible explanations but they do not, in themselves, provide the answer to historical questions. Only the historian's interpretation of the results can do that.

Computers, by facilitating and speeding up the process of statistical manipulation, have often resulted in bad as well as good statistical practice. It is now so easy to run a set of figures against several different series of causal variables that the temptation is to do this and then to seek explanations for statistically significant relationships which appear. This is putting the cart before the horse: the hypothesis that there may be a causal connection between two or more variables (based on a sound historical argument or judgement) must come first, before the statistical analysis of that connection. Also, the hypothesis must be capable of falsification (of being proved incorrect).[36] If our statistical testing of a hypothesis does not yield supporting evidence we must be prepared to reject the hypothesis or to introduce another variable, on the basis of another reasoned conjecture, rather than to tinker around with the hypothesis just to make the data fit. Statistics may serve to reveal or to clarify a particular tendency, but how we interpret that tendency, its significance, and the causal connections it may indicate are matters for seasoned historical judgement. The historical significance of results may also vary depending upon their use in an argument. If a minor and supportive piece of evidence is sought, the quantitative result may be accepted more readily than in a case where the quantitative analysis is the foundation stone of a whole argument or thesis.

Pitfalls of modelling

When we move from the use of descriptive statistics and simple statistical analysis of data to the use of quantitative techniques married to theoretical models of the functioning of variables, a whole new set of problems arise. In addition to those pitfalls already discussed, the model applied must also be scrutinised. If a model is applied to the past, one must ask: does it embody a valid approximation of the behaviour of variables and actors at that time? Sometimes a neoclassical economic model is applied which has a supply–demand, free-market basis, a limited number of variables derived from knowledge of the functioning of modern industrialised societies and a whole set of present-centred assumptions. (Most prominent of these is the rationality postulate which assumes that economic actors will always act to maximise their profits or individual economic interests.) Such models generally assume that markets will move towards clearing at a certain level of price and hence of supply and demand. Sufficient information for buyers and sellers to act in such a way as to achieve this (in the medium term at least) is assumed. Even where the assumptions underlying models are questionable, a theory may be defended by its ability to make reasonably good predictions about changes to variables under particular sets of circumstances (such a justification is normally termed 'instrumental'). It is nevertheless always wise to justify the applicability of any model to the case in question, and if an instrumental justification is to be used this should be clearly stated. Most models also elevate those variables which are measurable to the most important in any analysis as these are the ones which can be integrated into the model. Non-measurables are given little attention, and the implications of this should always be borne in mind.

Studies of railway innovation have commonly used econometric tools. However, to evaluate railway systems with any precision it is necessary to place a monetary value on every effect of railway innovation. This is difficult in itself but also creates the problem of where to draw the line. Similarly, in national income estimations made within a national accounts framework (which relies on counting inputs and outputs and drawing a balance) there are major problems in constructing indices of economic growth for the eighteenth and nineteenth centuries. Surviving data from a sample of industries must be multiplied on the basis of what we know of the sectoral composition of the economy and of the relative growth rates of different sectors. There is a major problem of weighting the evidence which we have so that it can be used to estimate growth rates across the economy. Even if we manage to achieve a reasonably accurate estimate for this, it must be remembered that it is difficult to allow for changes in the weights over time and impossible to allow for the impact of innovations in the quality or design of goods, or for such important aspects of economic development as improvements in working hours and conditions.

Conclusion

At the simplest level, quantification can bring to history the ability to summarise large bodies of data, to display such data effectively and to express typical measures and values. In many cases quantification also results both in clearer specification and in more rigorous testing of hypotheses about historical causation or relationships between variables. Statistical techniques may enable us to uncover important characteristics which are not apparent in the raw data and to confirm that relationships and patterns in the data are not present merely by chance. At the same time, vigilance is required in examining the source and reliability of data and the degree to which it may have been distorted by collection and prior processing. The danger of comparing statistical categories across time and space are legion and one should always therefore be on the lookout for 'results' of research which may merely be the irrelevant products of varying categories or statistical conventions. Above all, one must beware the dual sins of spurious attempts at statistical accuracy (where the data are insufficiently robust to support this) and the confusion of statistical measures of significance with a rounded evaluation of the historical importance of findings.

According to Burke:

> The introduction into historical discourse of large numbers of statistics has tended to polarise the profession into supporters and opponents. Both sides have tended to exaggerate the novelty posed by the use of figures. Statistics can be faked, but so can texts. Statistics are easy to misinterpret, but so are texts. Machine readable data are not user friendly, but the same goes for many manuscripts, written in illegible hands or on the verge of disintegration.[37]

History is not an easy subject whether the historian chooses a quantitative or a qualitative approach or, as is often most appropriate, a mixture of the two. Neither should it be, and the paramount requirement for all historians is to think hard about what they are doing and to be vigilant in interpreting evidence. Issues of the appropriateness of evidence for addressing the questions being posed – of reliability, representativeness and comparability – must be uppermost in all kinds of historical research. In quantitative work, these issues must be examined and specified very precisely, but once this is done the potential benefits of applying a range of statistical and quantitative techniques are great.

Notes

1 Darrell Huff, *How to lie with statistics* (London, 1973) p.10.
2 Some common statistical techniques are mentioned in this chapter. They will all be more fully explained later in the book. If difficulties are experienced in understanding the arguments made here, use of the glossary is recommended.
3 François Furet, 'Quantitative history' *Daedalus, C* quoted by Carlo Ginzburg, *The cheese and the worms*, (London, 1971), p. xx.
4 E. Le Roy Ladurie, *The peasants of Languedoc* (English translation, London, 1974); this is only one of many Annaliste examples of detailed research on different French regions which incorporated much use of statistical series.
5 A. L. Bowley, *Wages in the United Kingdom in the nineteenth century* (Cambridge, 1900); G. H. Wood, *The history of wages in the cotton trade during the past one hundred years* (Manchester, 1910); E. H. Phelps Brown and S. V. Hopkins, 'Seven centuries of the price of consumables compared with builders' wage rates', in E. M. Carus Wilson (ed.), *Essays in economic history 11* (London, 1954), pp. 179–96; B. R. Mitchell and P. Deane, *Abstract of British historical statistics* (Cambridge, 1962).
6 For a contemporary survey and collection of examples, see Peter Temin, *The new economic history: selected readings* (Harmondsworth, 1973).
7 Lawrence Stone, *The past and the present revisited* (London, 1987), p. 94. For a longer sustained attack on the quantifiers, see J. Barzun, *Clio and the doctors* (Chicago, IL, 1974).
8 These attempts have come from both sides. Economic sociologists have developed some very interesting sophistications of 'economic' theory, most of which have been virtually ignored by economists. See, for example, N. J. Smelser and R. Swedberg, *Handbook of economic sociology* (New York, 1994). A significant grouping of economists, on the other hand, have reached out to 'colonise' areas of social and cultural history in the past few decades, investigating many topics, from family relationships to crime and drugs, through the prism of supply-and-demand theory. For a recent collection, see M. Tommasi and K. Lerulli, *The new economics of human behaviour* (Cambridge, 1995).
9 Carl Bridenbaugh, 'The great mutation', *American Historical Review*, 68 (1963), p. 326; quoted by J. Tosh, in *The pursuit of history*, 2nd edn (London, 1991), p. 202.
10 Tony Judt, 'A clown in regal purple: social history and the historians', *History Workshop Journal*, 7 (1979), p. 74
11 The phrase is from Stone, *The past and the present revisited* (London, 1987), p. 94 who also quotes Liam Hudson.
12 Richard Cobb, 'Historians in white coats' (1971), quoted in Charles Tilly, *As sociology meets history* (New York, 1981), p. 72.
13 For further discussion, see Chapter 9 and R. Middleton and P. Wardley, 'Information technology in economic and social history: the computer as philosopher's stone or Pandora's box?', *Economic History Review*, 43, 4 (1990), pp 667–96.
14 Compare L. Stone, *The Family, sex and marriage in England, 1500–1800* (London, 1977), a study of elites using diary evidence, with E. A. Wrigley and R. S. Schofield, *The population history of England, 1541–1871* (London, 1981), which derived statistics from more than 400 parish registers.
15 See, for example, Julian Hoppitt, *Risk and failure in English business, 1700–1800* (Cambridge, 1987); R. Lloyd Jones and M. J. Lewis, *Manchester and the age of the factory: the business structure of cottonopolis in the industrial revolution* (London, 1988).
16 Paul Thompson, *The Edwardians* (St Albans, 1977).

17 Michael Anderson, *Family structure in nineteenth-century Lancashire* (London, 1971).

18 The Cambridge Group have followed up the 1981 volume, in which they analysed aggregate demographic indices, with a collection of their reconstitutions studies: E. A. Wrigley, R. Davies, J. Oeppen and R. Schofield (eds), *English population history from family reconstitution, 1580–1837* (Cambridge, 1997).

19 One of the best of these is S. Szreter, *Fertility, class and gender in Britain, 1860–1940* (Cambridge, 1996).

20 For a collection of articles which includes several of these sorts of studies, see R. Floud and D. N. McCloskey (eds), *The economic history of Britain since 1700*, 3 vols, 2nd edn (Cambridge, 1994). The *Journal of Economic History* and *Explorations in Economic History* also have a significant proportion of articles which employ models alongside quantification.

21 For an introduction to such history, see D. N. McCloskey, *Econometric history* (London, 1987). For extended but equally accessible and more recent discussion, see T. G. Rawski (ed.), *Economics and the historian* (London, 1996).

22 They have been discussed in this way, as part of the rhetoric of economics alongside other devices, such as storytelling and metaphor, by D. N. McCloskey, in *If you're so smart: the narrative of economic expertise* (Chicago, IL, 1990).

23 For discussion of the pitfalls of official values in measuring foreign trade, see G. N. Clark, *Guide to English commercial statistics, 1696–1782* (London, 1938); R. Davis, *The Industrial Revolution and English overseas trade* (Leicester, 1979).

24 Fear of tax or social security implications continued to prevent women declaring paid work on official forms in the late twentieth century.

25 For full discussion of these issues, see E. Higgs, 'Women, occupations and work in the nineteenth-century censuses', *History Workshop Journal*, 23 (1987), pp. 59–80.

26 This built upon the revisions of D. V. Glass: E. A. Wrigley and R. S. Schofield, *The population history of England, 1541–1871: a reconstruction* (London, 1981), pp. 159, 175, 181, 575.

27 B. R. Wilson, *Religion in secular society* (London, 1966); M. Vovelle, *Piété baroque et déchristianisation en Provence au 18è siècle* (Paris, 1973); both quoted by Peter Burke, *Sociology and History* (London, 1980), p. 40.

28 D. C. Coleman, 'History, economic history and the numbers game', *Historical Journal*, 38, 3 (1995), p. 641.

29 This was pointed out by Peter Lindert, in 'English living standards, population growth and Wrigley and Schofield', *Explorations in Economic History*, 20 (1983), pp. 385–408.

30 T. M. Porter, 'Making things quantitative', *Science in Context*, 7, 3 (1994), p. 401.

31 The problem of increasing the distortion the closer one tries to observe and to measure has been much discussed and is generally referred to as the Heisenberg indeterminacy principle. This stresses the errors inherent in the sensitive scientific measuring implements required for very close observation in the natural sciences. Werner Heisenberg, *Physics and philosophy: the revolution in modern science* (London, 1959).

32 T. M. Porter, *Trust in numbers: the pursuit of objectivity in science and public life* (Princeton, NJ, 1995), p. 35.

33 This is pointed out by N. F. R. Crafts, in *British economic growth during the industrial revolution* (Oxford, 1985).

34 For a classic treatment of the potential misuses of statistics, see D. Huff, *How to lie with statistics* (London, 1954).

35 Stephen J. Gould, *The mismeasure of man* (Harmondsworth, 1981).

36 The need for a falsifiable hypothesis was stressed by Karl Popper as a way of defending the hypothetico deductive approach to data and as a way of seeking a mechanical objectivity in scientific enquiry: as free from bias and subjective manipulation as possible. K. Popper, *Conjectures and refutations: the growth of scientific knowledge* (London, 1963).
37 Peter Burke (ed.), *New perspectives on historical writing* (Cambridge, 1991), p. 15.

Further Reading

A. Green and K. Troup (eds), *The houses of history: a critical reader in twentieth-century history and theory* (Manchester, 1999), Chapter 6.
C. H. Lee, *The quantitative approach to economic history* (London, 1977).
T. K. Rabb, 'The development of quantification in historical research', *Journal of Interdisciplinary History*, XIII, 4 (1983).
J. Tosh, *The pursuit of history* (London 1984; 3rd edn 1999), Chapter 9.
E. R. Tufte, *Visual explanations: images and quantities, evidence and narrative* (Cheshire, CT, 1997)

For some examples of interpreting statistics see:
E. M. Higgs, *Making sense of the Census* (London, 1989)
C. Johnson and S. Briscoe, *Measuring the economy: a guide to understanding official statistics* (Harmondsworth, 1995)
E. A. Wrigley (ed.), *Identifying people in the past* (London, 1973)

For a guide to statistical methods for historians see later bibliographies and especially:
R. Darcy and R. C. Rohrs, *A guide to quantitative history* (Westport, CT, 1995)
R. Floud, *An introduction to quantitative methods for historians* (London, 1973; 2nd edn 1979)
L. Haskins and K. Jeffreys, *Understanding quantitative history* (Cambridge, MA, 1991)

For the impact of computers in historical work and the range of methods involved see Chapter 9 and:
D. I. Greenstein, *A historian's guide to computing* (Oxford, 1994)
R. Jensen, 'The micro-computer revolution for historians', *Journal of Interdisciplinary History*, XIV, 1 (1983)
R. Lloyd-Jones and M. J. Lewis, *Using computers in history: a practical guide* (London, 1996)

E. Mawdsley and T. Munck, *Computing for historians: an introductory guide* (Manchester, 1993)

R. Middleton and P. Wardley, 'Information technology in economic and social history: the computer as philosopher's stone or Pandora's box?', *Economic History Review*, 43, 4 (1990), pp 667–96

2

The origins and nature of quantitative thinking

Quantification is not merely a strategy for describing the social and natural worlds but a means of reconfiguring them. It entails the imposition of new meanings and the disappearance of old ones. Often it is allied to systems of experimental or administrative control, and in fact considerable feats of human organisation are generally required even to create stable, reasonably standardised measures.

. . . Many social qualities have already been successfully quantified in a variety of ways. Those who seek to do it differently, or to spread the net of quantified qualities wider, need to consider not only epistemological questions but also moral and political ones. There is strength in numbers, and anyone who proposes to wield them more effectively must ask not only about their validity but also about how the world might be changed by adopting new forms of quantification.[1]

Study of the history of statistical approaches yields some important insights into the nature of the data collected by individuals and by private and public bodies in the past. As with any other type of historical evidence, statistical information is always specified and gathered in relation to some particular commercial, legal, political, economic, moral or personal goal. The resultant figures with their assumptions, omissions, categories, biases and inconsistencies are the legacy with which historians grapple in their effort to interpret the past and to ask their own, very different, questions. Furthermore, just as the data collected in the past have been socially constructed by those who sought particular information for their own purposes or for purposes of state, so also the evolution of statistical methods and theories has been driven and moulded by particular social, political, moral or commercial goals. As we shall see, statistical thinking and statistical method have evolved within a social, economic and intellectual environment which conditioned their nature. Unless this is understood it is very difficult to comprehend both the opportunities and the controversies which surround quantification in the human sciences today.[2]

The account which follows concentrates upon the history of quantification and of statistical methods and theories in Britain, but the story has some direct parallels and overlaps with developments in other Western countries, especially France, Italy and the United States.[3]

2.1 Origins of the statistical movement in Britain

Although the foundations of empirical social research in Britain are rightly associated with the Victorian statistical movement, the origin of quantitative study of economic social and political problems can be identified much earlier. It should be seen as part of the Enlightenment attempts to understand and to control society through rational, scientific enquiry and analysis. Some of the earliest work in this tradition in Britain is associated with John Graunt and William Petty in the 1650s and 1660s.[4] In a series of papers William Petty argued the need for accounts of inhabitants in order to discover occupational structure and religious observance in England and Ireland. He also called for a general registration of details of births, deaths and marriages in order to reveal age structures, religion, occupations and wealth in different parts of the kingdom. He established a new way of viewing society and of analysing social and political issues using *political arithmetic*. The foundation of political arithmetic was the idea that the prosperity and strength of the state rested on the number and condition of its subjects.[5] Petty had been personal secretary to Thomas Hobbes in the 1640s and he may have been influenced in applying mechanical and statistical methods to social and political analysis by Hobbes's atheistic and authoritarian approach. He was also influenced in scientific method by the ideas of Francis Bacon.[6] Petty's political arithmetic developed further during his time as Surveyor General in Ireland when he organised a detailed survey of County Down. Like his nineteenth-century successors, Petty saw the collection of statistical data and the analysis of that data as an indispensable preliminary to a scientific understanding of the functioning of society and to the achievement of social and political reforms. He also saw numbers as a way to become more objective, 'sensible' and less subjective and passionate:

> The method I take to do this is not yet very usual; for instead of using only comparative and superlative Words and intellectual Arguments, I have taken the course (as a specimen of the Political Arithmetick I have long aimed at) to express myself in terms of Number, Weight and measure; to use only Arguments of Sense, and to consider only such Causes as have visible Foundations in Nature; leaving those that depend upon the mutable minds, Opinions, Appetites and Passions of particular Men, to the Consideration of others.[7]

At much the same time, John Graunt was working on some of the earliest historical demography. His *Natural and political observations on the bills of mortality*, published in 1662, analysed the London bills to consider urban and rural death rates, infant mortality rates, the excess of female births over deaths and the formation of life tables.[8] Graunt, significantly, also discussed the reliability of social data, in particular whether different figures were sufficiently accurate to justify manipulation. He thus highlighted a consideration which remains central today in quantitative approaches to society.

Measures of demographic change and of the social, political and moral determinants of population growth were a key focus of numerical thinking long before Thomas Malthus published his famous *Essay on the principle of population* in 1798.[9] Petty's followers in the statistical tradition in the late seventeenth and early eighteenth centuries, most notably Gregory King, concentrated on population and upon social structure, although trade and public finance was a growing concern. King's estimate of the numbers and wealth of each rank of society in 1688 has become well known and used as a historical source, as in Table 3.2 (although it was not published in full until 1802). Charles Davenant and others concentrated at this time upon the statistics of trade with a view to efficient public finance and accounting. Davenant's definition of political arithmetic as 'the art of reasoning by figures upon things relating to government'[10] has endured to show how literally statistical, that is 'state-thinking', this approach originally was and was to remain for some time. There was a pragmatic force at work: the needs of an expanding and centralising state bureaucracy for accurate estimates of wealth and revenues.

Many writers in the eighteenth century extolled the virtues of quantitative thinking and calculation, especially in areas of public finance, including war finance, customs and excise, imports and exports.[11] There were 15 different estimates of national income alone between Petty's research and that of Patrick Colquhoun in the 1790s. In the same period progress was also made towards standardising the myriad local and customary weights and measures in England in the interests of internal trade.[12] This can be seen as vital in establishing the conditions of an exchange society with a common discourse and common understandings about the weights and qualities of goods being transacted. It is an illustration of one of the main purposes of the evolution of commonly understood statistical measures and methods: that they function as a form of common discourse across geographical space and differing local cultures.

Improvements in the natural sciences, in the measurement of longitude, time, pressure and temperature, were matched by calendar reform and the Ordnance Survey (from 1791).[13] The eighteenth century also saw major progress in developing the principles of life insurance with use of life tables which had been introduced in Graunt's *Natural and political observations on the bills of mortality* and developed in 1686 by Edmund Halley (of comet fame).[14] Additional work done for the Scottish Ministers' Widows Fund, founded in 1744 by Alexander Webster and Robert Wallace, development of the mathematical theories of chance by de Moivre and Simpson in the 1760s and progress made under the auspices of the Equitable Assurances for Lives and Survivorships (founded in 1762) were particularly significant.[15] Probability theory was being advanced in the physical sciences as well as in relation to the insurance industry. Laplace built on the work of de Moivre, and both he and the Reverend Thomas Bayes (apparently independently) contributed to modern probability theory by developing the *a posteriori* technique. This enabled the prediction of events in the future, or the inference of causation from a record of past occurrences.[16] Interestingly, the Gambling Act of 1774, which attempted to define insurance and chance as opposites, can be seen to have marked an important transition in the acceptance of actuarial 'certainties'. Life insurance was no longer viewed as a gamble, nor length of life seen as random: both were coming to be seen as calculable mathematical probabilities. The insurance of sickness, where it was so much more difficult to calculate the odds, remained much more risky and more a matter for subjective assessments, usually based on interviews, until well into the nineteenth century. Chance was being tamed, but the general drive for objective rules to replace subjective evaluations in life assurance and in other fields (an important element in the rise of statistical thought and method) was a slow process.[17]

2.2 The meaning of statistics

The word *statistics* probably first entered the English language in 1770 with W. Hooper's translation from the German of a book by J. F. von Bielefeld.[18] The meaning of statistics here was linked to the notion of statesmanship and defined as 'the science which teaches us ... the political arrangement of all the modern states of the known world'.[19] This *Staatenkunde* notion can be traced back to Aristotle, but it became a serious, albeit contested, academic discipline in Germany in the eighteenth century.[20] The word *statistics* was firmly situated in the English language by Sir John Sinclair. The first volume of his massive survey, *A statistical account of Scotland*, appeared 1791. Sinclair defined statistical enquiries as those 'respecting the population, political circumstances and production of a country and other matters of State', and he was so convinced of their importance that he advocated sending statistical 'missionaries' around the country.[21]

By the end of the eighteenth century a shift had started to occur in the definition of statistics in Britain away from the idea of ordered facts (both numerical and non-numerical), which would reveal the condition of the state, in the direction of more narrowly defined quantitative evidence, but change was slow. The 1797 edition of the *Encyclopedia Britannica* still defined *statistics* as 'a word lately introduced to express a view or survey of any kingdom, county or parish',[22] but the association of statistics with description or display of numerical data was developing. Statistics in France was identified by Charles Dupin as numerical information about society, as early as 1820,[23] and in his *The statistical breviary* of 1801 William Playfair implied that statistical works should be limited to quantitative data.[24] Yet as late as 1842 J. R. McCulloch rejected the idea 'that everything in statistics may be estimated in figures'.[25] It was not until the twentieth century that the word *statistics* came specifically to mean the arrangement and manipulation of purely quantitative evidence: a development which had involved the 'displacement of concepts by quantities'.[26] Thus the notion of statistics, from its inception in the English language, and for at least a century after, exhibited a fluidity of meaning which lay at the core of competing claims to its importance and precision. The scope, purpose and methods of statistics were by no means fixed: to some extent this remains a foundation of controversy to this day.

2.3 Data display and collection

Important developments in the display and collection of statistics occurred in the late eighteenth and early nineteenth centuries. The use of graphs and visual representation date from this time although, after their first development by the Dundee businessman William Playfair in his *The commercial and political atlas* of 1787, they virtually disappeared to re-emerge only slowly in this country from the late nineteenth century. Playfair's *Atlas* was well ahead of its time in including graphs of exports and imports and of English and French annual revenues and the size of the national debt, 1688–1800. His later *Lineal arithmetic* (1798) contained 37 coloured graphs covering a wider array of economic issues.[27]

The early nineteenth century also saw the extended collection of statistical data in a variety of fields. Medical statistics were developed, largely in the work of William Black, Gilbert Stone and James Annesley and in the more disparate efforts of a number of provincial medical statisticians who gathered data as a prelude for campaigning for public health reforms. National criminal statistics were published from 1810, regularly from 1832, partly because of contemporary controversy over capital punishment. Interestingly, from the major debates over criminal commitments which surrounded the Select Committee of 1828 it was generally agreed that most of the apparent increase in crime (which was based on the rise of commitments) arose from more effective law enforcement and from changes in the classification of crimes than it did from any real increase in offenses.[28] Thus one of the most enduring problems of many sorts of statistics, particularly those relating to crime, was starkly exposed: the problem of distinguishing real changes from apparent shifts which arise because the numbers collected relate only indirectly to the main object of study or because the definitions or parameters of statistical measures change over time.

There were also various official surveys in the early nineteenth century, which included quantitative analysis of education (1818, 1833), for example, and of factory employment (1816 Select Committee). But the most obvious and important developments in the early nineteenth-century collection and use of social statistics were the establishment of the census (from 1801) and Civil Registration (from 1837). The census was seen as essential for effective government, for revenue raising and for recruitment of armed forces. John Rickman, who supervised the first four censuses, had argued for the first census to demonstrate population increase and growing prosperity and thus to assuage the domestic discontent which characterised the inflationary and high tax years of the Napoleonic Wars.

Alongside the first census Rickman collected returns from the clergy of decennial baptism and burial figures, 1700–80, and yearly figures thereafter. These formed a basis for some of the earliest (and much subsequent) work in historical demography.[29] But the early censuses themselves contained only limited information derived from questions which were poorly framed. They relied on the voluntary labour of parish officials and they were inevitably highly inaccurate not least because data were collected over several days, which left scope for double counting and omissions.[30]

As in the mid-eighteenth century, it was commercial actuarial work which provided the greatest impetus to the development of statistical techniques in the early nineteenth century. This was associated particularly with Joshua Milne of the Sun Life Assurance Society.[31] Discontent with prevailing life tables, recognition that parish registers could not be used to rectify them because of their exclusions (particularly of dissenters) and growing demands for more accurate information about health and causes of death created major pressure for civil registration. The General Register Office was established in 1837 to administer both Civil Registration and the census and this became one of the most active government departments undertaking statistical study of social problems. By the 1840s and 1850s it was joined in the production of social and economic statistics by the Home Office, the War Office, the Board of Trade, the Admiralty and the Poor Law Commission. The statistical movement associated with the Victorian era was now well underway.

The desire for more, and more accurate, figures to aid government and the state had parallels in France in particular. Attempts had been made to gather detailed social statistics in 1800–01 by the *Bureau de Statistique* working through local *intendents* who in turn relied upon local elites and savants to provide information. The result was a wonderful archive of diverse information about local landscapes, peoples, customs, festivals, dress and habits. But Napoleon Bonaparte closed the Bureau in 1811 because he needed different, more focused and uniform information for purposes of conscription, taxation and managing the war economy.[32] This is a good illustration of wider trends in statistical developments: a narrowing of interest to features which could more easily be categorised, quantified and compared with precision across time and space in the interests of state policy but often at the expense of variety, richness and accuracy.[33]

2.4 The Victorian statistical movement

The rise of an industrialised, urbanised and commercial society was accompanied by the urge to measure, to engineer and to control. The statistical urge came partly from anxiety about social change and instability. Apart from the various offices of government busy with the production of statistical data, there developed a large number of private and voluntary associations in London such as the Statistical Society of London, the Central Society of Education, the Health of Towns Association and the Society for the Diffusion of Useful Knowledge. A plethora of reform and statistical societies and associations also sprang up in provincial towns and cities. They often promoted local initiative as a counterweight to what was seen as central government interference and attendant high taxation. However, a widely held set of social attitudes and a common view of the needs and purposes of social reform underpinned these associations and much of the activity of the state. The statistical movement as a whole and the nature of data collected and classified in the nineteenth century whether by public or voluntary agencies shared a common purpose: to assist economic and social engineering and social reform.[34]

Historians have been bequeathed a great deal more quantitative information for the nineteenth century than for earlier periods, but there is little uniformity, standardisation or sophistication in the way in which information was gathered or initially processed from the raw data. Publications of the period give a flavour of the statistical urge, the interest in trifles and oddities and the sort of discipline and innovation with which statistics were collected and arranged. Figures 2.1 and 2.2 are extracts from *Mulhall's Dictionary of Statistics* (London, 1884) which reads like a mixture of the *Guiness Book of Records* and a railway timetable on 'speed'.

Much of the raw data and original evidence upon which such publications as Mulhall's was based have not survived, which means that the many printed summary figures and extracts cannot be checked. In addition, the social, political and economic preoccupations of nineteenth-century bureaucrats, civil servants and reformers conditioned and controlled the nature of the information gathered and of that left out. Even the very act of quantification itself, across the many areas of social and economic data, necessarily ignored the array of meanings and connotations which attached to things measured. As Nietzsche pronounced: 'The form of life epitomized by quantification depends on the art of forgetting'.[35] Thus the statistical legacy which the Victorian state and voluntary associations have left for historians is a patchy one and generally difficult to use for historians' purposes. As the

Source: Michael G. Mulhall FSS, *Mulhall's dictionary of statistics* (London, 1884), pp. 152–3.

F.—INCREASE IN FRANCE AND BELGIUM.

DIVORCES, PER 1000 MARRIAGES.

Period	France	Paris	Belgium	Brussels.
1826–30	1·1	4·0	1·0	4·1
1831–40	1·8	7·0	1·4	5·8
1841–50	3·8	9·9	1·4	6·6
1851–60	4·3	15·6	2·4	9·9
1861–70	5·6	22·9	2·9	11·2
1871–78	6·3	24·9	5·1	12·4

G.—DIVORCE AND SUICIDE COMPARED.

	Divorces, per 1000 Marriages.	Suicides, per 100,000 Inhab.		Divorces, per 1000 Marriages.	Suicides, per 100,000 Inhab.
Ireland	1	1·7	Germany	17	14·3
England	2	6·7	Denmark	30	28·2
Scotland	2	4·0	Switzerland	51	20·2
Russia	3	2·5	London	4	8·6
Italy	3	3·7	Berlin	10	17·0
Sweden	7	8·1	Brussels	14	27·1
Belgium	7	7·1	Vienna	23	28·7
Holland	8	9·6	Paris	25	42·2
France	9	15·6	Stockholm	28	35·4
Austria	10	9·6	Copenhagen	29	30·2

DOCKS.—Those of London comprise 690, those of Liverpool 543, those of Cardiff 113 acres.

COST IN MILLIONS £.

London	20 1	Antwerp.	6·5	Hull	1·2
Liverpool	18 2	Cherbourg	3·5	Bristol.	0·9
Glasgow	7·6	Holyhead	2·0	Dundee	0·8

The new docks at Hamburg will cost 5½ millions sterling. Dock-dues as a rule average 2 shillings a ton in European ports, the charges on a vessel of 1000 tons being as follows:—

Liverpool.	£133	Hamburg	£110	Amsterdam.	£81
London.	125	Antwerp	93	General average	100

The largest lock in the world is that of Cardiff, 600 feet long by 80 in width, ordinary depth of water 36 feet.

DOGS.

A.—DOGS OF ALL KINDS.

	Number Licensed.	Per 1000 Inhabitants.
Great Britain	1,128,000	38
Ireland	368,000	73
France	1,864,000	49
Germany	1,432,000	31

Sheep-dogs are not taxed in the United Kingdom, and the total number of dogs in the kingdom is at least 2,000,000, say 55 per 1000 inhabitants, worth £800,000. It is found that 100 male dogs go mad, as compared with 14 female. A dog accidentally locked up at Metz passed 39 days without food, and recovered.

B.—HUNTING-DOGS IN UNITED KINGDOM.

	England.	Ireland.	Scotland.	U. Kingdom.
Stag-hounds	604	246	...	850
Fox-hounds	12,866	1,522	660	15,048
Harriers	3,258	1,516	...	4,774
Beagles	448	...	74	522
Total	17,176	3,284	734	21,194

C.—TRAIN OF DOGS, IN DRAMS.

Sheep-dog	29·5	Retriever	25·7	Greyhound	23·4
Fox-hound	29·2	Collie	25·4	Terrier	20·0
Setter	26·1	Bull-dog	24·0	Spaniel	18·1
Mastiff	26·1	Newfoundland	24·0	Lap-dog	18·0

As compared with the above, the wolf has 42, the jackal 15, the fox 13 drams.

DRAINAGE.—Subsoil drainage in England costs on an average £5 per acre, and produces 5 bushels more wheat, say 20 per cent. extra. Reclaiming land in Scotland costs about £17 per acre.

For drainage of towns, see *Sewers.*

DRINK.

A.—CONSUMPTION IN UNITED KINGDOM.

MILLIONS OF GALLONS.

Year.	Beer.	Spirits.	Wine.	Equivalent in Alcohol.
1840	640	25·7	6·5	44·3
1860	770	27·2	7·5	49·9
1871	980	33·6	16·1	63·9
1881	1,007	37·0	15·6	67·2

B.—CONSUMPTION PER INHABITANT.

GALLONS.

Year.	Beer.	Spirits.	Wine.	Equivalent in Alcohol.
1840	24·2	0·97	0·25	1·64
1860	26·5	0·93	0·26	1·72
1871	30·6	1·06	0·51	2·02
1881	28·6	1·05	0·44	1·92

Fig. 2.1 Divorce, docks, dogs, drainage and drink: a page from *Mulhall's dictionary*, 1884.

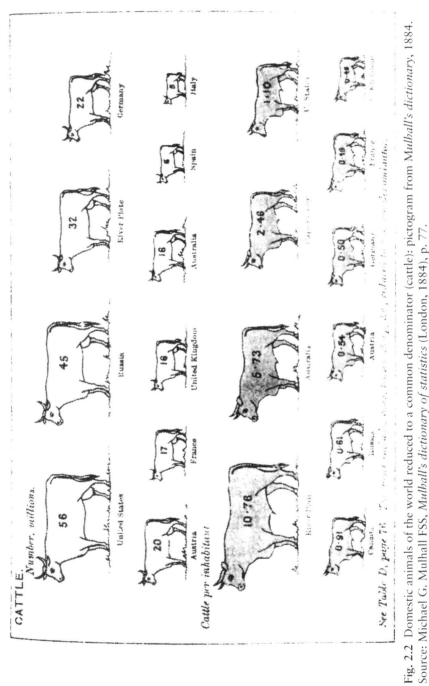

Fig. 2.2 Domestic animals of the world reduced to a common denominator (cattle): pictogram from *Mulhall's dictionary*, 1884.
Source: Michael G. Mulhall FSS, *Mulhall's dictionary of statistics* (London, 1884), p. 77.

techniques of statistical analysis remained very primitive until the late nineteenth century, it was relatively easy for interested parties to manipulate the figures to fit particular opinions or predispositions and it is these statements (in parliamentary papers and in other contemporary accounts), backed by a selection of the quantitative evidence, which have most often survived.[36] One of the major biases of statistics gathered at this time came from the tendency amongst reformers to vindicate industrial progress by blaming social problems on other causes such as the growth of cities, alcohol consumption, the moral weakness of the poor or the evils of Anglicanism.[37]

The Board of Trade, for example, under its first director, the businessman G. R. Porter, was charged with gathering and analysing information on the trade, manufactures and economic distress of provincial England: a reaction to the commercial and social dislocation which characterised the 1830s and 1840s. But local chambers of commerce were unable (and sometimes unwilling) to provide comprehensive or consistent information, and Porter was forced to rely upon his contacts amongst merchants and manufacturers and other 'well-informed gentlemen' and upon work done in similar vein already by the London Statistical Society.[38] Furthermore, his brief was too disparate: it cast wide to include criminal statistics, police figures and hospital returns, and there was little understanding of the value or potential of analysis and display of the figures in the form of graphs and charts. The result was a vast mass of often impenetrable, inconsistent, partial and biased numerical information of which best use was never made in the nineteenth century and with which historians still struggle.

By 1846 the General Register Office cost £73 000 a year and employed 80 staff centrally with a further 2800 local registrars.[39] This was big bureaucracy by nineteenth-century standards. William Farr was in charge of the Office and of organising and planning the census from 1851, which was the first to include a welter of occupational and social questions. Farr's personal preoccupation with mortality and diseases, sanitary reform and improvements in occupational health drove a great deal of the statistical analysis undertaken by the Office and also determined the structure and nature of the questions framed in the census schedules and the priorities absorbed by the enumerators responsible for ensuring 'accurate' returns. Farr's work from the 1840s anticipated later developments as it included 'statistically controlled experiments' designed to enable him to separate out the influences of sex, location, climate and occupation upon epidemics and mortality rates. He was also interested in the age of marriage and rate of remarriage and in the production of new life tables. Because of this the late nineteenth-century censuses have been generally of more use and interest to demographic and medical historians than to historians interested in the family economy or the nature of work and employment of men and women, as the information on these is patchy and very unreliable, especially for women.[40]

Farr represented a much wider nineteenth-century obsession with health which made itself felt in major collections of statistical information, from the heights and weights of members of the armed forces and transported convicts to local and large-scale surveys of urban disease and living conditions. These have subsequently informed the history of medicine as well as demographic research. At the time, however, the figures were often collected and used specifically to confirm contemporary prejudices and beliefs, such as the miasmic theory of disease transmission, and to condemn the sorts of 'thoughtless extravagance' and 'ignorance of domestic economy' which were widely thought to lie behind the high disease and death rates of the urban working classes. Historians have to be aware and make allowances for the ways in which bias and purpose enter into the evidence which they are forced to use. Chadwick's important surveys of urban conditions fit this pattern. Assisted in the provinces by Southwood Smith, Neil Arnott and J. P. Kay, Chadwick highlighted the 'condition of England question' which was seen to lie primarily in the improvidence of the poor. His analysis was a mixture of moralism and environmentalism, seen in different mixes in the work of many of his contemporaries, especially those considering the health of towns. W. H. Duncan on Liverpool, J. Clay on Preston, Thomas Laycock on York and Lionel Playfair on Lancashire: all stressed the moral and spiritual as well as the environmental causes of ill health, including depraved domestic habits, improvidence and the abuse of alcohol and opiates. The term 'moral statistics' was widely used in the first two thirds of the nineteenth century, highlighting the moral preoccupations of the Victorian statistical movement, preoccupations which ran through the collection and interpretation of figures on crime, education and religion as much as they did through the statistics of health.[41] Michelle Perrot has characterised the French moral statisticians of the time as bourgeois reformers, seeking to control deviant behaviour of all sorts by using the power of numbers.[42]

2.5 Statistical theory

The late nineteenth and early twentieth century saw not just the continued collection of masses of socially constructed and socially interpreted quantitative data but also witnessed major developments in statistical theory and analysis which, with relatively minor refinements, are still the central elements in statistics to this day. Understanding how and why these new techniques arose is interesting in itself but it is also important in illustrating that statistical and other 'scientific' procedures cannot be seen as separate from the environment in which they were formed and the purposes which they were geared to serve.

By the mid-nineteenth century there was growing recognition of the regularities which were emerging in social data. In his opening address to the Royal Statistical Society, published in 1860, Nassau Senior (who had been instrumental in investigating and transforming the Poor Law in 1834) suggested that 'the human will obeys laws nearly as certain as those which regulate matter'.[43] The most influential thinker to pursue a numerical social *science* which stressed the regularities and periodicities to be found in social data, and the use of probability theory in understanding these, was the astronomer Adolphe Quetelet.[44] He drew parallels between statistics and astronomy and studied aggregated phenomena such as mortality, crime and suicide. He saw statistical regularity as providing the key to social science and promoted the 'law of large numbers' which implied that general effects in society are always produced by general causes, accidental or chance factors having no influence when a mass are considered collectively. His most celebrated construct was *L'homme moyen*, or average man, an abstract being who exhibited all human attributes in a given country. Quetelet's belief that statistical laws can prevail for a mass even when the constituent individuals are too numerous or too inscrutable for their actions to be understood individually became the foundation of much later social science theory, especially in economics, and was also important in influencing ideas in the natural sciences.

In history it was most immediately taken up in the work of Henry Thomas Buckle, who denounced the mediocre presentation of chronicles of kings and battles and aimed to inject some science, order, symmetry and law into history. Marx used Quetelet's notion of the average man in defining the labour theory of value, and, most notably, Emile Durkheim used the statistical ideas of Quetelet and others in his research on suicide. In *Suicide* (1897), the first great sociological work based upon quantification, Durkheim used statistics to show that individuals were dominated by collective impulses which could not be reduced to the particular circumstances which individuals cite to rationalise their deeds.[45]

During the late nineteenth century confidence in the value and reliability of statistical laws spread from the social to the physical and biological sciences, and the analogies and similes of social science were used frequently in thermodynamics and heredity. Approaches in these disciplines were united by the idea that the greatest variability and chaos at one level was consistent with remarkable stability at the aggregate level which manifested itself in the statistical laws of large numbers. The development of statistical procedures for dealing with aggregated phenomena which came to dominate the field for a century in the natural and social sciences was associated with the work of three men in particular: Francis Galton (1822–1911), Karl Pearson (1857–1936) and R. A. Fisher (1890–1962). Galton was a cousin of Charles Darwin; he invented correlation and regression analysis, providing the major breakthrough which enabled the simultaneous analysis of more than one variable. Pearson, a Fabian socialist and atheist, developed and systematised Galton's insights, gave his name to the product moment coefficient of correlation, produced the chi-squared (χ^2) distribution and founded the biometric school (more will be said about these various techniques later in this book). His son Egon Pearson continued this role as he also continued the friction which had developed over method between his father and

Ronald Fisher. Fisher reshaped the basis of statistical theorising by systematising the analysis of variance and by creating tests to indicate the significance of research results based on evidence from discrete experiments or samples. He was actively involved in agricultural and biological experiments.

All three, despite their different orientations, were eugenicists. They were from a much wider body of influential scientists and politicians and other professionals of the time who claimed that the most important biological characteristics, including human traits such as mental ability, were inherited and that ancestry rather than environment or mutation was the crucial variable in determining both intelligence and behaviour. It is possible that moral statistics was an influence in this line of argument but the conclusions drawn went beyond the moral condemnations of Chadwick and others to suggest that the only long-term way to solve the problems of an expanding commercial society was to improve the bloodstock to ensure that those with good characteristics (the fit) had more children than those with bad characteristics (the unfit). At the root of this was the view that the urban poor were morally degenerate as well as dangerous. Natural selection had failed to root them out because of the intervention of charity, medicine and sanitary reform. This body of ideas became notorious and controversial in the twentieth century, in large part, but not solely, because of the racial and ethnic policies of the Nazi Party in Germany, which relied heavily upon eugenicist ideas.[46] Debates about race, class and intelligence quotient (IQ) continue to spark vitriolic debate, especially where supported by quantitative data.[47]

The racial and class assumptions of eugenics were deeply embedded in late nineteenth-century social and scientific ideas, particularly amongst the professional middle class, in law, medicine and academic life. Karl Pearson, for example, was elected to the new Chair in Eugenics at University College, London, in 1911. The manipulation of numbers in seemingly objective scientific enquiry assisted in placing eugenics in a respectable light and indicates how dangerous numbers can be unless their use is policed and questioned by people unafraid to get involved in disputes over seemingly uncontrovertible, scientific evidence. Galton and Pearson developed statistical theory to apply to their eugenics research for studies of twins, correlations of intelligence between relatives, measures of hereditability and racial inferiority. It has been argued, particularly by Donald A. Mackenzie, that eugenics not only motivated their statistical work but also affected both its content and its methods. The shape of the science they developed was partially determined by eugenic objectives, and these objectives also determined new ways of collecting and storing data.[48] Because their central concern was with the impact of characteristics of one generation on the next, the statistical dependence of human variables (height, intelligence or whatever) were central to their research. For example, Pearson's work on statistical association clashed with his former pupil Yule's approach to this subject largely because of Pearson's commitment to eugenic research. Pearson's need for the measurability of associations between variables which might be inherited differed from Yule's desire merely to indicate whether there was any indication of an association or not.[49]

There was a bitter personal controversy between Pearson and Fisher. Unlike Pearson, the much more conservative Fisher believed that heredibility of characteristics was entirely a result of genetics and that this vindicated the rigour of a statistical, probability-based approach to the subject, termed 'biometric eugenics'.[50] Arguably, the most important element of statistical theory developed by Fisher was in relation to statistical inference, that is, the ability to infer from the known and the examined to the unknown and the unexamined. The most widely employed idea concerning statistical inference before Fisher had been Bayes's theorem, known as the method of inverse probability. Bayes's theorem had suggested that we should change our belief in a theory in the light of new evidence and its effects on the probability that an initial idea was correct. The main problem for Fisher and others was that prior probabilities and existing beliefs in relationships or theories varied from person to person and were hard to pin down. This struck at the heart of the scientific community's fear of subjectivity. Fisher claimed to provide an objective alternative. In his view, the accuracy of a scientific finding should be judged in relation to the probability of getting results at least as impressive as those obtained assuming they had occurred entirely by chance. A probability value, P, of 0.05 (i.e. 1 in 20), was arbitrarily accepted as reasonable, and this probability has assumed enormous importance in statistical inference ever since even though it has been argued that the technique 'routinely exaggerates the size and significance of implausible findings'.[51] Whereas Bayes's theorem took account of context, prior knowledge and plausibility, Fisher's test has no means of taking subjective elements, including plausibility, into account. Yet it is still Fisher's test which is dominant today in this field.[52] It has been modified by researchers to include confidence intervals (i.e. likely ranges of error in the results), but this still does not factor in plausibility. This underlines the fact that statistical tests should be undertaken when and only when there is a highly plausible reason for doing so (based on experience and prior knowledge) and that statistical significance should *never* be equated with substantive or real significance.

The drive to quantify and record so many aspects of economic and social life in the nineteenth and twentieth centuries – to know and thus to control society as well as the natural and physical world – was reflected in the nature of economics and sociology as they emerged as academic subjects in the late nineteenth and early twentieth century. It predisposed them, from the outset, to use quantitative methods. In history, however, much less emphasis was placed upon statistical and mathematical analysis, outside of economic history, until well into the twentieth century. This is because quantification, from its inception, has been closely associated with a particular understanding about knowledge and its construction – positivism – which suited social science, economics and social policy orientations far better than history.

2.6 Positivism

Positivism assumes that the only true knowledge is scientific knowledge which describes and explains observable phenomena. The assumption behind positivism is the possibility of a neutral and meticulous observation of facts which eventually reveals regularities and even laws of behaviour. In the nineteenth century the dominant belief within the scientific and intellectual community was that close observation of the recorded facts would lead, by a process of induction, to an understanding of 'laws' about the workings of the economy, society and historical development, in the same was as such observation in the natural sciences. The approach of Darwin's *The origin of species* could be followed in the study of human social evolution. The idea was that scientists of society, like those of physics or chemistry, approached their task without preconceptions or moral involvement, gathered evidence neutrally, applied rules and criteria to interpret the evidence and drew their conclusions from this. Through study and induction the idea was that positive knowledge of social phenomena would provide the basis for scientifically-grounded intervention in economic and social affairs to the benefit of society as a whole. The positivist desire for quantification had such power because of the widely shared social ambitions for science.

Nowadays scientific knowledge is seen less as the build up of some all-encompassing body of realist and objective knowledge than of the rise and decline of successive ways of theorising about the physical world (the rise and decline of paradigms of thought). It is also regarded as the study of probabilities rather than of laws or absolute truths. This is partly because of the influence of statistical approaches in both natural science and social science. The meaning of objectivity has shifted at the same time. It is now uncommon to believe that objectivity can be identified with 'truth' or knowledge congruent with the real. Instead, objectivity is applied to knowledge which meets criteria of validity and reliability that are held to be as free from bias as possible. It indicates the avoidance of subjectivity by following 'impartial' rules of measurement, observation and experiment. This is in no sense unrelated to the disciplines of quantification and statistics. Karl Pearson was the type of positivist who argued that there is no knowable thing in itself underlying our perceptions, and that perceptions provide the whole basis of knowledge. But for him and for others this made the rigour and objectivity of testing perceptions for their accuracy all the more important. Statistics and statistical theory gained ground and became a prominent discourse in many fields of enquiry not despite the shift from belief in underlying truths but because of it.

The notion that there is an internal logic of scientific development un-affected by its social context may have been popular in the nineteenth century but it is now regarded with great scepticism. Similarly in history there is now greater recognition of historical relativism: the acceptance that historians are deeply influenced by their own culture and environment and that this fundamentally conditions the history which they write. Thus, it is generally acknowledged that all history is to a greater or lesser extent contemporary history in that it reflects the views and interests of contempo-rary writers as much if not more than it tells us about the past. History is researched and written through the eyes, the preoccupations and the language of later periods. Despite or because of these changes in perspective there is still a great deal of friction amongst historians and social scientists about the degree to which they are involved in a scientific methodology, and this friction has increased in recent years with the growing influence of postmodernism, post-structuralism and an emphasis upon language and discourse as the beginning and the end point of knowledge. Some social scientists and historians now claim that we have left behind the old modernist certainties of building up a knowledge of social life, past or present, from our attempted observations of 'reality'. Instead they empha-sise the role of ideas and discourse in creating knowledge and deny any direct relationship between knowledge and reality.[53]

The association of quantitative approaches with positivistic scientific enquiry and with attempts to mould society along particular lines has made them a brunt of postmodern condemnation. For postmodern critics, numbers represent the cutting edge of modernity. Numbers have been seen as acting on people and exercising power over them particularly through the creation of statistically verifiable behavioural norms against which an oppressive category of abnormality is created.[54] Yet this is perhaps unfair, because quantification shares with other 'languages' many of the same characteristics in helping to create the society it purports to describe or to mediate. Other languages also share, with quantification, the production of oppressive categories which promote or extol individuals or behaviours by condemning their opposites. The fact that quantification appears, and is promoted as, more objective and more rigorous in its hold on reality than qualitative accounts, and that it is potentially more hegemonic across time and space than other languages, are dangers and call for vigilance. But these should not blind us to problems which occur with other approaches to history. The force of linguistic structures, manners of delivery, rhetoric, style and narrative need similar evaluation, care and reflexivity. One could argue that words carry subtleties of connotation and context and fertile ambigui-ties which allow one to communicate more effectively than in numbers. But what words gain in flexibility they lose *vis-à-vis* numbers in 'precision'. Both carry problems and a mix of the two appears desirable. Unfortunately, we are too often presented with a mutually exclusive choice between words and numbers (qualitative and quantitative) as if each represents an entirely different approach to knowledge. As Giddens has argued 'all quantitative data, when scrutinised, turn out to be composites of "qualitative" . . . interpretations, produced by situated researchers, coders, government officials and others'.[55] The problems which quantification shares with other discourses is one of degree rather than kind. As Porter states, 'the credibility of numbers, like the credibility of knowledge in any form, is a social and moral problem'.[56]

2.7 Objectivity and prejudice

Objectivity and the desirability of objectivity are a key to understanding what numbers and their disciplined application have in common with words within a linguistic structure. The term 'objectivity' is sometimes understood to refer to accounts of the external world which are held to represent the world as it exists independently of our conceptions. But a much more frequent usage is in reference to knowledge claimed to meet criteria of validity and reliability and held to be free from bias. As few intellectuals these days would subscribe to the view that objectivity means truth or an unclouded appreciation of reality, the second meaning (mechanical objectivity) is the one which should concern us here, and it is largely its use in this sense which has driven quantifiers in their endeavours and which has helped to secure the authority both of science and of numbers. In this sense 'objectivity' means personal restraint and the following of rules. This encapsulates the way in which statistical methodology has evolved, particularly amongst its positivist practitioners and pioneers in the late nineteenth and early twentieth centuries. Pearson, for example, was wedded to the subordination of personal interests and prejudices to public standards and to the moral training and self denial which this involved. He believed that mathematical statistics should be the language of reasoning in all areas of human activity, especially in government, which he believed had for so long been in the hands of scientifically illiterate aristocrats. Pearson's goal, and one which he saw as more important than any idea of objectivity as truth, was the spread to all aspects of life of an ordered method of investigation and the taming of individual subjectivity and bias in the interests of society. This attitude can be seen pervading the growth of quantification in the nineteenth and twentieth centuries. Often the accuracy of observations, which might employ experience and intuition, have been subordinated to the need for comparability, a common set of categories of analysis, a common language and comparability of results.

    This background helps one to understand both the advantages of quantification and why there has been, and still is, so much bad feeling between the more rigorous exponents of quantitative history and those who condemn much of the work done in this area. The clash over quantification can be seen as philosophical as well as practical, covering the nature of history as well as of appropriate research techniques. But antipathies are also fuelled by mutual misunderstandings, ignorance and prejudice. Quantitative history in itself need be no less nor no more positivistic or scientific than an analysis based on qualitative data. Indeed the two approaches are by no means as methodologically separate or distinctive as much debate has made them out to be. In opposing exchanges between those who support and those who deride quantification in history it is frequently the case that each side creates a caricature of the other. In particular, those opposing quantification too often imply that all quantitative history (where it is not pure mystification) is an attempt to impose an inappropriate scientific methodology upon the analysis of complex human behaviour in the past: to force evidence into classificatory straightjackets which allow too little for diversity or unpredictability. Alternatively, it is claimed that the statistical techniques themselves are so imbued with the values and prejudices of those who were responsible for creating them that they are of little use in wider contexts. But it would be a mistake to think that theories and techniques of statistics are any more tainted in this way than other sorts of theories, ideas and concepts used in social study. In fact, some recent thawing of the qualitative–quantitative conflict in the social sciences owes much to discussion of the reflexive, subjective and normative nature of qualitative approaches and of the problems inherent in language and linguistic structures which circumscribe and define what is said, written and thought. Whether we communicate with each other in words or in numbers or in a mixture of the two, many of the problems are the same. The so called 'linguistic turn' which has involved historians looking closely at the values, beliefs, assumptions and categories embedded in the language of documents and the language used by historians has a counterpart in an older critique of quantification and its power to restrict understanding by narrowing the scope of discourse to things neatly and subjectively categorised and enumerated.

Many statistical applications are a useful aid to display or to summarise facts relevant to an argument. They are often used alongside other sorts of approaches in which qualitative evidence is used and are no more scientific or positivistic for being numerical than would be a descriptive section of prose used in the same context. At the opposite extreme the application of a model of human behaviour to the past and the empirical testing of such a model would constitute a 'scientific' methodology whether or not the model and its testing were framed in quantitative terms. More often than not, social science models, especially those derived from economics, do involve numerical analysis, hence the common but often mistaken identification of positivistic scientific approaches with quantification. But the debate about whether history can be regarded as a (social) science is not the same as that concerning the advantages or otherwise of quantitative and non-quantitative history. Although some quantitative historians make extreme claims to greater objectivity and analytical rigour than can be possible with other techniques, this is not necessarily a hallmark of quantification in itself.

Conclusion

From this chapter we have learned about the rise of data collection, quantitative thinking and analysis and we have considered the close connection between these and the goals and assumptions of their creators and the worlds in which they lived. We have learned that quantification is not only concerned with describing the world but also with engineering it in particular ways. But qualitative approaches are not intrinsically superior in this respect because, like quantification, they also use socially constructed categories and rules of communication. Qualitative approaches may be less precise and more multivalent than quantitative approaches but neither has an intrinsically superior claim to distance from the predispositions and beliefs of their creators despite their protestations to the contrary.

There are no easy answers these days to the question 'What is history?' But, in their efforts to understand the past, historians are not helped by a polarisation of opinion about quantitative and non-quantitative methods. There is a wide spectrum of quantitative evidence, and many useful, often simple, techniques which can be used in historical research, providing one remains aware of the pitfalls and biases of the evidence. There is a similar spectrum of sources, concepts, theories, methods and pitfalls which underpin qualitative history. Each piece of research, whether relying heavily on numbers or not, must be judged on its own merits: by the consistency and cogency of arguments in relation to a critical use of the available evidence. A critical approach to the social construction of evidence and 'knowledge' and a reflexive attitude on the part of the historian are essential whether we are considering quantitative or qualitative history. But this involves leaving behind what has become a rather sterile and unhelpful debate about the inherent superiority of one approach over the other.

Notes

1 T. M. Porter, 'Making things quantitative', *Science in Context*, 7, 3 (1994), pp. 389, 404.
2 This chapter is largely free of statistical terminology. If necessary, use the glossary, and if any parts of the argument of this chapter appear unclear at this point do not worry as they will be more fully explained in subsequent sections of the book which deal with specific techniques of quantitative investigation.
3 National variations in the pace and degree of development of statistical concerns in relation to practical problems of state, of economic and social reform, national intellectual cultures, and the development of different academic subjects from physics and astronomy to eugenics, geography and economics is a fascinating subject and explored to some degree in T. M. Porter, *The rise of statistical*

thinking, 1820–1900 (Princeton, NJ, 1986); T. M. Porter, *Trust in numbers: the pursuit of objectivity in science and public life* (Princeton, NJ, 1995), especially Part 3. For the British experience, see J. R. N. Stone, *Some British empiricists in the social sciences, 1650–1900* (Cambridge, 1997); M. J. Cullen, *The statistical movement in early Victorian Britain: the foundations of empirical social research* (Sussex, 1975), and D. A. Mackenzie, *Statistics in Britain, 1865–1930: the social construction of scientific knowledge* (Edinburgh, 1981). For Italian developments see S. Patriarca, *Numbers and nationhood: writing statistics in nineteenth-century Italy* (Cambridge, 1996).

4 Cullen, *The statistical movement in early Victorian Britain* (1975), pp. 1–16.

5 P. Deane, 'Political arithmetic', in J., Eatwell, M. Milgate, and P. Newman (eds), *The new Palgrave: a dictionary of economics*, 4 volumes (1987), pp. 990–3. There were strong authoritarian undertones in this. Petty, for example, proposed that, because the value of an English life could be calculated as far surpassing that of an Irish life, the wealth of Britain would be augmented by forcibly transporting all Irish men, except a few cowherds, to England. W. Petty, 'A treatise on Ireland'(1687), in C. H. Hull (ed.), *The economic writings of Sir William Petty together with the observations on the Bills of mortality more probably by Captain John Graunt* (Cambridge, 1899), vol. 2, p. 554.

6 Q. Skinner, 'History and ideology in the English revolution', *Historical Journal*, 8 (1965), pp. 171, 129; Q. Skinner, 'Thomas Hobbes and his disciples in England and France', *Comparative Studies in Society and History*, 8 (1965–6), pp. 153–67; Porter, *The rise of statistical thinking* (1986), p. 19.

7 William Petty, *Political arithmetic*, preface in C. H. Hull (ed.), *The economic writings of Sir William Petty*, 2 volumes (Cambridge, 1899), vol. 1, p. 244.

8 Whether Graunt or Petty wrote this work is a matter of some dispute: see Cullen, *The statistical movement in early Victorian Britain* (1975), p 2.

9 This and the later version of Malthus's essay are included in E. A. Wrigley, and D. Souden (eds), *The works of Thomas Robert Malthus*, 8 vols (London, 1986). For commentary on the early development of demographic statistics, see D. V. Glass, *Numbering the people: the eighteenth-century population controversy and the development of census and vital statistics in Britain* (Farnborough, 1973).

10 This was the dominant definition of political arithmetic in the eighteenth century. C. Davenant, *The political and commercial works* (1771), vol. 1, p. 128, quoted by J. Hoppit, 'Political arithmetic in eighteenth-century England', *Economic History Review*, 49, 3 (1996), pp. 516–40.

11 Hoppit, 'Political arithmetic in eighteenth-century England' (1996), pp. 516–40; The philosophy of algebraic analysis was also gaining ground in these fields. See W. J. Ashworth, 'Memory, efficiency, and symbolic analysis. Charles Babbage, John Herschel and the industrial mind', *ISIS*, 87, 4 (1996), pp. 629–53.

12 This was a protracted business – a struggle between scientific ideals and administrative practicalities: J. Hoppit, 'Reforming Britain's weights and measures, 1660–1824', *English Historical Review*, 1 (1993), pp. 82–104. It met with considerable opposition, see, for example, R. Sheldon, A. Randall, A. Charlesworth and D. Walsh, 'Popular protest and the persistence of the customary corn measures: resistance to the Winchester Bushel in the English West', in A. Randall, and A. Charlesworth (eds), *Markets, market culture and popular protest in eighteenth-century Britain and Ireland* (Liverpool, 1996), pp. 25–45. The French Revolution gave a stimulus to similar advances in unifying weights and measures on the continent, but the process in France alone took over 40 years: Ken Alder, 'A revolution to measure: the political economy of the metric system in France', in M. Norton Wise (ed.), *The values of precision* (Princeton, NJ, 1995), 39–71. Kula has linked moves to unify measures with political revolutions more generally, stressing the connection between metrolog-

ical and juridical equality. In China and Russia as well as France moves to unify measurement helped to shift the economies away from an order based on privilege to one based on law, which had the added advantage of greater efficiency in administration and taxation: W. Kula, *Measures and men* (Princeton, NJ, 1986).

13 Hoppit, 'Political arithmetic in eighteenth-century England' (1996); Cullen, *The statistical movement in early Victorian Britain* (1975); Porter, *Trust in numbers* (1995), pp. viii–ix.

14 Cullen, *The statistical movement in early Victorian Britain* (1975), p. 7. The links between astronomy (both as inspiration and training) and statistical and model-building ideas applied to social phenomena were very strong. Most major quantitative social theorists of the period either started out as astronomers or were involved with astronomy, most notably Adolphe Quetelet. See W. J. Ashworth, 'The calculating eye: Baily, Herschel, Babbage and the business of astronomy', *British Journal of Historical Studies*, 27 (1994), pp. 409–41. Life tables were named after places in just the same way as astronomical tables were named after constellations.

15 Cullen, *The statistical movement in early Victorian Britain* (1975), p. 8.

16 Bayes's work was published in 1763 (two years after his death). Unfortunately, his ideas proved less powerful for much of the twentieth century than those of his successors (as we shall see) even though some would argue that Bayes's theorem is a more sophisticated way of gauging the significance of experimental results. R. Matthews, 'Flukes and flaws', *Prospect* (November 1998), pp. 20–24. For the history of probability theory, see T. M. Porter, *The rise of statistical thinking 1820–1900* (1986), but, more particularly, see I. Todhunter, *A history of the mathematical theory of probability* (New York, 1949), Ian Hacking, *The taming of chance* (Cambridge, 1990), and L. Daston, *Classical probability in the enlightenment* (Princeton, NJ, 1988).

17 Daston, *Classical probability in the enlightenment* (1988); Hacking, *The taming of chance* (1990).

18 J. F. Von Bielfeld, *The elements of universal erudition* (translated by W. Hooper) 3 vols (London, 1770); Cullen, *The statistical movement in early Victorian Britain* (1975), p. 10.

19 Bielfeld, *The elements of universal erudition* (1770), p. 269, quoted by Cullen, p. 10.

20 Cullen, *The statistical movement in early Victorian Britain* (1975), p. 10.

21 Sir John Sinclair, *The statistical account of Scotland*, vol. XX (Edinburgh, 1798), p. xix n.

22 *Encyclopedia Britannica*, 3rd edn (Edinburgh 1797), vol. XII, p. 731, quoted by Cullen, *The statistical movement in early Victorian Britain* (1975), pp. 10–11.

23 Porter, *The rise of statistical thinking* (1986), p. 24.

24 Cullen, *The statistical movement in early Victorian Britain* (1975), p. 11, referring to William Playfair, *The statistical breviary* (London, 1801), p. 4.

25 Cullen, *The statistical movement in early Victorian Britain* (1975), p. 11, quoting from W. T. Brande (ed.), *A dictionary of science, literature and art* (London, 1842), p. 1150.

26 A phrase used by T. M. Porter, 'Making things quantitative', *Science in Context*, 7, 3 (1994), p. 397. By this time a shift had also occurred in statistical method which became wrapped up in the meaning of statistics itself as the study of 'laws' of error and variation in large numbers. See also Mackenzie, *Statistics in Britain* (1981), p. 8 *ff*.

27 Cullen, *The statistical movement in early Victorian Britain* (1975), p. 11.

28 Cullen, *The statistical movement in early Victorian Britain* (1975), p. 14.

29 Rickman's death and the establishment of the General Register Office in 1837 meant that categories in the 1841 Census, and, gradually, in those thereafter,

became more detailed and clearly defined. Interestingly, Rickman's conclusions about the timing of population change in the eighteenth century, based on the clerical data he had requested, have not been seriously undermined by later more sophisticated work. D. V. Glass, 'Some aspects of the development of demography', *Journal of the Royal Society of Arts*, 104 (1955–6), pp. 854–69; E. A. Wrigley and R. S. Schofield, *The population history of England and Wales, 1541–1871* (Cambridge, 1981).

30 Census night was introduced in 1841 by Lister. E. Higgs, *Making sense of the census* (London, 1989), p. 9.

31 Milne developed the Carlisle tables of mortality which were thereafter often used in preference to the Northampton tables, though the Select Committee on Laws respecting Friendly Societies (III, 1826–7, p. 11) still thought fit to call for more accurate and extensive collections of facts for the construction of such tables.

32 Porter, *Trust in numbers* (1995), p. 36.

33 M. Norton Wise (ed.), *The values of precision* (1995), introduction.

34 Cullen, *The statistical movement in early Victorian Britain* (1975), pp. 135–49; cf. Porter, *The rise of statistical thinking*, (1986), pp. 23–39.

35 Nietzsche, quoted by Porter, in 'Making things quantitative' (1994), p. 396.

36 The tendency to destroy the original quantitative data once they have been processed, summarised or analysed is not unique to the nineteenth century. Materials from twentieth-century social surveys and questionnaires have often similarly been discarded. This is indicative of both carelessness and an embedded idea that data collection is done for one purpose only and cannot or should not be re-analysed later for asking different questions or for use with other techniques. An exception to the general story of destruction of original raw data is the 1929–31 New London Survey which has been computerised, is deposited at the Economic and Social Research Council Date Archive (no. SN 3758) and is now providing research material for a number of British economic and social historians. See, for example, D. Baines and P. Johnson, 'In search of the "traditional" working class: social mobility and occupational continuity in inter-war London', *Economic History Review*, 52, 4 (1999), pp. 692–713.

37 Cullen, *The statistical movement in early Victorian Britain* (1975), p. 144 and *passim*. Tirades against Anglicanism were not characteristic of the statistical movement generally but were prominent in the influential work of G. R. Porter at the Board of Trade. Porter, *The rise of statistical thinking* (1986), p. 34.

38 Cullen, *The statistical movement in early Victorian Britain* (1975), chapter 1.

39 Cullen, *The statistical movement in early Victorian Britain* (1975), chapter 2.

40 Cullen, *The statistical movement in early Victorian Britain* (1975), chapter 2; E. Higgs, 'Women, occupations and work in the nineteenth-century census' *History Workshop Journal*, 23 (1987), pp. 59–80. For suggested corrections to the female participation rate figures, see J. Humphries, 'Women and work', in J. Purvis, (ed.), *Women's history, 1850–1914: an introduction* (London, 1995), pp. 85–105.

41 Crime rates, suicide rates and rates of ill health did, however, gradually contribute to an acknowledgement that these were features of society and not solely reflective of individual failings; Cullen, *The statistical movement in early Victorian Britain* (1975), chapters 4 and 5. Such figures were used enthusiastically by late nineteenth-century social reformers, Fabian socialists and early collectivists, and figure importantly in the origins of social work as a profession.

42 Michelle Perrot, 'Premières measures des faits sociaux: les débuts de la statistique criminelle en France (1790–1830)', in *Pour une histoire*, cited by Porter, *The rise of statistical thinking* (1986), p. 30.

43 Nassau W. Senior, Opening address, *Journal of the Royal Statistical Society*, 23, (1860), p. 359, quoted in Porter, *The rise of statistical thinking*, p. 57.

44 The best discussion of Quetelet appears in A. Desrosières, *The politics of large numbers* (Cambridge, MA, 1998). See also Porter, *The rise of statistical thinking*, pp. 41–50.

45 Porter, *The rise of statistical thinking* (1986), pp. 60–69. See also A. Desrosières, *The politics of large numbers*, pp. 186–7, 95–101.

46 Such beliefs were prevalent throughout Europe even after the Second World War and influenced social and health programmes in many countries. A policy of sterilising the 'unfit' and conducting medical experiments on the mentally ill was, for example, followed in Sweden as recently as the 1950s and 1960s under the Social Democratic Party.

47 See S. J. Gould, *The mismeasure of man* (Harmondsworth, 1981).

48 Mackenzie probably overplays this analysis a bit as his commitment to the social construction of knowledge is rather mechanistic. D. A. Mackenzie, *Statistics in Britain, 1865–1930: the social construction of scientific knowledge* (Edinburgh, 1981).

49 Pearson was committed to correlation and regression so that the degree of association between variables, especially hereditability, could be predicted in populations yet to be measured. For correlation and regression see Chapter 6; for discussion of this, see Mackenzie, *Statistics in Britain* (1981), especially chapter 7: 'The politics of the contingency table'. Here, Mackenzie argues that the desire for precise predictability led Pearson to extend the theory of correlation from interval variables such as height and IQ measures to nominal variables such as eye and hair colour. This is how the Pearson correlation coefficient came to be developed and accepted.

50 This belief was termed Mendelism after Gregor Mendel (1822–84). Mendel was an Austrian monk who observed the changes produced in successive generations of pea plants by cross-fertilising plants with different characteristics. Fisher continued these sorts of experiments and was resolutely set against attaching importance to mutationism or 'random drift' in evolution. Mackenzie, *Statistics in Britain* (1981), p. 191. Fisher argued in the 1930s that clergymen's stipends should be varied according to their fertility in order to ensure reproduction of the best genes for service of the Church.

51 Why did Fisher set 0.05 as the crucial dividing line for significance? Apparently for no other reason than that it was 'convenient'. See Robert Matthews, 'Flukes and flaws', *Prospect* (November 1998). Acceptance of the 0.05 significance level is geared to setting a uniform standard so that results can be compared. Acceptance did not imply setting any sort of absolute standard regarding the importance and reliability of results, but this is often forgotten.

52 There has been a growing popularity of the Bayesian alternative in recent years in many disciplines. One example is in carbon dating in archaeology, where Bayesian techniques have recently been advanced by Dr Caitlin Buck of Cardiff University (web address:http://bcal.cf.ac.uk). Interestingly, because of the complex calculations involved in Bayesian reasoning, it is only with the advent of computer-assisted calculation that the extension of the technique has been possible.

53 The growth of historical relativism is usually associated with the ideas of the Italian philosopher Bernedetto Croce in the 1920s. Extreme relativism is associated with postmodernism, and particularly with the writings of Hayden White. White cites Croce as a major influence. For an introduction to these developments and further reading, see Anna Green and Kathleen Troup, *The houses of history: a critical reader in 20th-century history and theory* (Manchester, 1999), chapters 8–12.

54 See, for example M. Foucault, *The order of things* (New York, 1973); R. Rorty, *Objectivity, relativism and truth* (Cambridge, 1991); Nikolas Rose, *Governing the soul* (London, 1990).

55 A. Giddens, *The constitution of society* (Cambridge, 1984), p. 333. I am grateful to Kevin Passmore for this quote.
56 Porter, *Trust in numbers* (1995), p. 11. Jurgen Habermas, in particular, makes a distinction between the instrumentality of the empirical analytical sciences and the less problematic hermeneutic sciences: the latter are seen as oriented around meaningful communication, involving techniques such as the interpretation of documents. J. Habermas, *The structural transformation of the public sphere* (English translation, Cambridge, MA, 1962). But these categories are, in practice, inextricably intertwined in what researchers do. A shared framework of meanings and assumptions, sustained by consensus and authority, is present whether we are primarily quantitative in our approach to historical research or not.

Further reading

M. J. Cullen, *The statistical movement in early Victorian Britain* (Hassocks, 1975)

L. Daston, *Classicial probability in the Enlightenment* (Princeton, NJ, 1988)

P. Deane, 'Political arithmetic', in J. Eatwell, M. Milgate and P. Newman (eds), *The new Palgrave: a dictionary of economics*, 4 vols (1987)

Alain Desrosières, *The politics of large numbers. A history of statistical reasoning* (Cambridge, MA, 1998)

T. Fragssmyr, J. L. Heilbron and R. E. Rider (eds), *The quantifying spirit in the eighteenth century* (Berkely and Los Angeles, 1990), especially essays by Heilbron

D. V. Glass, *Numbering the people: the eighteenth-century population controversy and the development of census and vital statistics in Britain* (Farnborough, 1973)

I. Hacking, *The taming of chance* (Cambridge, 1990)

E. M. Higgs, *Making sense of the Census* (London, 1989)

J. Hoppit, 'Political arithmetic in eighteenth-century England', *Economic History Review*, 49, 3 (1996), pp. 516–40

J. Hoppit, 'Reforming Britain's weights and measures, 1660–1824' *English Historical Review*, 1 (1993), pp. 82–104

W. Kula, *Measures and men* (Princeton, NJ, 1986)

D. A. Mackenzie, *Statistics in Britain, 1865–1930: the social construction of scientific knowledge* (Edinburgh, 1981)

R. Matthews, 'Flukes and flaws', *Prospect* (November 1998), pp. 20–24

M. Norton Wise (ed.), *The values of precision* (Princeton, NJ, 1995)

Silvana Patriarca, *Numbers and nationhood: writing statistics in nineteenth-century Italy* (Cambridge, 1996)

K. Pearson, *The history of statistics in the seventeenth and eighteenth centuries against the changing background of intellectual, scientific and religious thought*, ed. E. S. Pearson (London, 1936–8; reissued London, 1978)

M. Poovey, *A history of the modern fact* (Chicago, IL, 1998)

T. M. Porter, *The rise of statistical thinking, 1820–1900* (Princeton, NJ, 1986)

T. M. Porter, *Trust in numbers: the pursuit of objectivity in science and public life* (Princeton, NJ, 1995)

J. R. N. Stone, *Some British empiricists in the social sciences, 1650–1900* (Cambridge, 1997)

PART
II

DESCRIPTIVE AND
ANALYTICAL STATISTICS
FOR HISTORIANS

|3|

Arranging, rearranging and displaying data

. . . what we call our data are really our own constructions of other people's constructions of what they and their compatriots are up to.[1]

After gathering data relevant to the research issues in question, the first thing that a historian, or anyone else concerned with quantitative data, will usually need to do is to look closely at the nature of the evidence. This is assisted by arranging and rearranging the material into an easily understandable and accessible format which addresses the research questions posed. Much can be learned simply from the arrangement and display of data into clearly labelled tables and figures of various kinds but care must be taken to avoid introducing additional or deliberate distortions. As we discussed in Chapter 1, and as Geertz reminds us in the quote above, the data set itself will inevitably be the construction of those responsible for its collection and our further rearrangment will inject additional interpretive elements into the evidence. Distortion is unavoidable – the most we can aim for is an honest professionalism – and this should always be borne in mind in quantitative as well as in qualitative analysis.

The purpose of this chapter and the next is to introduce the historian to the nature of different sorts of quantitative evidence and to ways of arranging and studying that evidence so that basic questions can immediately be asked and answered. This aspect of quantitative method is generally referred to as 'elementary descriptive statistics'. It is concerned with identifying the most important features of the data through rearrangement and presentation.

3.1 Types of data

It is important at the outset to classify data by type because quantitative analysis can be undertaken with some sorts of data and not others. There are two main types of data, **categorical data** and **numeric data**, and it is common to recognise two subclasses in each of these, as highlighted in Table 3.1.

Table 3.1 Types of variables

Variable type	Description	Examples
Categorical		
Nominal (unordered)	Gives only qualitative information	Names, occupations, nationalities, sex, religion
Ordinal (ordered)	Ranking or order is important	Social status, economic class
Numeric		
Interval	Distance between values has meaning	Year, temperature
Ratio	Ratio of two values has meaning	Wealth, age, prices, wages

Source: based on Loren Haskins and Kirk Jeffrey, *Understanding quantitative history* (Cambridge, MA, 1990), p. 211, Table 6.1.

NOMINAL DATA

The term 'nominal' comes from the word *name*. Common nominal variables are names of persons, places, possessions, nationalities, religions. Dichotomous variables such as sex may also be nominal. (A dichotomous variable is one which can take only two 'values'.) The defining character of nominal data is that the variable cannot be rank ordered: rearranging the order does not affect the level of information provided. Also, it is not possible to add up a list of nominal data as the units are varied and mutually exclusive. Lists of individuals, business enterprises or occupations are commonly given as nominal data, but if they are ranked in any definable order by wealth, importance or size they should more properly be seen as ordinal.

Sometimes **nominal data** are coded to make processing easier (e.g. nationalities might be coded as Swedish 1, Canadian 2, French 3, German 4, and so on, with no significance attached to the numerical order or magnitude). Where this occurs the data remain categorical even though they are expressed numerically. This can cause some confusion, but a quick rule of thumb is to ask 'Would it make any sense at all to take an average of these numbers?' If the answer is no then the series of numbers are merely codes representing a categorical variable.

ORDINAL DATA

The term 'ordinal' comes from the word *order*. Ordinal data are generally more informative than are nominal data because the order is important. The order indicates relative size, status, age or some other hierarchical feature. In other words, ordinal data represent a hierarchy of information (e.g. listings of occupations in order of social status, of wealth holding by value of assets, of income or earnings hierarchies). An example of ordinal data is provided in Table 3.2, which reproduces Gregory King's hierarchy of income in 1688. Unlike nominal data, if the order here were to be disturbed an important additional piece of information would be lost: the social status hierarchy.

Table 3.2 Numbers in social classes, *c.* 1688

Class	Number of families
Temporal lords	160
Spiritual lords	26
Baronets	800
Knights	600
Esquires	3 000
Gentlemen	12 000
Persons in greater offices and places	5 000
Persons in lesser offices and places	5 000
Eminent merchants and traders by sea	2 000
Lesser merchants and traders by sea	8 000
Persons in the law	10 000
Eminent clergymen	2 000
Lesser clergymen	8 000

Source: Gregory King, quoted in L. Soltow, 'Long run changes in British income inequality', *Economic History Review*, XXI, 1 (1968) p. 18. © Economic History Society

INTERVAL DATA

Interval data are numeric. With interval data the distances between the numbers have meaning. Examples of interval data include dates.[2]

RATIO DATA

Ratio data are interval data where the ratio of two values has meaning (e.g. ages or incomes). Ratio variables have a zero value on their scale. Most data used in quantitative analysis are of ratio type because the additional information (common units of measure and known intervals between classes) is a necessary prerequisite for most further statistical procedures (e.g.yields of crops in bushels or some other common unit of measure; wages or earnings data in pounds, shillings and pence; price movements over time for particular goods or services; series of imports or exports, values or volumes, over time; prison sentences for different crimes or from different courts). Interval data are either counted in whole numbers (e.g. numbers of people), termed discrete data, or measured on a continuous scale (e.g. heights, weights or wages), termed continuous data.

Sometimes it is hard at first to spot the type of data. Nominal data arranged in a meaningful order become ordinal data. Similarly, the dividing line between ordinal and ratio data is sometimes confusing: the guiding point should be that *in ratio data there must be common units of measure which can be added, divided and averaged.*

3.2 Some definitions involved in regrouping data

Once the nature of the data has been identified, reclassifying and regrouping is a common first step which the historian takes in order to display the information more effectively and before undertaking any sort of statistical analysis. Some definitions are important here.

- **Data set:** a data set is a group of data selected or gathered by the historian to help him or her answer a particular question. A data set usually consists of a series of cases.
- **Case:** a case consists of one or more pieces of information relating to a particular unit of investigation. For example, if one had a list of men with their names, ages and occupations, each distinct male with the information pertaining to him would constitute a case.
- **Variable:** each piece of information relating to a case is called a variable. In other words, a variable is a measure associated with each case in the data set. The measure is likely to vary from one case to the next, hence the term variable. In the list of men and their ages and occupations the variables are names (nominal), ages (ratio) and occupations (nominal, provided they are not ranked in order of prestige or income, in which case they would be ordinal).
- **Data matrix:** a data matrix is a convenient way of organising and tabulating a data set. In a data matrix each case has a row to itself and each variable has a column.
- **Vector:** a vector is a column or row of information from a data matrix.
- **Field:** a vector is sometimes also referred to as a field of information.
- **Cell:** a cell is a single unit of information in a data matrix.

In the example in Table 3.3 the data set is arranged in matrix form (note: the matrix consists of the entries only, not the headings). It is this form of arrangement and display of data which lies behind the formation of a spreadsheet on a computer. The cases (in this example, data relating to individual trade areas and countries) can be read across the rows, and the variables (imports, exports and re-exports) are shown in successive columns.

Table 3.3 UK imports from, and exports and re-exports to, various regional groups and countries, 1965 (current prices in £millions)

Region (case)	Variable		
	Imports	Exports	Re-exports
EFTA[a]	666.9	555.0	18.2
EEC[b]	994.7	904.8	75.4
Eastern Europe	222.4	125.2	3.7
Southern Europe and West Africa	202.9	195.0	4.4
Turkey and the Middle East	325.4	243.1	4.6
Rest of Africa	604.7	550.8	7.4
Asia	456.5	473.3	9.8
West Indies	98.7	97.1	1.8
Central and South America	289.7	157.7	3.0
Russia	118.8	46.9	0.5
Germany	265.4	255.0	30.4
Netherlands	270.8	193.1	9.9
Belgium	121.8	169.2	4.6
France	190.5	177.2	16.2
Republic of Ireland	170.4	175.8	9.9
India	128.3	114.1	2.3
Australia	219.5	281.4	3.0
New Zealand	208.2	125.0	1.1
United States	671.4	493.7	21.0
Canada	458.2	200.6	7.4
Argentina	71.5	26.8	0.7
South Africa	199.8	263.5	3.9

[a]European Free Trade Association: Austria, Denmark (including Greenland), Liechtenstein, Norway, Portugal, Sweden and Switzerland.
[b]European Economic Community: Belgium, France, West Germany, Italy, Luxembourg, Netherlands.
Source: B. R. Mitchell and H. G. Jones, *Second abstract of British historical statistics* (London, 1971), pp. 136–40.

It is worth noting that matrix notation is sometimes used as a shorthand way of indicating the information to be found in a particular cell of a specific data matrix. For matrix notation each matrix is assigned a letter of the alphabet, each row and column a number. Let us call the matrix contained in Table 3.3 matrix **A**; $a_{1,2}$ denotes row 1, column 2 (i.e. exports to members of the European Free Trade Association (EFTA)]; $a_{4,3}$ denotes

Table 3.4 The ratio of non-caps to caps and of seats to spittoons in the best room of four pubs in Bolton, 24–28 January, unknown year in the 1930s

Pub	Seats per spittoon	Non-caps to caps	Condition of spittoons
A	8	1.5	Dry
B	5	0.5	Wet
C	4	0.6	Wet
D	7	1.0	Slightly wet

Source: Mass Observation, *The pub and the people: a Worktown study* (London, 1987 edn), p. 205.

row 4, column 3 (i.e. re-exports to Southern Europe and West Africa). In Table 3.4 information about the social nature of four pubs is given in matrix form. If we call the matrix contained within Table 3.4 matrix **B**, $b_{4,3}$ denotes the condition of spittoons in pub D ('slightly wet'!). Note that in matrix notation, the name is generally given as a bold capital letter, whereas each element is represented by the same letter but as italic lower-case; the row number is always given first in the subscript, before the column number. A matrix with i rows and j columns is called an $i \times j$ matrix (i.e. the matrix in Table 3.3 is a 22×3 matrix).

The historian beginning a project in quantitative analysis must often decide which unit he or she will treat as cases and which as variables relative to those cases which form the study. This decision will be based upon the nature of the enquiry or analysis. In the case of matrix **A** the focus of research is to be UK trade with specific trading partners. As a result, the countries and trading blocks are made the cases, and exports, imports and re-exports are the variables. Had the focus been re-exports, different re-exported goods may have become the cases, with country and trade block destinations forming the variables. Had the focus of enquiry been traded commodities, different sorts of goods may have been selected as the cases, with relevant export and import quantities and/or values as the variables. Once a decision has been made on the basis of research priorities, the information can then be arranged in a way suitable for clarity of display and/or further statistical or computer analysis.

3.3 The presentation of tables and figures

It is important to note at this point some important but simple rules about the professional presentation and layout of all tables and figures.

• All tables and figures must have a title which briefly describes their content, indicates the time period covered and the units of measurement which are used.

- All tables and figures must give details of the precise source or sources of the information which they contain. This is very important because it is necessary to give readers an opportunity to check figures or to seek further information about the derivation of figures from the sources quoted. Without the opportunity for readers to do this the statistics themselves and any analysis or conclusions based upon them will always be open to question. Without detailed source notes, people will rightly think that the initial figures could have come from anywhere or have been manufactured, and no one will be interested in the analysis based upon them.
- Column and row headings should be brief but self-explanatory, with units of measurement clearly shown.
- Vectors of data which are to be compared should be close together, and derived statistics such as percentages and averages should be next to the figures to which they relate (either in brackets within the same cell or in an adjacent vector).

3.4 Initial questions about the data

As soon as a historian or social scientist is faced with quantitative data it is a healthy sign if there are immediately many questions to ask. How were the data collected and what errors might they contain? Is the same sort of evidence available for each case or is the evidence patchy? For what purpose was the data selected and how does that purpose line up with our interests as historians? If, for example, Table 3.3 was to be used as a source for investigating the economic arguments for joining or opposing membership of the European Economic Community (EEC) in the late 1960s, the historian may well feel frustrated. The overlaps (between trading blocks and countries), as well as omissions and inconsistencies of the data collected from British official trade records, would be problematic. We might also wish to question whether a matrix for a single year would be representative. Was 1965 unusual in any way or was the UK consistently heavily tied by trade to the Commonwealth, EFTA, North America and South Africa before joining the EEC? Figures for other years would certainly be needed if the focus of research hinged upon the EEC entry debates. It would be necessary to get a sense of any growth or change in the direction of trade over time, and a breakdown of trade by type of goods would be vital in assessing whether any losses which might occur from EEC entry could be substituted easily by trade within the EEC.

Similarly, we know that the material in Table 3.4 was gathered by volunteers organised by upper middle-class academics involved in the Mass Observation group and anxious to investigate the culture and leisure habits of the industrial working classes.[3] Should we be sceptical about their findings or the basis and validity of their research? Why were spittoons such a source of interest and were these academics correct in thinking that the level of spitting might tell us something about the 'social class' nature of the pub? As historians, rather than as statisticians, we should be always questioning the origins and reliability of the data for our purposes and asking what other sorts of data we would ideally need for our research. These questions are the essential prerequisite of quantitative analysis.

Apart from the data matrix, there are several other commonly used tools of descriptive statistics. Each shares with the matrix the attempt to impose order on information. We must bear in mind that the process of ordering and classification always results in loss of some of the richness and detail of the original source. This should always be appreciated and, where necessary, discussed as part of the research. But we here concentrate upon the benefit of careful choice of descriptive statistics which will assist with immediate visual appreciation of the data, in summarising large data sets and in providing the basis for further statistical analysis.

3.5 Grouping data in a frequency distribution

Before we discuss frequency distributions, some definitions may be needed.

- **Distribution:** a distribution is the full range of values for any one variable (e.g. the range of values in a column vector).
- **Frequency:** the frequency is the number of times any one value of the variable occurs.
- **Frequency distribution:** a frequency distribution is a tabulation which shows the frequency with which a particular variable occurs.

There are three types of frequency distribution:

- simple
- grouped
- cumulative

Each can be expressed in original units of measurement or in percentages. The choice of which frequency distribution to use depends upon which aspect of the data needs to be highlighted or examined.

The best way to illustrate the formation and use of frequency distributions is to use some examples. Consider the data contained in Table 3.5, which is an extract from the return of convicts confined in Portland Prison, 1849. We can quickly and clearly demonstrate features of the data, such as sentence lengths, ages of prisoners, and geographical origins of prisoners by drawing up some frequency distributions.

In the simplest form we can add up the number of cases experiencing discrete sentence lengths. 'Discrete' in statistical parlance means separate, discontinuous and referring to distinct objects, as do sentence lengths in Table 3.6

Table 3.5 Return of convicts confined in Portland prison, 1849

Name	Age (years)	Offence	Place of committal	Sentence (years)
James Hackett	21	Felony	Salford	7
John Taylor	20	Stealing a file and monies	Leicester	7
John Brown	20	Larceny (PC)	CC Court	7
James Barker	47	Stealing fowls, two indictments	Exeter	14
William Johnson	25	Setting fire to sacks of straw	Stafford	20
James Sweeney	58	Uttering counterfeit coin (PC)	Caernarvon	15
George Williams	21	Burglary (PC)	CC Court	10
Francis Best	35	Housebreaking, larceny	Worcester	15
John Henry	36	Uttering forged notes	Glasgow	20
Thomas Hartshorn	33	Robbery with violence	Liverpool	15
Samuel Laughton	22	Burglary, stealing silver spoons, etc.	Nottingham	14
Thomas Robinson	23	Burglary and theft, two indictments	Maidstone	14
Martin Stone	22	Horse stealing	Dorchester	15
Richard Ashford	58	Stealing 3lbs of pork	Exeter	10
John Dobson	28	Stealing money from the person (PC)	Stafford	14
Samuel Diggle	36	Burglary	Liverpool	15
George Goult	22	Robbery (PC)	Chelmsford	12
Robert Holder	23	Stealing from a dwelling £15 and pair of pistols	Portsmouth	15
Richard Jones	36	Warehouse breaking, and stealing malt and hops	Reading	15
Hugh King alias Cameron	36	Theft by housebreaking	Glasgow	14
Austin Montroe	34	Larceny in a dwelling to the value £5 (PC)	CC Court	15

Note: PC = previous conviction; CC Court = Central Criminal Court, London.
Source: based on an extract from the Public Record Office, Home Office, 8/102, Public Record Office, Kew.

Table 3.6 Simple frequency distribution of
sentence lengths (unrelated to type of crime) of
prisoners in Portland Prison, 1849

Sentence length (years)	Number of prisoners
7	3
10	2
12	1
14	5
15	8
20	2
Total	21

Source: see Table 3.5.

It is often clearer to group the data into particular bands, as in Table 3.7.
With just this short extract from the Portland Prison data this represents no
major advantage over Table 3.6 because there are only six discrete categories of sentence, but if the data were more extensive, with many different
sentence lengths, the grouped distribution would represent a major advantage in terms of clarity in conveying the character of a lot of information
very clearly and simply.

Table 3.7 Grouped frequency distribution of
sentence lengths (unrelated to type of crime)
of prisoners in Portland Prison, 1849

Sentence length (years)	Number of prisoners
0–6	0
7–13	6
14–20	15
21–27	0
Total	21

Source: see Table 3.5.

In Table 3.8 information concerning prisoners' origins is given in a
grouped frequency distribution. If left in the original discrete categories the
frequency distribution would convey little more than Table 3.5. In grouped
form Table 3.8 provides immediate clarity in conveying the distinctive
regional pattern of prisoners' origins as indicated by place of committal.
Table 3.8 also includes a percentage column. Percentages are often more
useful than the original units in enabling one to see, at a glance, the shape of

the distribution. Percentages are also invaluable if one wishes to compare the distribution of two or more data sets of different sizes (e.g. of different groups of Portland prisoners at different dates) or of different data (such as male and female prisoners).

Table 3.8 Grouped frequency distribution of prisoners origins as indicated by place of committal

| UK area | Prisoners | |
	number	per cent
London	3	14
Midlands	3	14
East	1	5
South	7	29
North	7	38
Total	21	100

Source: see Table 3.5.
This can of course give only a rough indication by geographical region and ignores the fact that prisoners may originate from outside the region of their committal.

Of course, the regional pattern of prisoners' origins may not accurately be estimated from the places of committal not least because Central Criminal Court cases are likely to have come from further afield. In addition, of course, no account can be taken of the degree to which crime and committal took place away from a prisoner's normal place of residence nor can we allow for possibly very high geographical mobility of criminals. These are the sorts of points which it is important to add in order to qualify results or to draw attention to the weaknesses of any conclusions which might be drawn from Table 3.8.

Table 3.9 Cumulative grouped frequency distribution of prisoners' ages, Portland Prison, 1849

Age (years)	Number of prisoners
<20	0
<25	9
<30	11
<35	13
<40	18
<45	18
<50	19
<55	19
<60	21

Source: see Table 3.5.
Note: the sign '<' means 'less than'.

Table 3.10 Percentage cumulative grouped frequency distribution of prisoners' ages, Portland Prison, 1849

Age (years)	Prisoners	
	number	per cent
≥50	2	9.5
≥40	3	14.3
≥30	10	47.6
≥20	21	100

Source: see Table 3.5.
Note: the sign '≥' means 'greater than or equal to'.

Sometimes a cumulative frequency distribution is the most useful choice, as in Tables 3.9 and 3.10, because these distributions convey an easier appreciation of the character of the data. Prisoners' ages are probably better expressed in this way than in a simple grouped distribution. Again, percentages are especially useful when comparing the distribution of two data sets of differing size and composition. Note that in the percentage frequency table the percentages have been rounded to one decimal place. In most circumstances it is good practice to round to the nearest whole number or to one decimal place. Any greater precision would result in the sort of spurious 'accuracy' which can get quantitative historical work a bad name.

Table 3.11 shows various frequency distributions for Hearth Tax payers in two Yorkshire townships in the 1660s. The Hearth Tax returns give the names of heads of households with the numbers of hearths on which they paid tax. Percentage frequency distributions enable comparisons to be made between the two townships.

Similarly, the Land Tax payers of the West Yorkshire township of Sowerby, listed in Table 3.12, can be regrouped to provide a clearer indication of the distribution of landholdings than it is possible to see from the raw data set itself (see Table 3.13). The choice of class intervals here is of course dependent upon the researcher and in turn this should be determined by the level of detail required to address the research questions posed.

The nominal data in the occupation field could also be grouped as the basis for asking questions about a possible relationship between occupation and value of landholding.

Both the Hearth Tax and the Land Tax returns have been the subject of extensive debate as to their accuracy and potential uses for the historian. The 1662 return for Yorkshire included exempt households and is therefore more useful than other returns which did not. The accuracy and completeness with respect to names and numbers of householders is debatable, but the Hearth Tax is a key source, especially for demographic history, and

Table 3.11 Analysis of Hearth Tax returns, in the Yorkshire townships of Sowerby (including Soyland) and Calverley, 1664

Number of hearths	Household heads	
	number	per cent
Sowerby		
Exempt	140	30
0	3	1
1	185	39
2	72	15
3	29	6
4	27	6
5	10	2
6	2	<1
7	1	<1
8	1	<1
9	1	<1
Total	471	100
Calverley		
Exempt	43	34
0	0	0
1	58	46
2	18	14
3	6	5
4	1	1
5		
⋮	⋮	⋮
14	1	1
Total	127	100

Source: P. Hudson, 'Landholding and the organisation of textile manufacture in Yorkshire rural townships *c.* 1660–1810', in M. Berg, ed., *Markets and manufacture in early industrial Europe* (London, 1991), p. 272. Original source: Hearth tax returns, E179/210/393, 16 Charles II, Lady Day 1664, PRO.

many attempts have been made to estimate population totals from Hearth Tax figures by using multipliers to represent the average household size.The Land Tax returns hold similar pitfalls for the historian. Their accuracy appears to have varied greatly from one region to another, and acreages are rarely given, which is frustrating for historians wishing to use the returns to investigate the distribution of landholdings rather than levels of taxation. Because of differing land values across the country (upon which taxation was generally based) it is very difficult to calculate acreage equivalents from the tax assessments. Furthermore, it is difficult to use the returns to look at wealth structures in terms of landownership because many people owned

Table 3.12 Land Tax payers, Sowerby, West Yorkshire, 1782

Name	Occupation	£	s	d
			Land Tax paid	
John Batty	Clothier	1	3	6
Benjamin Bramley	Fuller	2	0	6
John Butterworth	Clothier		19	6
Abraham Clegg	Weaver		3	6
Thomas Cockcroft	Weaver		5	6
William Crossley	Clothier	1	8	0
John Derden	Merchant	5	0	0
Henry Dyson (3)	Yeoman	9	10	0
William Ellis	Yeoman	12	6	0
Eli Fielding	Weaver		2	6
Abe Gibson	Yeoman	5	0	0
John Gledhill	Clothier		15	6
David Greenwood	Clothier	1	13	6
John Greenwood	Miller	1	0	6
John Greenwood (3)	Merchant	12	0	0
Thomas Greenwood	Inn keeper		7	6
Cornelius Haigh	Fuller	2	0	6
John Hanson	Weaver		5	6
John Howarth	Clothier	1	10	0
Richard Hinscliffe	Clothier		17	6
Joshua Horton	Victualler		10	6
Wats Horton (24)	Gentleman	46	17	6
John Hoyle	Clothier		19	6
Richard Ingham	Clothier	1	4	0
John Irving	Woodcutter		2	6
John Lea (2)	Merchant	4	10	0
William Moore	Yeoman	2	5	0
Grace Ogden	Widow		2	6
Robert Parker (6)	Attorney	17	8	0
Danile Phillips	Clothier		5	0
Elizabeth Pimley	Widow		17	6
James Riley	Butcher	2	10	6
Joshua Riley	Clothier		7	6
Matthew Scott	Weaver		3	6
George Stansfield (15)	Merchant	30	2	6
Will Walker	Merchant	12	0	0
John Swain	Clothier		12	0
Ann Swain	Clothier	1	0	0
Matthew Tillotson	Weaver		10	0
Richard Thomas	Clerk	2	0	0
Sir John Deardon	Gentleman	7	10	0
John Walker	Weaver		3	6
John Walker	Clothier		15	0
Samuel Waterhouse	Merchant	8	0	0
John Whitaker	Clothier		19	6
Mary Whitworth	Weaver		4	6
Samuel Wood	Apothecary	2	0	0

Note: where a proprietor was liable to tax on more than one property the number of properties is given in brackets after the name.
Source: Land Tax returns, 1782, West Yorkshire Archive Service, Halifax, with hypothetical occupational data.

Table 3.13 Grouped and percentage grouped frequency distribution of Land Tax payers in Sowerby, West Yorkshire, 1782

Tax paid	Number	Per cent
< 5 s	7	15
5 s–< £1	15	32
£1–< £5	14	30
£5–< £10	5	11
£10–< £20	4	8
≥ £20	2	4
Total	47	100

Source: see Table 3.12.

and rented land across several different Land Tax assessment boundaries. One must also be wary about studying change over time in landownership or occupancy from the returns because the Land Tax often went unrevised from year to year.[4]

There are four important things to remember about the formation and presentation of frequency distributions:

- Each needs both a correct heading indicating its content and/or purpose and details of the source of the information.
- Columns must always have an appropriate heading.
- Simple and grouped frequency distributions should always include a total figure (this is useful anyway as a check that all the cases have been included).
- Most importantly, grouped distributions must be sure to have *no overlap* between the categories or class intervals.

3.6 Bar charts

Bar charts and histograms are both ways of displaying the sort of data collected in frequency distributions. Bar charts and histograms present the information in the form of a figure rather than a table. Their advantage is that they often give a clearer and more immediate visual representation of the data than that given in a frequency table.

Bar charts can be used for nominal, ordinal or interval data. The bars are usually separated from one another, and the variables can appear in any order. The length (or height) of the bars is proportional to the observed frequencies. The width and area of the bars can vary and is not important. Examples of bar charts are given in Figures 3.1–3.3.

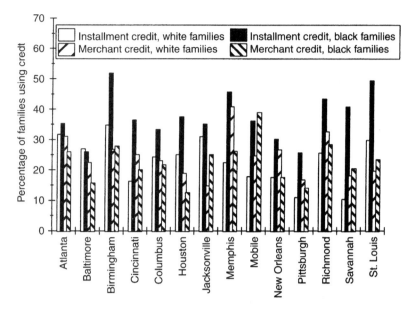

Fig. 3.1 Use of credit in US cities, 1917–19.
Source: Martha L. Olney, 'When your word is not enough: race, collateral and household credit', *Journal of Economic History*, 58, 2 (1998), p. 419.

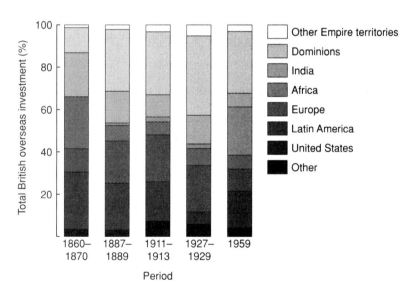

Fig. 3.2 Geographical distribution of British foreign investments, 1860–1959.
Source: based upon E. J. Hobsbawm, *Industry and Empire* (London, 1968), p. 303.

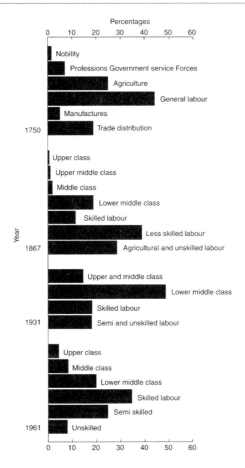

Fig. 3.3 Bar charts of class structure (%), 1750–1961.
Source: based upon E. J. Hobsbawm, *Industry and Empire* (London, 1968), p. 303.

It is common to display the frequencies of different variables side by side as in Figure 3.1. Each bar can also be divided to represent further features of the data, as in Figure 3.2 (a component bar chart, in which the components are expressed as a percentage of the whole). The bars in a bar chart can be arranged vertically or horizontally; the latter is sometimes preferred when hierarchical data are being displayed, as in Figure 3.3.

Figure 3.4(a) contains a mass of raw data which is difficult to interpret in that form. Place-of-birth data for Glasgow have been extracted from the table to produce the barchart of Figure 3.4(b). This is a good indication of the level of clarity and efficiency of communication which can be achieved with the aid of a computer graphics package, allowing the production of a barchart in three dimensions, with categories side by side for comparative purposes.

PRESENT IN

BIRTH-PLACE	*Galashiels (Municipal or Police Burgh).				Glasgow (Parliamentary Burgh).				*Glasgow (Municipal Burgh).				*Govan (Police Burgh).			
	MALES.		FEMALES.		MALES.		FEMALES.		MALES.		FEMALES.		MALES.		FEMALES.	
	Under 20 Yrs.	Above 20 Yrs.	Under 20 Yrs.	Above 20 Yrs.	Under 20 Yrs.	Above 20 Yrs.	Under 20 Yrs.	Above 20 Yrs.	Under 20 Yrs.	Above 20 Yrs.	Under 20 Yrs.	Above 20 Yrs.	Under 20 Yrs.	Above 20 Yrs.	Under 20 Yrs.	Above 20 Yrs.
SCOTLAND	3,564	3,235	3,467	4,149	100,763	93,409	101,870	110,201	105,739	97,145	106,791	113,923	10,954	9,143	10,688	9,462

Fig. 3.4 (a) Facsimile of 1881 Census, Glasgow, Govern and Galashields
Source: E. Mawdsley and T. Munck, *Computing for historians*
(Manchester, 1993), p. 132.

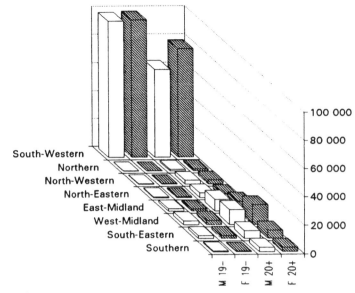

Fig. 3.4 **(b)** Bar chart showing Glasgow population (municipal burgh) by place of birth, 1881.
Source: E. Mawdsley and T. Munck, *Computing for historians* (Manchester, 1993), p. 134.

3.7 Histograms

Interval data are more usually represented by a histogram. A histogram is a diagrammatic representation of a frequency distribution consisting of a series of rectangles or bars with a width proportional to the class interval and an area proportional to the frequency.

In a histogram data values are continuous rather than discrete and appear next to one another, usually along the horizontal axis. The width of each bar of a histogram is usually the same (providing that the data values or range of values for each bar are the same) though this can be varied if class intervals are of unequal size. The area covered by the bars (and the height if the class intervals are equal in size) is always proportional to the frequency being represented. Examples of histograms are given in Figures 3.5 and 3.6. Figure 3.5 has the additional feature of being placed on its side with two histograms back to back, allowing immediate comparison between male and female populations. This form is known as an age pyramid. Using the facilities provided by a computer software package, histograms, like bar charts, can be drawn in three dimensions, in which case the volume as well as the height of the bars is proportional to the frequencies represented, which can give further visual clarity to the data.

Sometimes the midpoints of the tops of histogram blocks are joined by

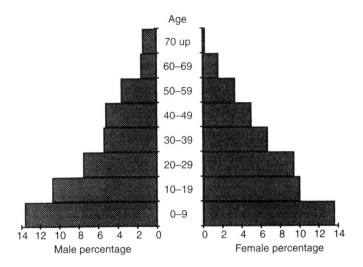

Fig. 3.5 Age pyramid of Bristol, Rhode Island, 1774.
Source: based on John Demos, 'Families in colonial Bristol, Rhode Island: an exercise in historical demography', *William and Mary Quarterly* 3rd series, 25, (1968), p. 53. Taken from L. Haskins and K. Jeffrey, *Understanding quantitative history* (Cambridge, MA, 1990), p. 52.

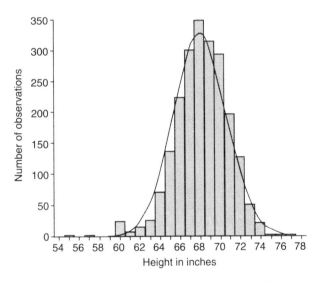

Fig. 3.6 Height distribution of US passport applicants, 1830–57.
Source: John Komlos, 'On the nature of the Malthusian threat in the eighteenth century', *Economic History Review*, 52, 4 (1999), p. 736. © Economic History Society. In this figure the histogram is compared for analytical purposes with the shape of the normal distribution (see pp. 103–4, 175–6).

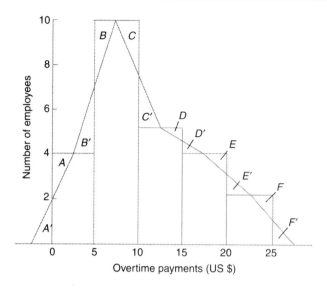

Fig. 3.7 Frequency polygon formed from a histogram, showing average weekly overtime payments in a New York dry cleaning firm, 1968–72. Note: the areas of histogram 'lost' above the curve of the polygon (areas A–F) are 'regained' by the inclusion of equal 'extra' areas below the curve of the polygon (areas A′–F′, respectively), so that the area of the histogram and the area under the curve are equal. Source: hypothetical data.

straight lines to form a frequency polygon, as in Figure 3.7. Note that the area under the 'curve' remains the same as the area covered by the histogram. Sometimes the histogram or polygon is smoothed into a frequency curve by using much smaller class intervals.

The purpose of frequency polygons and frequency curves is to provide a clearer visual picture of the character of the frequency distribution. They also have the advantage over the histogram that several can be plotted on the same axis, making their comparison much easier. In Figure 3.8 frequency polygons for different years have two different horizontal class intervals because of the different way in which the age figures were reported in the Royal Commission on Children in Factories, 1834, and in the Census of 1851. This does not prevent a visual comparison being made.

It is important to note:

- in bar charts and histograms the variables or frequencies represented by the bars must be labelled clearly at the base of the bars themselves or by shading the bars and providing a key;
- the vertical and horizontal axes must be clearly labelled.

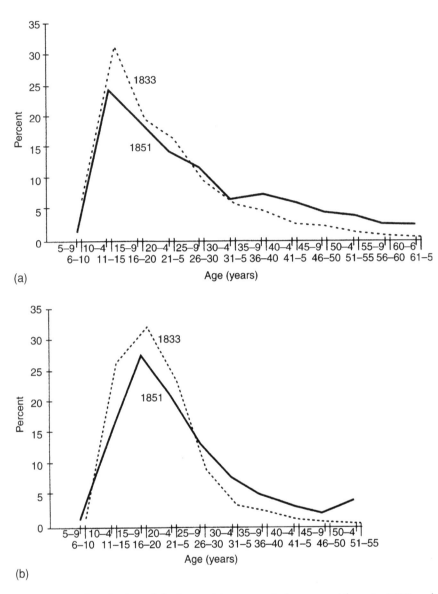

(a)

(b)

Fig. 3.8 Age distribution of the Lancashire cotton industry workforce in 1833 and 1851: (a) males; (b) females.
Source: H. M. Boot, 'How skilled were Lancashire cotton factory workers in 1833?' *Economic History Review*, 48, 2 (1995), p. 286. (c) Economic History Society

3.8 Pie charts and pyramid charts

These provide a clear representation of the proportions of different categories or values found in a data set. A pie chart is a circle or shallow cylinder divided into sectors to represent each item or variable. The sizes of the sectors (number of degrees of the circle) are exactly proportional to the distribution of the data. Each sector is usually shaded and labelled with a percentage, and a key is also provided to identify the units or cases represented by the sectors. Figure 3.9 is a pie chart showing the proportions of UK re-exports by geographical or trading area in 1965. It is derived from the data in Table 3.3 on page 57. The size of the sectors is calculated and measured by dividing the 360 degrees (360") of a circle into the same proportions as those of the data. For example, the size of the sector (in terms of the angle α, illustrated in Figure 3.9) for EFTA was calculated in the following way:

$$\text{angle } \alpha = \frac{\text{total EFTA re-exports}}{\text{total re-exports, excluding double counting}} \times 360"$$

$$= \frac{£18.2 \text{ million}}{£160 \text{ million}} \times 360"$$

$$= 41" \text{ (to nearest degree)}$$

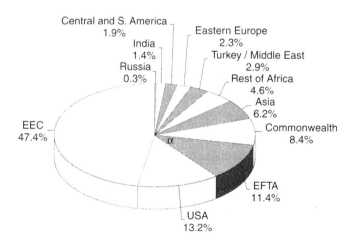

Fig. 3.9 Pie chart: proportions of UK re-exports by geographical or trading area, 1965. (Note: $\alpha = 41°$).
Source: see Table 3.3.

The sector for EFTA is therefore drawn so that the angle α at the centre of the circle is 41°. Note that in this example care has been taken not to overlap or double count the re-export figures by including trade blocks in the pie chart alongside countries which are part of those trade blocks.

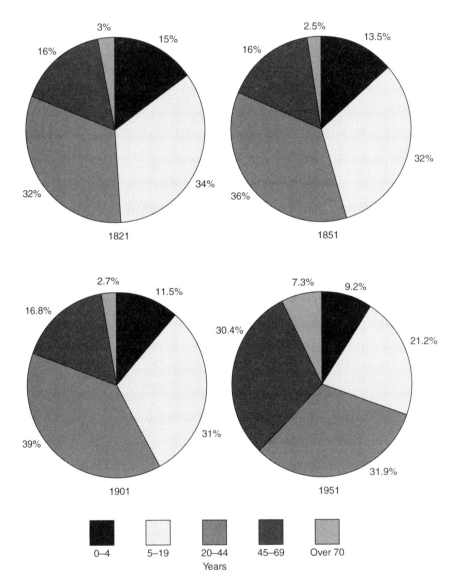

Fig. 3.10 Pie charts showing the age composition of the British population for various years.
Source: based upon E. J. Hobsbawn, *Industry and Empire* (London, 1968), p. 303.

In the old days pie charts were drawn by using a protractor and compass. Nowadays, computer software can processes the information and produce the pie chart very easily. Often the software produces pie charts in three dimensions, which can give further visual impact to the data display. Pie charts can be used side by side to give a rapid indication of change over time, as in Figure 3.10. From Figure 3.10 it is easy to see the advantage of comparative pie charts over the display of these data in a table.

Pie charts are useful where there are relatively few variables which make up proportions of the whole, where it is more important to convey the proportions than the numerical values and where a strong visual emphasis is required.

Where data proportions reflect a marked hierarchy, a triangular chart is sometimes used, with the same principle as the pie chart. This is called a pyramid chart. An example is given in Figure 3.11. Just as in a pie chart, the area represented by the sections of the triangle are drawn so that they are proportional to the data distribution. In this case this is easily calculated by using the formula for the area of a triangle. (i.e. half the length of the base multiplied by the perpendicular height); nowadays one can simply feed the data into a computer software package and give the appropriate instructions.

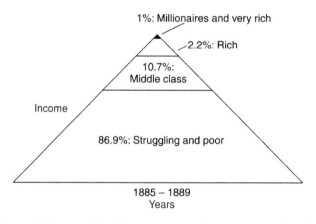

Fig. 3.11 Pyramid chart of the Victorian rich and poor. Source: based upon E. J. Hobsbawm, *Industry and Empire* (London, 1968), p. 308.

3.9 Graphs: time-series

Line graphs are especially useful for displaying time-series data (i.e. data which vary over time). They are therefore particularly common in historical use. They have a wide variety of other functions particularly where it is

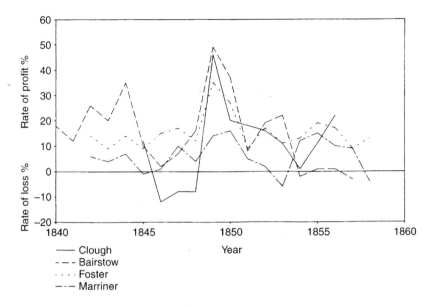

Fig. 3.12 Profit rates in the worsted industry, 1840–58.
Source: Pat Hudson, *The genesis of industrial capital* (Cambridge, 1986), p. 239.

desired to represent the relationship between the movement of two or more variables.

In a time-series graph time is usually measured on the horizontal axis (usually referred to as the *x* axis) which is marked out in months, years or another unit of time. The movement of one or more variables can then be drawn with respect to a scaled vertical axis (or *y* axis). If more than one variable is depicted, a key or legend must be provided to indicate clearly which line represents which variable. Figure 3.12 shows the yearly profit rates for four firms in the worsted industry, in the nineteenth century, which I researched in the early 1980s. Three firms ran at a loss in some years so I placed the horizontal axis accordingly. It does not have to be at the bottom of the graph. The vertical axis of a graph is also moveable if it is necessary to depict negative values.

Sometimes the different variables which we wish to depict on the same time-series graph for comparative purposes have a different unit of measurement. In this case it is necessary to provide two or more separate scales on the same vertical axis or to have a second vertical axis with a separate scale on the right-hand side of the figure. If different variables have the same unit of measure but one is very much smaller than the others, the smaller measure may be expressed in a multiple so that lines can be compared on the same graph or, as in the case of Figure 3.13, a second scale can start at a higher point on the *y* axis.

Fig. 3.13 Absolute and real per capita poor relief expenditure in two parishes, 1770–1835.
Source: K. D. M. Snell, *Annals of the labouring poor* (Cambridge, 1985), p. 89.

If the variables to be depicted grow slowly at first but then accelerate rapidly logarithmic scale (log scale) may be used on the vertical axis to create a semi-logarithmic graph. A semi-logarithmic graph is one in which the measures on the vertical axis decrease successively at the upper end of the range of values because they are expressed in logarithms rather than the original units. The curve is thus made to fit on a page and be easily visible, as in Figure 3.14. The purpose of the semi-logarithmic graph is to show the rate of change of data rather than changes in the actual amounts: the slope of the curve indicates the rate of change because each point shows the percentage change from the last point. Alternatively, if the variable exhibits exponential growth, the vertical scale can increase in units which are successively the square roots of the previous unit. This is termed an **exponential scale**. Both logarithmic and exponential scales have the same purpose in allowing the graphing of rapidly growing variables of different kinds.[5] One must, of course, be on the lookout for vertical scales of this kind because at first sight they may give a misleading impression of the rate of growth of the data.

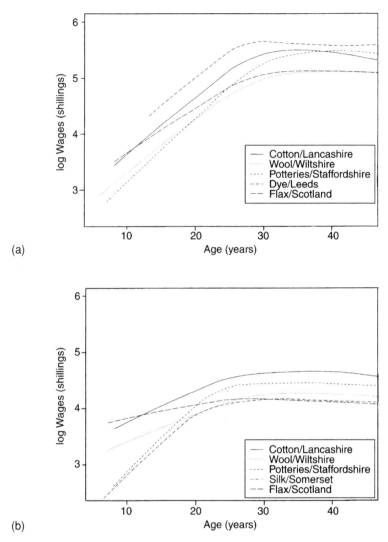

Fig. 3.14 Semi-logarithmic graphs of earnings and age profiles (smoothed) of factory workers from selected industrial centres: (a) males; (b) females.
Source: based on H. M. Boot, 'How skilled were Lancashire cotton factory workers in 1833?', *Economic History Review*, 48, 2 (1995), p. 298. © Economic History Society

3.10 Other graphs

Graphs have many other uses apart from time-series. A common use is in graphing pairs of case variables. In such a graph, which is designed to indicate the relationship between the movement of two variables with respect to one another (e.g. height and weight of army recruits, exports and imports), it is not crucial which axis is used for which variable. However, if one is analysing the movement of two variables whereby one is suspected to be a prime cause of the movement of the other (e.g. the price of corn and incidence of rural protest or the movement of real wages and meat consumption) the causal variable or so-called independent variable is normally located on the horizontal axis, with the dependent variable on the vertical axis. Thus, in the first example, where high food prices may have been partly responsible for social unrest, corn prices would generally be placed on the horizontal axis and the number of protest incidents on the vertical axis. Real wage movements (as a possible cause of variation in the consumption of meat) would be on the horizontal axis, with meat consumption on the vertical scale. These so-called scatter graphs (also called scatter diagrams or scatter plots) are more fully explored in Chapter 6, pp. 143–7, 156–7.

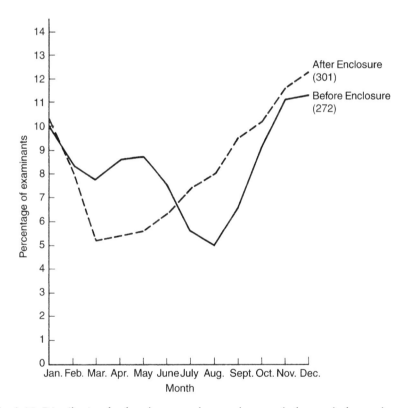

Fig. 3.15 Distribution for female seasonal unemployment before and after enclosure in the counties of Bedfordshire, Cambridgeshire, Essex, Hertfordshire, Huntingdonshire, Norfolk and Suffolk. Unemployment is measured as a three-month moving average.
Source: K. D. M. Snell, *Annals of the labouring poor* (Cambridge, 1985), p. 156. For moving averages see pp. 129–31, 266.

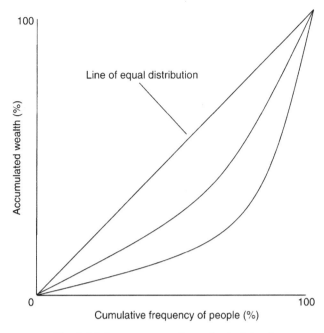

Fig. 3.16 Lorenz curves (hypothetical data)

Graphs can also be used to represent more novel or complex relationships. Figure 3.15 is one of many interesting graphs appearing in K. D. M.
Snell's *Annals of the labouring poor* (1985). It shows an unusual use of
graphical representation to demonstrate seasonal variation, in this case in
female unemployment before and after enclosure. This excellent use of
graphical representation was very effective in supporting Snell's analysis of
the impact of enclosure upon women's work in the countryside, although
his assumption that the timing of settlement examinations and certificates
would accurately reflect the timing of unemployment has received some
criticism.[6]

A type of graph very commonly used in economics and in economic and
social history is the Lorenz curve. The Lorenz curve is a cumulative percentage curve which plots accumulated wealth (%) on the *y* axis against
cumulative population or households (%) on the *x* axis. The Lorenz curve
gives an immediate impression of the level of inequality in wealth terms. It
is used for comparisons between countries, or between different time-periods,
rather than as a quantitative measure of inequality. Figure 3.16 shows two
Lorenz curves of different shapes indicating contrasting inequalities. The
Lorenz curve nearer to the straight line represents a society in which income
distribution is more equal than is the case in the society represented by the
Lorenz curve which is more distant from the line of equal distribution.

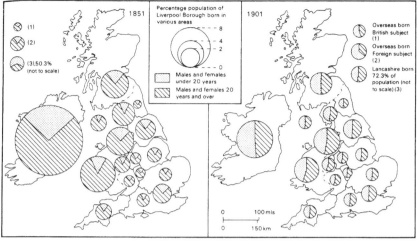

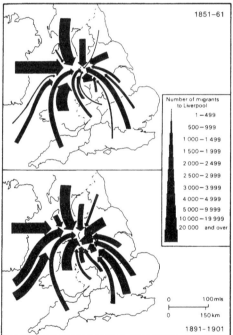

Fig. 3.17 Cartograms showing age and origin of immigrants to Liverpool, 1851–1901.
Source: R. J. Lawton 'Population', in J. Langton and R. J. Morris (eds), *Atlas of industrialising Britain 1780–1914* (London, 1986), p. 29.

3.11 Cartograms

The role of cartograms (maps onto which graphs, symbols, pie charts, etc., are superimposed to represent different variables) have grown increasingly popular in recent years, especially with the expansion of computer software, notably geographical information systems (GIS), which makes them much easier to prepare. Figure 3.17 illustrates a historical use. It is drawn from *An atlas of industrialising Britain 1780–1914*, which contains many such examples.[7]

Conclusion

This conclusion starts with a **WARNING**. The reordering, reclassification, regrouping and visual display of statistical information in charts, graphs or tables carries a heavy responsibility because it is easy to distort the appearance of series or runs of figures by choosing inappropriate display techniques, distorting classifications, or inappropriate scales of measurement (on the axes of a graph, for example). These can either exaggerate or underplay the character of the original data and create a misleading impression of the evidence. It must also be remembered that all rearranging and classifying of data loses something of the integrity and richness of the original source, and this is something which should always be borne in mind. Even at this simple level of descriptive statistics, the important first step is always to look closely at the figures and their origin and to consider, as a historian, the likely omissions, biases and distortions of the evidence. Such problems need to be thought about in relation to the purpose for which the data will be employed (i.e. the research questions being asked). Careful judgements at this point are important in determining whether further manipulation or analysis is wise or worth doing.

Having sounded the alarms, one can also say that elementary descriptive statistics, when employed with care and attention, can be a very useful tool for the initial summary and display of raw data. Manipulation into a matrix, frequency distribution, chart or graph can go a long way to highlighting clearly the characteristics of the data, to answering simple questions and helping to create further analytical interrogations.

Notes

1 C. Geertz, *The interpretation of cultures* (1973), New York, p.9.
2 Mathematically speaking, with interval data there is no zero measure (as in measures of temperature in Kelvin, where the zero is expostulated rather than real).
3 Mass Observation was a movement founded in the 1920s. Its aim was to gather on-the-spot accounts, by participants and observers, of history as it was

happening. The 'movement' resulted in a large and valuable collection of diaries, notebooks, surveys and interviews relating to the war period in particular. Several books were also written by Tom Harrison and others responsible for initiating the archive. The collection is now housed at the University of Sussex.

4   For details of the Land Tax as a source, see M. Turner and D. Mills (eds), *Land and property: the English Land Tax 1692–1832* (Gloucester, 1986).

5   Logarithmic and exponential scales have a different theoretical basis, appropriate to different patterns of growth.

6   K. D. M. Snell, *Annals of the labouring poor* (Cambridge, 1985).

7   J. Langton and R. J. Morris, *An atlas of industrialising Britain 1780–1914* (London, 1986).

Further reading

F. Daly, D. J. Hand, M. C. Jones, A. D. Lunn and K. J. McConway, *Elements of statistics* (Harlow, 1995), Chapter 1. A very well produced and detailed Open University text.

R. Floud, *An introduction to quantitative methods for historians* (London, 1973, 2nd edn 1979), Chapters 1–4.

L. Haskins and K. Jeffrey, *Understanding quantitative history* (Cambridge, MA, 1991), Chapters 1 and 2. The best of the American publications in this field.

T. Hannagan, *Mastering statistics* (London, 1982, 3rd edn 1997) Chapters 4 and 5. The clearest of the short general statistics texts available.

E. Tufte, *Visual explanations: images and quantities, evidence and narrative* (Cheshire, CT, 1997). A mind-blowing exposition of quantitative imagery.

4

Summarising data: averages and distributions

After his study of heights, Quetelet continued his measurements of other physical attributes: arms and legs, skulls and weights, for which he still observed distributions in accordance with binomial law. From this he inferred the existence of an ideal average man, in whom all average characteristics were combined and who consituted the Creator's goal – perfection.[1]

Many measures occurring in nature such as the human physical attributes, which caught the attention of quantifiers such as Quetelet in the nineteenth century, cluster evenly (above and below) an average measure, with very few measures lying outside of a certain range. This type of finite and symmetrical (binomial) distribution is a common one, but other values and variables which historians are interested in examining are often distributed in other ways. This chapter considers the nature of data sets and vectors within them. It suggests simple ways in which distributions of values can be described, summarised and analysed. Remember, a distribution is the full range of values observed for any one variable. Most column vectors in data sets consist of a distribution of values.

4.1 Measures of central tendency

One of the first things which one may wish to do with a distribution of values is to calculate the **average** value. The average is an important summary characteristic but, as we shall see, averages must be chosen with care.

An average provides a value around which a set of data is located. It is a measure of central tendency in the data and is often the first stage of an investigation. There are three commonly-used measures of average:

- the **arithmetic mean,** usually referred to simply as the **mean;**

- the **median**;
- the **mode**.

Each of these measures the average or central tendency of a distribution in a different way. *The choice of measure depends upon the nature of the distribution and the purpose for which the average is being calculated.*

The mean

The **mean** is the average as it is most commonly understood and calculated: formed by adding all the values together and dividing by the number of observations. It is used only for interval data.

The *advantages* of the mean are that:

- it takes account of all of the values;
- there are measures of dispersion which can be used with it (see pp. 93–8).

The major *disadvantage* is that it is sensitive to untypical extreme values: the value of the mean may be badly distorted away from the typical experience by the presence of one or two unusually large or small outlying values.

In the pictogram in Figure 4.1, showing average incomes in a business firm in the early 1950s, the mean would be a poor indicator of average experience because its value is inflated by the income of one man (the boss?) at the pinnacle of the earnings pyramid.

The mean is usually represented by the symbol $\bar{X}$ (pronounced X bar) and the formula for calculating the mean is given as:

$$\bar{X} = \frac{\sum_{i=1}^{N} X_i}{N}$$

where

$\bar{X}$ is the mean of vector X;
X_i is the value of the variable for case i;
N is the number of observations.
Σ is 'the sum of'

The mean of land tax payments shown in Table 3.12 on page 66, for example, can be calculated as:

$$\text{mean} = \frac{\text{sum of all payments}}{\text{number of tax payers}} = \frac{£202\ 10s\ 0d}{47}$$

$$= £4\ 6s\ 1d$$

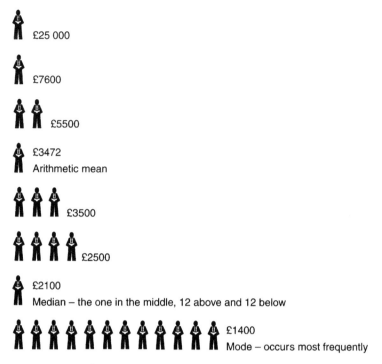

£25 000

£7600

£5500

£3472
Arithmetic mean

£3500

£2500

£2100
Median – the one in the middle, 12 above and 12 below

£1400
Mode – occurs most frequently

Fig. 4.1 Pictogram of white-collar salaries in a firm in the 1950s. Source: based on Darrel Huff, *How to lie with statistics* (London, 1973), p. 33.

It should be noted that in this case the mean is again not a very good measure of the average or typical payment because of the existence of one or two atypically large payers. (Atypically large or small values in a distribution are usually referred to as outliers).

The mean can also be calculated from a frequency distribution by using the formula:

$$\overline{X} = \frac{\sum_{i=1}^{k} f_i X_i}{N}$$

where

X_i is the value of the variable for group i;
f_i is the frequency with which that value occurs;
k is the number of groups;
N is the number of cases from which the frequency distribution has been compiled.

[The mean can also be estimated from a grouped frequency distribution by taking the mean of the class interval as X_i.]

Thus, if we take the frequency distribution shown in Table 3.6, page 62 drawn from Table 3.5, page 61, we can calculate the mean prison sentence as:

$$
\begin{aligned}
\overline{X} &= \frac{\sum_{i=1}^{6} f_i X_i}{N} \\
&= \frac{[(3 \times 7) + (2 \times 10) + (1 \times 12) + (5 \times 14) + (8 \times 15) + (2 \times 20)]}{21} \\
&= \frac{(21 + 20 + 12 + 70 + 120 + 40)}{21} \\
&= \frac{283}{21} \\
&= 13.5
\end{aligned}
$$

where f_i in this case is the number of prisoners, X_i is the sentence length, N is the total number of prisoners, and k is the number of different sentence lengths represented.

Yet again the mean is not really the best measure of the average for this distribution because no prisoner is serving a 13.5 year sentence. All sentences are in whole years and, more importantly, there is an obvious candidate for the most typical experience, which is 15 (this is by far the most commonly occurring experience, known as the mode; see below).

The mean provides the most justified measure of average when a distribution has few outliers, which are likely to distort the mean, and when the values of the variable seem to be fairly evenly spread around a central value. Such bell-shaped distributions are common especially in biological data, such as distributions of heights and weights.

The median

The **median** is the observation which lies at the centre, or middle, of a distribution when all of the observations or values are ranked in size order. It can be used with ordinal or interval data. When there is an even number of cases the median is the mean of the two middle ranking values.

The advantages of using the median are:

- it is immune from the influence of extreme values;
- it has some measures of dispersion associated with it (see below).

The median is a better way of calculating the average level of tax paid from Table 3.12 on page 66 than was the calculation of the arithmetic mean, because it is immune from the influence of the two largest and untypical tax payers. The median tax payment is £1 0 s 6 d.

It is possible to estimate the median of a grouped frequency distribution by assuming that the values of items in the class containing the median are distributed evenly, that is, that the median falls in the middle of that class. Thus the median value of Land Tax paid in Sowerby in 1782 can be calculated roughly from Table 3.13, page 67 as £3, which may be a useful enough approximation, depending upon the nature of the enquiry.

The mode

The **mode** is the most commonly occurring observation. It can be used with nominal, ordinal or interval data and is the only average one can use with nominal data. The advantage of the mode is that it represents the most common experience or occurrence, but the disadvantage is that it takes no account of other observations, has no measure of dispersal associated with it and can be entirely misleading if there is more than one commonly occurring observation (as in a bimodal or trimodal distribution, of which more below). It is a useful measure when a distribution is not spread evenly around a central value but is of limited use when data are very dispersed.

In our example above concerning sentence lengths of prisoners, the mode is a better way of expressing the average prison sentence than is the mean as the distribution in not widely spread and there is a very obvious common experience of 15 years.

In a grouped frequency distribution the **modal class** is the one with the highest frequency. In Table 3.13, for example, the modal class is 5 s–< £1. In the pictogram illustrated in Figure 4.1 the mode (£1400) and the median (£2100) are both better expressions of average than is the mean.

The choice of which measure of average to take will depend on the purpose of the exercise.

The geometric mean

The **geometric mean** is another average but it is less commonly used than the mean, median or mode. The geometric mean is defined as the Nth root of the product of the distribution (where N is the number of items in the distribution).

The geometric mean is used only with interval data, mostly in averaging growth rates or indices of growth. (An **index**, plural *indices*, is a series expressed in percentage terms, as explained in Chapter 5.)

To calculate the geometric mean one multiplies all the N values of a variable, X, together and takes the Nth root:

$$\text{geometric mean} = \sqrt[N]{X_1 X_2 X_3 \dots X_N}$$

This may also be written as

$$\text{geometric mean} = (X_1 X_2 X_3 \ldots X_N)^{1/N}$$

Note: There is no need for multiplication signs: $X_1 X_2$ is the same as $X_1 \times X_2$.

EXAMPLE

If the price of commodity A rises from £25 to £50, this is an increase of 100 per cent.
If the price of commodity B rises from £80 to £100 this is an increase of 25 per cent.

Thus

$$\text{mean increase} = \frac{125 \text{ per cent}}{2} = 62.5 \text{ per cent}$$

$$\text{geometric mean} = \sqrt{100 \times 25} \text{ per cent} = 50 \text{ per cent}$$

[Note: there is no need to write the value of N by the root sign when the square root is being taken, (i.e. when $N = 2$).]

Which of these measures to accept is open to debate and depends upon the researcher's purpose. The geometric mean gives less weight to extreme values than does the arithmetic mean but there is no measure of dispersion associated with it. Growth rates can also be measured and expressed in other ways (see Chapter 5) and these methods are often preferred to the geometric mean.

Choice of average

It is not always easy to make a clear-cut decision about which measure of average (mean, median or mode) is the best reflection of the character of the data. Sometimes it will depend upon the questions that one is asking about the evidence. For example, in Table 4.1 taken from E. A. Wrigley's study of marriage ages in early modern Colyton, Devon, all three measures of average marriage age are given. This is because each highlights different features of the data upon which Wrigley comments and each gives useful additional information. Where the three measures of average are given together in this way an indication of the shape of the distribution as a whole can be visualised. The data on male and female average marriage ages in Table 4.1 can be seen to be 'skewed' because for men and women and for all of the time periods the mean is greater than the median, which in turn is greater than the mode. This is a positively skewed distribution (see Section

Table 4.1 Age at first marriage in Colyton, 1560–1837

	Number	Mean	Median	Mode[a]
Men				
1560–1646	258	27.2	25.8	23.0
1647–1719	109	27.7	26.4	23.8
1720–1769	90	25.7	25.1	23.9
1770–1837	219	26.5	25.8	24.4
Women				
1560–1646	371	27.0	25.9	23.7
1647–1719	136	29.6	27.5	23.3
1720–1769	104	26.8	25.7	23.5
1770–1837	275	25.1	24.0	21.8

[a]The mode is interpolated from the mean and the median and not derived directly from the data.
Source: E. A. Wrigley, 'Family limitation in pre-industrial England', *Economic History Review*, 19, 1 (1966), p. 86. © Economic History Society

4.3, pp. 104–6). The use of the mean with the median is a common way of roughly indicating the shape of a distribution.

A recent report from the Institute of Fiscal Studies demonstrated that 'average' wealth is growing in Britain but that the distribution is becoming more unequal.[2] Mean wealth (in accumulated savings and assets) of £7136 contrasted markedly with a median of only £750! In addition, 30 per cent

Table 4.2 Summary statistics of marriages in Cortona, 1415–36

	Mean	Median	Standard deviation
Dowry (florins)	125.5	70	105.9
Groom's age (years)	28.1	27	8.3
Bride's age (years)	18.8	18	4.7
Groom household's wealth (florins)	609.7	164	1692.84
Bride household's wealth (florins)	700.7	196	1997.66
Number of children in grooms' households	2.25	2	1.87
Percentage of daughters in grooms' households	0.08	0	0.17
Number of children in brides' households	3.14	3	2.33
Percentage of daughters in brides' households	0.65	0.6	0.27
N		224	

Note: the marriages refer to households living in the town of Cortona and in 44 villages in its countryside.
Source: M. Botticini, 'A loveless economy? Intergenerational altruism and the marriage market in a Tuscan town, 1415–1436', *Journal of Economic History*, 59, 1 (1999), p. 108. Original sources: Florence, State Archives, Catasto 213, 214, 215, 216, 252, 253 and 254; Notarile Antecosimiano 1143, 1144, 1145, 1146, 5441, 10038, 18905, 18906, 18907, 18908, 18909, 18910, 18911, 18912, 18913 and 18914.

of the population had no savings outside of their home and pension, and around 10 per cent (mostly single parents and out-of-work couples) had no savings at all. This is another example of a positively skewed distribution where the mean is biased upwards, away from average experience by the presence of a small number of very high values.

In Botticini's article on the marriage market in fifteenth-century Tuscany (which is included in the Appendix, Article 12, as an exercise), the median and the mean are used together for a number of different variables, as shown in Table 4.2. The means are higher than the medians for all of the variables, again indicating the presence of positively skewed distributions (see Section 4.3, pp. 104–6).

4.2 Measures of dispersion

An average on its own tells us very little about the entire population: in particular, it says nothing about how divergent from the average is the distribution of individual observations. All distributions are not only clustered around central points but also spread out, or dispersed, around them.

The range is a first indication of dispersal. The range of a set of data is the highest value of the distribution minus the lowest value. The range is often used with the mode but can be used with any interval data.

There are a number of more sophisticated measures of dispersion which can be used with the mean and the median.

Dispersion around the mean: standard deviation and variance

Many very different distributions can have the same mean. For example, all three of the distributions in Table 4.3 have a mean of 45.88 despite the fact that A is widely dispersed (range 99), C is closely clustered (range 4) and B is influenced by the presence of one extreme atypical value (an 'outlier') and has the largest range, 151.

Because the average on its own tells us little about the entire population it is almost always used with some indication of the spread of data. A measure of dispersion tells us to what extent the values of a distribution are, or are not, bunched around the average. The measures of dispersion most commonly used with the mean are the variance and the standard deviation.

The variance is the average of the squares of the deviations from the mean. It is calculated by adding the square of the deviations of the individual values from the mean of the distribution and dividing this sum by the number of items in the distribution. The following formula achieves this:

Table 4.3 Distribution of defamation cases in three
English courts, 1680–7

	Distribution		
Year	A	B	C
1680	100	20	48
1681	88	28	47
1682	70	22	46
1683	50	45	45
1684	30	16	45
1685	20	167	45
1686	8	40	44
1687	1	29	47
Total	367	367	367

Source: hypothetical data.

$$\text{variance} = \frac{\sum_{i=1}^{N}(X_i - \overline{X})^2}{N}$$

where

$\overline{X}$ is the mean;
X_i is the value of the variable for row i;
N is the number of observations.

The standard deviation is another measure of dispersion around the mean. It is usually represented by the letter s or by the abbreviation SD. It is found by applying the formula for the variance and then taking the square root:

$$s = \sqrt{\left(\frac{\sum_{i=1}^{N}(X_i - \overline{X})^2}{N}\right)}$$

where the variables $\overline{X}$, X_i, and N are as defined already. The variance is always equal to the square of the standard deviation (s^2).
If we look again at Table 4.3:

in distribution A, $s = 34.77$, and the variance is 1209.11;
in distribution B, $s = 46.69$, and the variance is 2180.36;
in distribution C, $s = 1.27$, and the variance is 1.61.

Table 4.4 Statistics relating to Table 4.3

Year	i	Distribution					
		A		B		C	
		X_i	$X_i{-}\overline{X}$	X_i	$X_i{-}\overline{X}$	X_i	$X_i{-}\overline{X}$
1680	1	100	54.1	20	−25.9	48	2.1
1681	2	88	42.1	28	−17.9	47	1.1
1682	3	70	24.1	22	−23.9	46	0.1
1683	4	50	4.1	45	−0.9	45	−0.9
1684	5	30	−15.9	16	−29.9	45	−0.9
1685	6	20	−25.9	167	121.1	45	−0.9
1686	7	8	−37.9	40	−5.9	44	−1.9
1687	8	1	−44.9	29	−16.9	47	1.1
$\displaystyle\sum_{i=1}^{N}(X_i-\overline{X})^2$		9673		17 442		12.88	
Variance		1209.12		2180.36		1.61	
Standard deviation		34.77		46.69		1.27	

Note: for all distributions, the number of observations, N, is 8, the number of court cases is 367, and the average, $\overline{X}$ is 45.9. Note also that the square of a negative number is positive (i.e. −15.9 squared = −15.9 × −15.9 = +252.81).
Source: hypothetical data.

(See Table 4.4 for a partial breakdown of the calculations.) The greater the dispersion the larger the standard deviation and the variance. In each case *s* is expressed in the original units, in this example in the number of court cases.

The standard deviation can also be calculated directly from a grouped frequency distribution by applying the formula:

$$SD = \sqrt{\frac{\sum fD\overline{x}^2}{\sum f} - \left(\frac{\sum fD\overline{x}}{\sum f}\right)^2} \times \text{class interval}$$

where f = frequency; $D\overline{x}$ = deviations from the mean (or the assumed mean). Statistical software makes this calculation very straightforward.

The formula for the standard deviation (*s*) takes into account the amount that each value deviates from the mean (the $X_i - \overline{X}$ part of the formula), which is what makes it so much more useful in most cases than the range.

THE Z SCORE

Use of a measure called the *Z* score is becoming increasingly common in the social science and historical literatures. A *Z* score is the number of standard deviations which an observation is above the mean (if it is positive) or below the mean (if it is negative). Where *Z* scores are used the standard deviation becomes a sort of yardstick for comparative purposes. Distributions of *Z* scores can be created which enable the dispersion of different distributions to be compared. The standard deviation itself is no good for this because it is expressed in the original units of measurement (e.g. dollars, persons, cows). Z scores provide a universal unit for measuring dispersion. Because Z scores have standard values they are sometimes called standard scores.

Dispersion around the mean: the coefficient of variation

The coefficient of variation is another measure of the extent to which a variable differs from its mean. It is simply the standard deviation s, divided by the mean and is generally expressed as a percentage:

$$\text{coefficient of variation} = \frac{s}{\overline{X}} \times 100 \text{ per cent}$$

Because it is expressed as a percentage it too can be used to compare the dispersion of distributions of different sorts of variables one with another. The coefficient of variation is usually calculated for this purpose only – to compare the degree to which two variables differ from their respective means. One cannot use standard deviations for this because standard deviations are expressed in the original units of the variable (e.g. persons, exports, strikes, ploughs, hearths, looms, etc.), whereas the coefficient of variation is always a percentage.

If one were told that the three distributions in Table 4.3 were not all court cases but that each distribution related to a different variable, one would need, for comparative purposes, to calculate the coefficient of variation. For example, if the data set described the assets of eight farmers in the early nineteenth century with:

- series A, the number of cows;
- series B, the value of seed on hand in pounds sterling;
- series C, the value of land and farm buildings in thousands of pounds sterling

one might calculate the coefficient of variation to see the extent to which the different sorts of assets of these farmers varied from the average experience.

The coefficients of variation of the three distributions are:

- distribution A, 0.76 per cent,
- distribution B, 1.02 per cent
- distribution C, 0.03 per cent

The coefficient of variation is also used in comparing the variation of certain measures at different time periods or for different countries because standard measures are far easier to compare than are original units. Tables 4.5 and 4.6 are drawn from an article by Jeffrey G. Williamson based on his

Table 4.5 Coefficients of variation of real wages, 1854–1939

Year	Full sample[a]			Full sample less North America[b]			Full sample less North America and Iberia[c]	
	C(13)	C(17)	C(16)	C(12)	C(15)	C(14)	C(10)	C(13)
1854	0.326			0.308			0.340	
1870	0.254	0.255		0.224	0.223		0.229	0.232
1890		0.199			0.114			0.102
1913		0.191			0.068			0.039
1914			0.103			0.085		0.068
1926			0.148			0.146		0.138
1927		0.188	0.147		0.186	0.142		0.131
1939		0.285			0.200			0.138

[a]The 'full sample' included the following 13 countries until 1870: Australia, the United States, Belgium, France, Germany, Great Britain, Ireland, Netherlands, Norway, Spain, Sweden, Brazil and Portugal; in 1870 the following four countries were added to the sample: Argentina, Canada, Denmark and Italy; Portugal dropped from the sample from 1914 to 1926 and then rejoined.
[b]'Full sample less North America' excludes Canada and the United States, implying that we start with 12 countries and then increase to 15 in 1870; again, Portugal dropped from the sample between 1914 and 1926.
[c]'Full sample less North America and Iberia' excludes the United States, Canada, Spain and Portugal, implying that we start with 10 countries and expand to 13 in 1870.
Note: the number of countries in the sample, x, is indicated by the column heading C(x).
Source: J. G. Williamson, 'Globalisation, convergence and history' *Journal of Economic History*, 56, 2 (1996), p. 280.

Table 4.6 Coefficients of variation of gross domestic product (GDP) per worker-hour, 1870–1938

Year	Full sample[a]	Full sample less North America[b]
	C(15)	C(13)
1870	0.153	0.169
1890	0.118	0.122
1913	0.107	0.088
1929	0.110	0.080
1938	0.090	0.054

[a]The 'full sample' includes Australia, Austria, Belgium, Canada, Denmark, Finland, France, Germany, Italy, the Netherlands, Norway, Sweden, Switzerland, the United Kingdom, and the United States; it does not include Japan.
[b]The 'full sample less North America' drops Canada and the United States from the full sample.
Source: J. G. Williamson, 'Globalisation, convergence and history', *Journal of Economic History*, 56, 2 (1996), p. 280.

presidential address to the Economic History Association, 1996, entitled 'Globalisation, convergence and history'. His estimates of coefficients of variation of real wages, 1854–1939, and of coefficients of variation of gross domestic product (GDP) per worker-hour, 1870–1938, for the members of the Organisation for Economic Cooperation and Development (OECD), support his argument that convergence is linked to globalisation and that convergence was arrested in the period 1914–50.

Rank order dispersal measures

Rank order dispersal measures are commonly used with the median. The median, which divides the ranked distribution in half, is only one of a range of measures that summarise data according to their rank order.

Others commonly used rank order measures are:

- **quartiles**, which divide the ranked distribution into 4 equal parts;
- **quintiles**, which divide the ranked distribution into 5 equal parts;
- **deciles**, which divide the ranked distribution into 10 equal parts;
- **percentiles**, which divide the ranked distribution into a hundred equal parts.

There are three quartiles, four quintiles, nine deciles and 99 percentiles. Consider the distribution of 20 observations, ranked in size order on page 99, which is part of a hypothetical Hearth Tax document.

The **median** can be expressed as the second quartile (Q2). The measure of dispersion often used with the median is the interquartile range. This is the difference between the first and the third quartiles (Q1 and Q3). Sometimes this is divided by 2 to form the semi-interquartile range, or quartile deviation which in this example is 3.

The ninth decile, for example, of the distribution is 11.5. This distribution is too small to have percentiles. Percentiles can be calculated only where there are at least a hundred observations.

The lower quartile (Q1), the median (Q2) and the upper quartile (Q3) are often shown and calculated graphically as in Figure 4.2 which shows the distribution of wages amongst the 50 employees of a dry cleaning firm in 1965:

Half the employees earn less than £17 per week, and half earn between that amount and £30;
Half of the employees earn between £12.00 and £22.00 (the interquartile range);
A quarter of the employees earn less than £12.00, and a quarter earn more than £22.

An advantage of the interquartile range and the quartile deviation is that they are immune from the influence of very small or very large values. This

Number of hearths:	Deciles	Quintiles	Quartiles Q	
2				
2				
←——— 1st = 2.5				
3				
4				
←——— 2nd = 4.0		1st = 4.0		
4				
←———————— 1st = 4.5				
5				
←——— 3rd = 5.5				
6				
6				
←——— 4th = 6.0		2nd = 6.0		
6				
7				
←——— 5th = 7.5			2nd (median) = 7.5	Interquartile range = 6 (10.5 − 4.5)
8				
8				
←——— 6th = 8.5		3rd = 8.5		
9				
9				
←——— 7th = 9.5				
10				
←———————— 3rd = 10.5				
11				
←——— 8th = 10.5		4th = 10.5		
11				
11				
←——— 9th = 11.5				
12				
23				

Spreadsheet functions give slightly different results from the above first approximations as they take account of any skew in the distribution. In the example above the first quartile is really 4.75. The third quartile is 10.25 and the ninth decile is 11.10. The interquartile range is 5.5.

can be an advantage if there are just a few extreme outliers which would seriously effect alternative measures of dispersal such as the standard deviation.

More examples from history

If we are researching a historical question which hinges upon the nature of a data set, choosing and applying the most appropriate measure of central tendency and dispersal are likely to be crucial to the arguments which may be made.

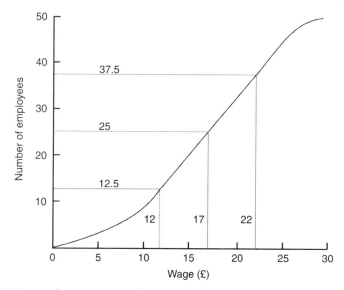

Fig. 4.2 Wages of SmartPants and Co., 1965, showing the graphical formation of Q1, Q2 and Q3.
Source: hypothetical data.

EXAMPLE 1

In considering the local impact of the Black Death in Birdbrook, Essex, and specifically the impact upon tenurial developments and the availability of customary land, Schofield employed mean, median and standard deviation measures to demonstrate change over time. Table 4.7 shows mean length of leasehold, where this indicates the period during which the tenement can be observed as remaining in the hands of the lessee by tracing it in the accounts from one year to the next. But the median is used to indicate the average term given at the inception of the lease to allow inclusion of terms granted for life (or lives) and to avoid replacing these with an arbitrary number of years. The standard deviation refers to leasehold lengths and relates to dispersal around the mean. Table 4.7 shows that the average length of time that a lessee remained in leasehold reduced dramatically in the first decade of the fifteenth century. Schofield argues that this reflected the replacement of a manorial economy based upon labour services with one based upon the money rent of farms and that a lot of the new tenants were incoming migrants.

EXAMPLE 2

In an example from more recent history, Figure 4.3 shows the effects of taxes and benefits upon quintile groups of households in Britain in 1987. It suggests that all five groups make direct and indirect tax contributions to

Table 4.7 Average length of occupation leaseholds commencing in each decade, from 1350 to 1409

Decade	Mean length of leasehold[a]	Standard deviation	Median length of term[b]	Number of leases entered[c]
1350–9	17.5	13.162	12	6
1360–9	18	12.675	9	3
1370–9	11.3	11.609	7	7
1380–9	15.2	9.441	9	12
1390–9	10.6	5.795	3	13
1400–9	4	3.210	1	27

[a]This is not the term given at the inception of the lease (see note b) but is the period during which the tenement can be observed as remaining in the hand of the lessee by tracing it through the accounts from one year to the next. Note also that the length of lease has been calculated as starting and ending in the first year of each account.
[b]This is the term actually given at the inception of the lease, which, in the case of longer terms, would be recorded in the court roll or, in the case of very short terms, in the 'farms' section of the account. The median value has been used here rather than the mean so as to allow inclusion of terms granted for life or for lives without replacing these with an arbitrary number of years.
[c]Three leaseholds entered in the decade 1380–9, four in that of 1390–9 and eight in that of 1400–9 had not expired by the accounting year 1409–10 (W.A.M. 25505). Only limited observation is possible after this date: the next surviving accounts date from accounting years 1412–3 (W.A.M. 25506), in which year the same lessees continue to hold, and 1426–7 (W.A.M. 25507), by which date all but one of these lessees of customary tenements had disappeared. The mean length of leasehold has been distorted as a result: in the case of 13 of the 14 lessees still holding in 1409–10 it has been assumed, for the basis of the calculation, that their tenure of the lease ended in 1412–13, and the lease of the individual still *in situ* in 1426–7 has been taken as ending in that accounting year. The effect of this is, obviously, to reduce the size of the mean, but the accuracy of the trend can be tested by artificially extending the length of those leases whose terminal date cannot be observed. By adding 3 years after 1412–13 for those leases commencing in 1380–9, 7.5 years for those commencing in 1390–9 and 10 years for those commencing in 1400–9 the following means ad standard deviations are obtained:

Decade	Mean	Standard deviation
1380–9	15.75	10.248
1390–9	13.30	7.289
1400–9	7.26	7.214

Source: Phillipp R. Schofield, 'Tenurial developments and the availability of customary land in a later medieval community', *Economic History Review*, 49, 2 (1996), p. 259. © Economic History Society

the welfare state and enjoy benefits in cash and kind. These taxes and benefits taken together make the distribution of final income considerably more equal than the distribution of original income.[3]

Quintiles are useful in Figure 4.4 in giving a clear idea of the differential effects of incomes, taxes and benefits across the spectrum of income distribution without clouding the diagram with an excessive amount of data which would add little to the point being made. What is actually being measured here are the Gini coefficients at each stage of the process relating to income, tax and benefits. The Gini coefficient is a summary measure of distributional

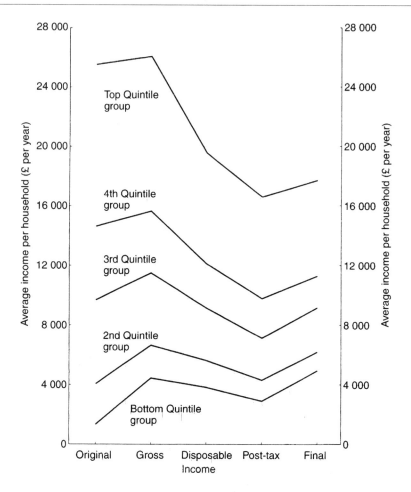

Fig. 4.3 The effects of taxes and benefits on quintile groups of households, 1987. Note: original income = employment and investment income before government intervention; gross income = original income plus cash benefits; disposable income = gross income minus direct taxes; post-tax income = disposable income minus indirect taxes; final income = post-tax income plus benefits in kind (e.g. health, education). Source: Paul Johnson, 'The welfare state' in R. Floud and D. N. McCloskey (eds), *The economic history of Britain since 1700*, Volume 3, 1939–1992 (2nd edn, Cambridge, 1994), p. 306. Original source: *Economic Trends* (1990), no. 439, p. 88.

equality between social groups. A Gini coefficient of 0 would denote absolute equality (the top 1 per cent, the bottom 1 per cent and all percentiles in between each receive 1 per cent of total income). A coefficient of 100 indicates total inequality (the top 1 per cent receive all the income, the rest get nothing).[4] The Gini coefficients relating to the data in Figure 4.3

are given in Table 4.8. They show that inequality grew between 1975 and 1987 and that this was a result of changes in original income (in turn affected by rising unemployment), rather than in the structure of taxes and benefits.

Table 4.8 Gini coefficients for the distribution of income at each stage of the tax-benefit system, 1975–87

	Year			
Gini coefficients (%)	1975	1979	1983	1987
Income type:				
original	43	45	49	52
gross	35	35	36	40
disposable	32	33	33	36
post-tax	33	35	36	40
final	31	32	33	36

Note: For definitions of income types, see Figure 4.3
Source: Paul Johnson, 'The welfare state', in R. Floud and D. N. McCloskey (eds), *The economic history of Britain since 1700*, Volume 3, 1939–1992 (2nd edn, Cambridge, 1994), p. 305. Original source: *Economic Trends* (1990), no. 439, p. 118.

4.3 Distributions

We have seen that distributions can cover a very wide range of values or that they can be made up of numbers which are clustered closely together. Distributions also take on different shapes, tending towards symmetry or a skew shape.

The normal distribution

There is an ideal type of distribution, known as the **normal distribution,** which is used in statistical theorising. The expression 'ideal type' is generally used to indicate a phenomenon which does not occur exactly in practice but which has those characteristics which are commonly found in real phenomena.[5] Normal distributions rarely occur exactly in social or historical data but in large-scale distributions and especially in the natural sciences it is found as a shape towards which distributions often tend. In the normal distribution the mean, the median and the mode have the same value, with an equal number of observations spread out symmetrically on either side. The normal distribution, as we shall see in Chapter 7, is also the basis of sampling theory in statistics. It is thus useful to know about the properties of the normal distribution.

In a normal distribution a constant proportion of cases lie between the mean and multipliers of the standard deviation from the mean:

- 68.26 per cent fall between one standard deviation above and below the mean;
- 95.46 per cent fall between 2 standard deviations above and below the mean;
- 99.7 per cent fall between 3 standard deviations above and below the mean.

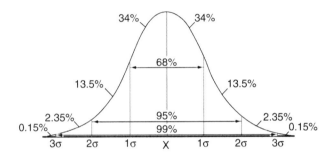

Fig. 4.4 The normal distribution. Note: σ = standard deviation; X = mean, median and mode.

The normal distribution can be represented graphically as in Figure 4.4. The bell-shaped curve of the normal distribution underlies much theorising about statistics and probability. The characteristics of Quetelet's average man were conceived and recorded in this way. Galton was influenced by Quetelet, by the social investigations of Charles Booth and by Darwinian theories of evolution in theorising the distribution of 'genetic worth' as a normal curve, see Figure 4.5

Skewed distributions

Other distributions commonly occur with historical and social data where the spread of observations is uneven, with more lying either above or below the mean. Where most observations lie below the mean the distribution is described as positively skewed. Where most observations lie above the mean the distribution is described as negatively skewed.

These distributions are represented graphically in Figure 4.6, with the relative positions of the mode and the median as well as the mean indicated. It is easy to see why the mean is not always a good measure to use for the

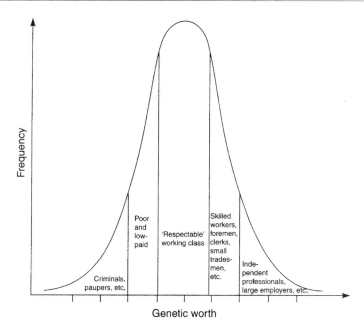

Fig. 4.5 Social classes and genetic worth (Galton, 1909).
Source: Alain Desrosières, *The politics of large numbers: a history of statistical reasoning* (Cambridge, MA, 1998), p. 114.

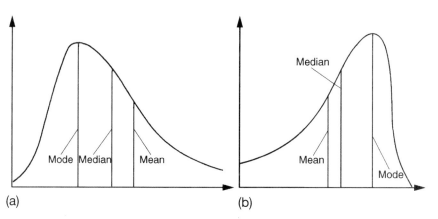

Fig. 4.6 Skewed distributions: (a) positive skew (mode and median less than mean); (b) negative skew (mode and median more than mean).

average of a skewed distribution, and it is usual in these cases to give the value of all three averages.

The distribution of the Land Tax payers of Sowerby given in Table 3.13, page 67, is skewed in favour of those paying under £5 and could be drawn roughly as in Figure 4.7.

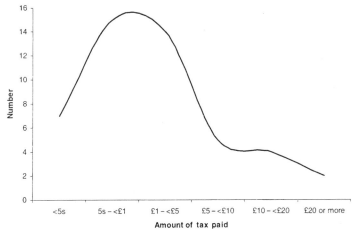

Fig. 4.7 Distribution of Land Tax payers, Sowerby, West Yorkshire, 1782.
Source: see Table 3.13, Chapter 3, page 67.

Other examples of skewed distributions can be found in Chapter 3 in Figures 3.6 and 3.8 (pages 72 and 74, respectively). The skew in Figure 3.6 is crucial to Komlos's argument that his critics have misunderstood the nature of height distributions historically. Figure 3.8 shows cotton industry employees by age in the nineteenth century. Young people were favoured as employees, with the female workforce appearing particularly youthful. There was, however, a long 'tail' of older workers.

The data in the pictogram in Figure 4.1, page 88, shows a positively skewed distribution, with the mean greater than the median, and the median greater than the mode.

Distributions with more than one mode

Sometimes distributions occur where there is more than one value around which observations cluster. The occurrence of such distributions illustrates

Fig. 4.8 Bimodal distribution.

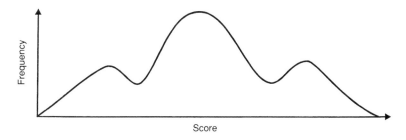

Fig. 4.9 Trimodal distribution.

the importance of studying the distribution carefully and perhaps graphing it or drawing a histogram or frequency polygon before rushing to select and calculate an average measure. Figures 4.8 and 4.9 show bimodal and trimodal distributions, respectively.

Conclusion

The most common piece of elementary statistical analysis involves summarising and considering the nature of a distribution or distributions of values. Measures of central tendency and of dispersion, together with the possibilities presented by graphing the distribution, go a long way toward making sense of data and enabling one to compare one distribution with another. These calculations and techniques are important in themselves but also as a preliminary to further, more sophisticated, analysis.

Notes

1 A. Desrosières, *The politics of large numbers* (Cambridge, MA, 1998), p. 76.
2 Reported in *The Independent*, 22 October 1999, p. 21.
3 Paul Johnson, 'The welfare state' in R. Floud and D. N. McCloskey (eds), *The economic history of Britain since 1700* Volume 3, 1939–1992 (2nd edn, Cambridge, 1994), pp. 284–317
4 The precise way of calculating the Gini coefficient varies. This can result in different absolute values even when the same data are being discussed, but the important thing to remember is that it is a measure used for comparison across countries or over time. As long as the same method of calculation is used, the absolute value of the Gini coefficient remains unimportant.
5 Ideal types are a useful aid to analysis, both quantitative and non-quantitative, because they enable the supposed underlying nature of real phenomena or data to be captured and discussed. Max Weber developed the use of ideal types in analysis, and they are widely adopted in social science, particularly in sociology.

Further reading

A. Aron and E. N. Aron, *Statistics for the behavioural and social sciences* (New Jersey, 1997), pp. 23–43.

F. Clegg, *Simple statistics: a coursebook for the social sciences* (Cambridge, 1982), pp. 13–43, 153–6. Lively and clear but is geared mainly to sociology and with limited coverage of the sort of statistical tools useful for history.

F. Daly, D. J. Hand, M. C. Jones, A. D. Lunn and K. J. McConway, *Elements of statistics* (Harlow, 1995), Chapters 3 and 5. A very well produced and detailed Open University text.

R. Darcy and R. C. Rohrs, *A guide to quantitative history* (Westport, CT, 1995), Chapter 3. An American text concentrating upon inferential statistics. Not as easy to follow as Haskins and Jeffrey for the novice but, geared to historical data, it does provide useful examples.

R. Floud, *An introduction to quantitative methods for historians* (London, 1973; 2nd edn, 1979), Chapter 5.

T. Hannagan, *Mastering statistics* (London 1982; 3rd edn 1997), Chapters 6 and 7. This is the clearest of the short general statistics texts available.

L. Haskins and K. Jeffrey, *Understanding quantitative history*, Cambridge, MA, 1991), Chapter 3.

R. Soloman and C. Winch, *Calculating and computing for social science and arts students* (Buckingham, 1994), Chapter 4. A short Open University social science text which includes a good introduction to basic calculations involving fractions, decimals, percentages, powers and forming algebraic equations.

|5|

Time-series and indices

For the historian time is of the essence; it embraces growth and decay, stagnation or adaptation, change in all its complexity.[1]

Where we start and where we end and how we get there do not lie implicit and latent in the manner of history itself waiting only to be teased out by the skilled historian. Such matters are constructed by historians themselves as they order the material within certain categories and declare certain chronologies 'periods'. In this process some things are suppressed, while others are privileged. It is sometimes thought that this allows historical statements only the status of fiction. Yet it is equally arguable that such artifices are enabling and empowering.[2]

Historians are often concerned with change over time and with chronological variation. They thus commonly need to collect and to consider chronological data or **time-series**. As the above quotations suggest, many of the most interesting historical questions concern growth or decline and fluctuations over time. Many interesting historical interpretations involve an appreciation of distinctive periods and turning points which historians create and justify. With this in mind this chapter considers the prospects and pitfalls involved in the collection, manipulation and analysis of time-series

A time-series consists of numerical data recorded at intervals of time in chronological order. It is thus a special case of a data vector in which measures of a variable are in chronological order. Time intervals can be yearly, monthly, quarterly, weekly or daily. As long as the intervals are regular, there are statistical techniques which we can use to analyse the series. The variable altering over time (e.g. exports, wages, capital investment, strikes, crimes, births, deaths) can be expressed as a monetary value, volume or quantity, or it might be converted into an index (also known as a **ratio value**).

5.1 Index numbers (indices)

An index number (or ratio value) is the value of a variable expressed as a percentage. The percentage is calculated as a proportion of the value which the variable holds in a so-called **base period** (most often a **base year**).

What are the advantages of using index numbers (or indices) rather than original data?

- Indices enable easier identification of trends and variations in the time-series especially where the original units are complicated (e.g. pounds, shillings and pence; tons and hundredweights; bushels; acres; rods and perches).
- Indices make it easy to compare the movement of two or more simultaneous time-series one with another, if they have the same base year. This is especially important where the original data values of the different series have different units (e.g. strikes and average wages, beer in millions of gallons produced and tobacco consumption in pounds per head).
- Indices enable the formation of composite and real indices (see below) which express the movement of weighted or adjusted variables.

5.2 The formation of indices

Indices are generally formed for prices, quantities or monetary values. To convert a time-series from original values to index numbers it is first necessary to select a base year (month or day, depending on the time intervals involved). The index value of 100 is given to the data value for that year. Every other year is then expressed as a percentage of the base year.[3] In Table 5.1 1766 was chosen as the base year. The index for 1765 ($I^{(1765)}$) is then calculated as follows.

Table 5.1 Strikes in France and index of strikes, 1760–70

Year	No. of strikes	Strike index (1766 = 100)
1760	20	67
1761	23	77
1762	22	73
1763	26	87
1764	29	97
1765	45	150
1766	30	100
1767	33	110
1768	35	117
1769	36	120
1770	38	127

Source: hypothetical data.

$$I^{(1765)} = \frac{\text{number of strikes in } 1765}{\text{number of strikes in base year } (1766)} \times 100$$

$$= \frac{45}{30} \times 100$$

$$= 150$$

Similarly, the index for 1761, is calculated as

$$I^{(1761)} = \frac{23}{30} \times 100$$

$$= 77$$

and so on. Note that once a base year has been chosen it should be indicated somewhere in the heading of the table or vector.

Table 5.2 gives beer output in barrels, tobacco consumption per head in pounds weight and net income per head, 1925–38. These are difficult to compare at face value because they are expressed in very different units. They are much easier to compare if one converts each series into indices with the same base year. Once this is done the remarkable feature which shows up in the indices is the extent to which the consumption of tobacco per head of the population held up during the low-income (high-unemployment) years of the early 1930s compared with beer output which remained consistently lower than base-year output in 1929. Of course, one immediately wonders whether the movement of beer output is likely to reflect beer

Table 5.2 Beer output (millions of barrels), tobacco consumption (pounds weight per head) and net income (pounds sterling per head), 1925–38

Year	Beer output	Tobacco consumption	Income	Indices (base year 1929)		
				beer	tobacco	income
1925	26.8	2.96	88.2	107	91	96
1926	25.2	3.00	86.6	100	93	95
1927	25.4	3.04	91.3	101	94	100
1928	24.6	3.11	91.1	98	96	100
1929	25.1	3.24	91.4	100	100	100
1930	23.9	3.31	86.2	95	102	94
1931	20.8	3.27	79.5	83	101	87
1932	18.0	3.23	77.1	72	100	84
1933	20.2	3.22	80.2	80	99	88
1934	20.9	3.41	83.1	83	105	91
1935	22.0	3.51	87.6	88	108	96
1936	22.7	3.72	93.2	90	115	102
1937	24.2	3.87	97.6	96	119	107
1938	24.7	4.00	98.3	98	123	108

Source: B. R. Mitchell, *British historical statistics* (Cambridge, 1988), pp. 709–11, 829.

consumption per head. If so an interesting comparison could be made about the impact of the conditions of the 1930s upon beer and tobacco consumption. Lower beer output figures might, however, reflect the loss of export markets, and this would have to be checked from other evidence before one could be sure that the output reflected domestic consumption, including the distribution of domestic consumption amongst different social classes as well as average consumption per head.

Converting raw data into indices with the same base year also enables them to be graphed together for comparative purposes. Figure 5.1 is reproduced from Charles Feinstein's recent article on the standard of living during the industrial revolution in Britain. It graphs the movements of a new food price index constructed by Feinstein with an older retail price index recorded by contemporaries for Oldham, Manchester and Staffordshire. The results are reassuringly similar although the fluctuations in the new index after 1820 are likely more accurately to reflect food prices paid by the mass of the population than is the older series.[4]

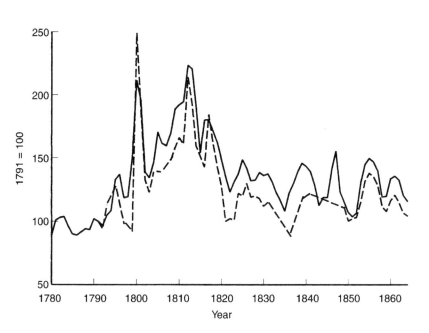

Fig. 5.1 Indices of food prices, 1780–1870. Solid line = Feinstein's food index; dashed line = retail price series.
Source: C. H. Feinstein, 'Pessimism perpetuated: real wages and the standard of living in Britain during and after the industrial revolution', *Journal of Economic History*, 58, 3 (1998), p. 637.

Choice of base year can be important in creating an impression of change in an index. If a low value near the start of the series is chosen, the index may appear at first glance to be growing much more significantly than if a later, higher figure is chosen. It is normally best to choose a base year near the middle of a series and a year which is not markedly out of line with the rest of the values or any perceivable trend.

From the data in Table 5.1 1766 was chosen as the base year because it is near the middle of the series and the value for that year is not markedly out of line (unlike 1765). In Table 5.2 1929 was chosen as the base year for each comsumption series for similar reasons. Feinstein chose 1791 (Figure 5.1) because it was the first year for which all the series were available but also because it is not out of line with other readings compared with values in the period 1798–1820. Once indices have been formed it is possible to go on to produce composite and real indices.

5.3 Composite indices

A **composite index** is an index combining the simultaneous movement of several variables in weighted combination. Composite indices are commonly used in estimates of the movement of average wages which are based upon figures for different occupational groups. They are also used a lot in estimates of the movement of the cost of living based upon price variation in the major components of family expenditure. Estimates of industrial output based on output figures from key sectors and estimates of change in agricultural prices based upon price series for individual crops and other products are further examples of the sort of information which composite indices can be formed to calculate.

To form a composite index one must follow four steps.

1. One must first decide which series to include in the composite. This is an especially important decision to be made when estimating the movement of living costs because there may be many different price series which could be included. It will be necessary first to decide what the main components of living costs are likely to have been. To do this a so-called basket of goods is compiled, with the major components represented. Price series evidence is then sought which will reflect the price movements of these components.
2. All of the separate indices which are to be included in the composite must have the same base year. If they do not already it is very easy to convert a series to a new base year, as shown in Table 5.3 and explained below.
3. Next one must make (often difficult) decisions about **weights** based on a judgement as to the relative importance of each individual series in the overall index. If for example one is estimating an index of the movement of living costs one will need to decide what proportion of the 'basket of

goods' comprises rent, fuel, clothing, food, transport, etc., so that one gives the changing prices of these items their due emphasis in the overall composite index. (See examples of calculation of weighted composite indices in Tables 5.4 and 5.5).

4. Finally, one must multiply each index number by its weight, add these together and then divide by the sum of the weights.

The common base year

Before giving an example of the construction of a composite index it is necessary to demonstrate how to convert indices to a common base year. Table 5.3 gives index numbers for the wages of agricultural and industrial workers in the Eastern seaboard of the United States in the late nineteenth century. Before attempting to create a composite index it is necessary to ensure that both series have the same base year. We here choose to convert the industrial wage series to base year 1890 to conform with the agricultural wage series. To convert the industrial wage index to a base year of 1890 each value of the old index was placed successively over the value for 1890 and multiplied by 100. For example, the new index number for the year 1870, $I^{(1870)}$, may be calculated as follows:

$$I^{(1870)} = \frac{\text{index of 1870 in existing index } (1880 = 100)}{\text{index of new base year (1890) in existing index } (1880 = 100)} \times 100$$

$$= \frac{93}{103} \times 100$$

$$= 90$$

Table 5.3 Indices of wages of industrial and agricultural workers (selected years)

Year	Indices of wages		
	agricultural 1890 = 100	industrial 1880 = 100	recalculated industrial 1890 = 100
1870	89	93	90
1875	88	95	92
1880	92	100	97
1885	96	98	95
1890	100	103	100
1900	98	99	96
1905	101	108	105
1910	99	110	107

Source: hypothetical data.

Similarly, for 1905,

$$I^{(1905)} = \frac{108}{103} \times 100$$

$$= 105$$

Conversion to the same base year enables much easier comparison between the two series, showing the industrial wage series to be more buoyant than the agricultural wage series.

5.4 Construction of composite indices: some examples

In the example in Table 5.4, the wage indices of four groups of workers in England and Wales are given for sample years 1780–1830. Once we have checked that they all have the same base year, to construct a composite index we must now give each component a weight. With an index of this kind we would need to make the best estimate we can (based on complementary historical evidence) of the balance of each group of workers in the working population overall. We would need to justify our decision about the weights and point to the evidence which we have used. Weights can be expressed in any numbers which give an indication of proportion in relation to the whole. They are usually expressed in numbers which add up to 10 or to 100, which makes calculation easier, but they do not have to add up to such round sums. In our example we might decide to assign weights as follows:

- agriculture, 3;
- skilled manufacture, 1;

- unskilled, 4;
- service sector, 2.

Table 5.4 Indices of average money earnings per week (1890 = 100) and the formation of a composite index for selected years in the period 1780–1830

Year	Index				Composite index
	agric.	skilled manu.	unskilled	service sector	
1780	65	69	55	53	59
1810	68	71	50	50	58
1815	72	73	64	52	65
1820	70	74	64	54	65
1830	73	78	68	58	69
Weight	3	1	4	2	

Note: agric. = agriculture; manu. = manufacturing.
Source: hypothetical data.

To form our composite index we now take each index number in turn and multiply it by its weight. We then add these and divide by the sum of the weights. Thus the composite index for 1780, $I_C^{(1780)}$, was formed as follows:

$$I_C^{(1780)} = \frac{(65 \times 3) + (69 \times 1) + (55 \times 4) + (53 \times 2)}{(3 + 1 + 4 + 2)}$$

$$= \frac{590}{10} = 59$$

The composite for 1820, $I_C^{(1820)}$, was formed as follows:

$$I_C^{(1820)} = \frac{(70 \times 3) + (74 \times 1) + (64 \times 4) + (54 \times 2)}{10} = 65$$

The main problem in forming an accurate composite index is getting the weights right. This is not a statistical issue at all but a matter of historical judgement. Weights are difficult to establish partly because of unreliable or partial evidence and the need to estimate proportions and partly because weights usually change over time. The wrong weights can considerably distort the composite index and make it meaningless. So central is this difficulty that it is referred to as 'the index number problem'.

In our examples in Tables 5.3 and 5.4, the bare figures disguise the many pitfalls in constructing wage indices even for one sector. Obtaining accurate money wage data is difficult when few wage books survive and when many workers were paid in family groups, by piece rates or in kind. There were also very significant regional and local wage differentials and variations between different occupations within each sector, to say nothing of the need to make allowance for female as well as male wages and for seasonal and more chronic unemployment and underemployment. From the patchy data available each sectoral wage series is itself inevitably already a composite, with the many problems which the construction of that composite has entailed.

Much debate amongst economic historians occurs over weighting decisions: 'the index number problem'. In revisions to indices of industrial output in Britain in the eighteenth and nineteenth century, for example, debates have hinged upon two things: choice of which industries to include (which in turn has related to the existence and reliability of the data) and what weights to assign to each industry. The choice of the weights radically affects the resulting calculation of the rate of growth of industrial output overall. One of the earliest indices of British industrial output since 1750 was compiled by Walther Hoffman in 1939 and this became a foundation for much theorising about the industrial revolution. In 1982 C. Knick Harley argued that Hoffman had overweighted the faster growing industries, especially the cotton industry, for the period 1770–1815.[5] Harley's revision suggested 40 per cent lower output growth for industry in the classic industrial revolution period and has ushered in a whole series of studies of slow growth and gradualism. Since 1982 further, more minor revisions have been suggested by Crafts and Harley and by Jackson, based on differing weights and compositions of the index, and there have been other challenges based upon revisions to the price data used.[6]

Most historians have chosen to weight according to the money value of the output. This is measured by multiplying unit prices by the quantities purchased in some base year (hence the importance of collecting accurate price data, which is difficult). But the choice of year upon which to base the weight is also a problem, because weights change over time. If values in 1850 are used as weights for British industrial output in the nineteenth century, cotton will loom very large. If the weights are based on 1913 values (after many years of much slower growth in cotton output than in other sectors), the role of cotton will be much smaller. There is no objectively correct way of adding up the elements in a composite index, especially where the weights are likely to change over the time period being studied. The choice must be made and justified according to the purposes of the research.

Various weighting schemes have been named after nineteenth-century investigators. A **Paasche index** uses estimates for the current or last year (or time period) as weights throughout the series. A Laspeyres index uses estimated weights for the initial year (or time period). In a period of significant economic, structural and technological change both the Paasche and Laspeyres weightings will introduce distortions, and it is common for both to be given so that upper and lower boundary measures may be compared. The Laspeyres index, for example, will tend to overstate price increases because no substitutions are allowed and because new goods and improvements in the quality of goods over time must be ignored. The Paasche index may have the opposite effect.

Some weighting systems use neither Paasche nor Laspeyres but attempt to change the weights over time, usually by averaging some component of the base and current indices. This is a difficult practice not only because it is difficult to estimate when or at what pace weights may change but also because important variations in the indices may occur simply as a result of a sudden shift in the weights applied, especially if this is not phased in very gradually.

Very often, composite indices are used to calculate change in the cost of living. The Retail Price Index measures the change from month to month in the average level of prices for the commodities and services purchased by nearly nine tenths of the households of the United Kingdom. The index is based on a stratified random sample of households whose basket of goods and the weights attached to various goods is researched in some detail. (See Chapter 8 for discussion of sampling techniques including stratified and random sampling.) A basket of goods is an assessment of the main goods and services purchased by households. Table 5.5 gives an example of the construction of a composite cost-of-living index.

Apart from the problems of obtaining reliable price data for periods in the past, the main difficulty in establishing a cost-of-living index is getting the 'basket of goods' right. Often the basket of goods is constrained by the data available or it encourages the use of unreliable proxy figures if price data for an important item in the basket of goods are missing. One of the earliest cost-of-living indices for the nineteenth century was produced by Silberling. J. H. Clapham used the Silberling index in 1926 in his estimates of the living standards of the working classes during the period of industrialisation, but, as T. S. Ashton pointed out, 'Silberling man' was a strange creature indeed:

> He did not occupy a house, or at least was not called upon to pay rent. He allowed himself only a moderate amount of bread and very little porridge, and he never touched potatoes or strong drink. On the other hand, he got though quite considerable quantities of beef and mutton and showed a fondness for butter. Perhaps he was a diabetic. The ordinary Englishman of the eighteenth century would have been puzzled by him.[7]

Silberling had relied upon those price series which were available to him at the time, but these gave a distorted view of the composition of living costs, the so-called 'basket of goods', and made Clapham's calculations easy for Ashton to deride.[8]

Table 5.5 Components of an index of living costs, 1890–1900 (1900 = 100)

Year	Food	Rent	Clothing	Fuel	Sundries	Composite index
1890	101	93	102	80	89	97.68
1891	103	94	102	78	85	98.72
1892	104	95	101	78	81	99.20
1893	99	96	100	85	81	96.80
1894	95	96	99	73	75	93.08
1895	92	97	98	71	75	91.16
1896	92	98	99	72	75	91.52
1897	95	98	98	73	75	93.28
1898	99	99	97	73	74	95.68
1899	95	99	96	79	76	93.72
1900	100	100	100	100	100	100.00
Weight	60	16	12	8	4	

Source: A. L. Bowley, *Wages and income in the United Kingdom since 1860* (Cambridge, 1937), pp. 120–1 Reproduced in R. Floud, *Introduction to quantitative methods for historians* (London, 1973), p. 126.

5.5 Real indices

A **real index** is the movement of a time-series, in index form, which has been adjusted to allow for the movement of another series, usually one of prices. This gives a measure of real change (with the effect of deflation or inflation taken into account) for example with real wages or real incomes or the values of exports or imports in constant prices.

To form a real index one must:

1. use the same base year for each component index;
2. divide the series to be adjusted (in the example below, the wage index) by the second series (in this example, the cost-of-living index) and multiply by 100 for each cell of information.

In Table 5.6 the composite earnings estimates from the calculations in Table 5.5 have been matched with a price series to produce a real index of 'living standards' (insofar as these are indicated by changes in the purchasing power of wages alone!). In Table 5.6, the two series did not originally have the same base year. The base year of the wage series was changed to 1900, as indicated on page 114.

A further example of real indices is provided in Table 5.7 which shows gate receipts and admission prices at English football league grounds, 1927–1994. Gate revenues and admission prices are given in the original units of measure (£) but they have also been converted into indices and deflated using the Retail Price Index. Indices make the figures easier to compare with one another, and the real indices convey change in the real cost of attendance at games for the fans and the purchasing power of revenues received by the clubs.

Table 5.6 Construction of an index of real wages, 1890–1900

Year	Money wages (1914 = 100)	Money wages (1900 = 100)	Cost of living (1900 = 100)	Real wages (1900 = 100)
1890	83	88.3	97.7	90.4
1891	83	88.3	998.7	89.5
1892	83	88.3	99.2	89.0
1893	83	88.3	96.8	91.2
1894	83	88.3	93.1	94.8
1895	83	88.3	91.2	96.8
1896	83	88.3	91.5	96.5
1897	84	89.4	93.3	95.8
1898	87	92.6	95.7	96.8
1899	89	94.7	93.7	101.1
1900	94	100.0	100.0	100.0

Source: based on, R. Floud, *Introduction to quantitative methods for historians* (London, 1973), p. 128. Original source: money wage index from E. C. Ramsbottom, reprinted in B. R. Mitchell and P. Deane, *Abstract of British historical statistics* (Cambridge, 1962), p. 345. Cost of living index is taken from Table 5.5.

Table 5.7 Aggregate league attendance, gate receipts, and average admission prices, 1927–1994

Year	Attendance[a]		Gate revenues[b]		Real gate revenue (1927 = 100)	Average admission price (£)	Real average admission price (1927 = 100)
	total	coef. var.	total	coef. var.			
1927	23.4	0.65	1 373	0.69	100	0.06	100
1932	21.8	0.66	1 263	0.73	110	0.06	118
1937	26.4	0.63	1 575	0.72	133	0.06	118
1947	35.4	0.61	2 933	0.70	183	0.08	121
1952	39.0	0.57	4 135	0.65	197	0.11	118
1957	32.7	0.57	4 311	0.67	171	0.13	122
1962	28.0	0.63	4 981	0.76	175	0.18	146
1967	28.9	0.73	6 931	0.90	205	0.24	166
1972	28.7	0.77	10 814	0.95	238	0.38	194
1973	25.4	0.85	11 823	1.00	241	0.46	222
1974	25.0	0.79	13 174	0.97	239	0.53	223
1975	25.6	0.81	15 180	0.98	228	0.59	209
1976	24.9	0.83	18 822	0.97	231	0.76	217
1977	26.0	0.82	22 220	0.97	234	0.85	210
1978	25.4	0.84	26 651	1.00	257	1.05	236
1979	24.5	0.83	28 960	0.95	254	1.18	243
1980	24.6	0.79	36 911	0.95	272	1.50	258
1981	21.9	0.82	40 239	1.02	264	1.84	281
1982	20.0	0.84	40 523	1.04	239	2.03	279
1983	18.8	0.82	42 096	1.03	236	2.24	294
1984	18.3	0.82	44 760	1.06	239	2.44	304
1985	17.8	0.92	49 276	1.17	249	2.77	327
1986	16.5	0.94	48 901	1.15	236	2.97	334
1987	17.4	0.89	55 844	1.08	259	3.21	348
1988	18.0	0.81	63 906	1.00	287	3.56	373
1989	18.5	0.77	72 885	0.98	304	3.95	384
1990	19.5	0.77	87 219	0.97	337	4.48	405
1991	19.5	0.81	103 691	1.04	369	5.32	442
1992	20.4	0.83	127 329	1.09	435	6.25	499
1993	20.6	0.77	146 238	1.10	485	7.09	549
1994	21.7	0.82	163 655	1.10	534	7.55	576

[a]Millions. [b]£Thousands.
Note: in order to keep the table to a manageable size, figures are given for every fifth year only, up to the early 1970s. Years are end-years of football seasons; i.e. 1927 is the 1926–7 season, and so on. Gate revenues and admission prices are deflated using the Retail Price Index. Coef. var. = coefficient of variation.
Source: S. Dobson and J. Goddard, 'Performance, revenue and cross subsidization in the Football League, 1927–1994', *Economic History Review*, 51, 4 (1998), p. 767.

5.6 Time-series: influences

There are several methods of statistical analysis of time-series. Most centre around the problem of separating out or isolating the various sorts of change and the component causes of change in the value of a variable over time. The methods of time-series analysis assume that there *may* be three types of influence affecting any time-series:

- *trend influences*, affecting long-term growth or decline;
- *regular fluctuations* around the long-term trend caused by seasonal or cyclical factors;
- *irregular fluctuations*, that are short-term, generally unrepeated, movements caused by, for example, wars, diseases and changes in government policy.

We must use historical judgement to ask if any or all of these three influences may be present in a series before we attempt to isolate and examine them. It is wise to graph the series to get an idea of its character before undertaking any more complex time-series analysis. In a time-series graph it is conventional to place time on the horizontal axis. In Figure 5.2 all three influences appear to be present. There is a weak and interrupted but perceptible upward trend in burials over time, there are fluctuations, which appear to have some regularity, and there are certainly one-off years of exceptionally high or low levels of death. The baptism series has a less obvious upward thrust until the late 1570s and, again, there appear to be some years where baptisms were excptionally high or low even allowing for the presence of defective registration. (Defective registration can be caused by a number of things, such as death of the incumbent, periods of war or social disturbance, lost pages from the register, illegibility of the register.)

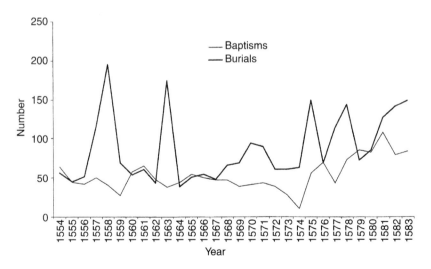

Fig. 5.2 Time-series graph of burials and baptisms, St Martin in the Fields, London, 1554–83. Source: parish registers, St Martin in the Fields, London, 1554–83.

5.7 Trends

There are several ways in which a **trend** may be identified and measured. As mentioned above, the simplest way to approach the nature of the time-series initially is to graph it. This alone may highlight the trend sufficiently for certain analytical purposes. If the time-series variable on the graph is generally upward sloping from left to right this indicates a positive trend (growth over time). If the time-series variable is generally downward sloping this indicates a negative trend (decline over time). The steeper the slope the greater the rate of growth or decline.

Not all trends in data are linear (i.e. tending towards a straight-line trajectory in one direction). Sometimes non-linear trends are present in data: the observations do not lie around a straight line but around a curve of some sort. These cannot be analysed in the manner described below and it is always wise to draw a rough graph of any time-series data before engaging in more sophisticated calculations in order to check that a linear trend may be present. It is possible to analyse time-series which embody non-linear trends, but these are less commonly applied and are largely beyond the scope of this volume. Graphing the data at the outset may also highlight a shift in the slope of the trend (growth rate) at a particular point in time: this suggests a need to measure growth rates for certain periods within the data rather than over the series as a whole.

Measures of trend: growth rates

Growth rates are often used as a general measure of the pace and direction of trend in a time-series. Growth rates can be positive (when the values of a series are generally increasing over time) or negative (when the values of a series are decreasing over time). There are several ways to measure growth rates but it is important with all of them to acknowledge at the outset that choice of period over which the growth rate is to be measured can make a big difference. Many time-series exhibit marked cyclical fluctuations. This is particularly true of national income and its components and determinants (e.g. gross domestic product, industrial output, exports). If we choose to measure growth rates from the depth of a slump at the start of the series to a major boom at the end, the growth rate is likely to be seriously inflated. If, conversely, we choose to measure from a boom year at the beginning to a slump year at the end the growth rate is likely seriously to underestimate growth in the period. Both should be avoided.

Two different growth rates are commonly used: mean increase per year and average percentage growth rate. The mean increase per year is calculated as follows:

$$\text{mean increase per year} = \frac{X_N - X_T}{N}$$

where

X_T is the value of the variable at the start of the series;
X_N is the value of the variable at the end of the series;
N is the number of yearly observations.

Table 5.8 and Figure 5.2 show a positive growth rate for burials. A less obvious positive growth for baptisms is present, especially from the 1570s. Despite some growth in the period 1578–82, marriages have a more stable

Table 5.8 Annual baptisms, marriages and burials, St Martin in the Fields, London, 1554–83

Year	Number of baptisms	Number of marriages	Number of burials	Plague deaths[a]
1554	64	25	56	
1555	44	15	45	
1556	42	12	52	
1557	50	24	115	3
1558	40	18	195	1
1559	27	23	69	
1560	58	25	54	
1561	65	16	61	
1562	48	19	43	
1563	38	23	175	145
1564	44	25	38	1
1565	55	29	51	
1566	50	28	55	
1567	47	22	48	
1568	47	23	66	
1569	39	28	69	
1570	41	23	94	
1571	43	29	90	
1572	39	26	61	
1573	28*	18*	61	
1574	11*	6*	63	
1575	56	29	150	51
1576	70	35	69	4
1577	43*	25	114	14
1578	74	41	144	
1579	86	39	73	
1580	83	26	86	
1581	109	30	128	
1582	80	30	142	
1583	84	25	150	

[a]Number of deaths said to be the result of the bubonic plague.
*Defective registration.
Source: parish registers, St Martin in the Fields, London, 1554–83.

character. The growth rate for burials, taking the first and the last observation, gives a result of 3.13 burials [(150 – 56)/30], but this probably exaggerates the underlying growth rate because the last observation is one of a group of particularly high numbers of deaths. The growth rate for marriages is 0 because the higher levels of the 1570s are not reflected in a measure which relies on the first and last observations only.

This is the problem with using the mean increase per year: the value of the first and last reading become all-important. It is a serious problem unless the series is growing or declining very steadily and without major fluctuations. If the trend is unstable the first or last reading may be markedly out of line with the general trend and will distort the growth-rate result. If, on graphing the data, it is obvious that the first or last reading is widely out of line it is wise to take another value near the start or end of the series instead. If this is done the value of N will need to be adjusted accordingly.

In the example given (Table 5.8) the first reading for baptisms is markedly out of line and it would give a more accurate measure of the growth rate for the whole baptism series if we took the second rather than the first observation. If we were to draw two lines on the baptism graph in Figure 5.2 from the first to the last observation and from the second to the last, the two, with their different gradients (hence different growth rates) would illustrate the difference made by choosing a start date which is markedly out of line with the trend of the series. Taking the second observation, the mean increase per year becomes 1.3 baptisms instead of 0.7 baptisms.

Note: the unit of measurement in which the mean is expressed is the original unit of the series (e.g. baptisms (in the case above), export values, number of people able to sign marriage registers, incidents of industrial sabotage and so on). It is thus impossible to compare one growth rate with the growth rate of other series which are expressed in different units. We may, for example, wish to compare: the growth rate of export values over time with the tonnage of the merchant fleet; the number of people able to sign marriage registers with investment levels in education or incidents of industrial sabotage with wage rates. For these sorts of growth rate comparisons, a different measure is needed. One possibility is the *average percentage growth rate.*

The average percentage growth rate is not simply the average of the growth rates from year to year in a series. Such a measure would overestimate growth because growth is cumulative. What is needed is a measure which expresses each year's growth as a percentage of the value of the previous year. This is the purpose of the average percentage growth rate: it measures the average of the increase of each year or period over the previous one (in other words, the compound growth rate), expressed as a percentage. It eliminates the problem of needing a common unit for comparison (as the growth rate is expressed as a percentage) but it still suffers from reliance upon only the first and last observations chosen.

The formula for the average percentage growth rate, r, is as follows:

$$r = \left[\sqrt[m]{\left(\frac{X_N}{X_T} \right)} - 1 \right] \times 100$$

This is exactly the same as:

$$r = \left[\left(\frac{X_N}{X_T} \right)^{1/m} - 1 \right] \times 100$$

which has the advantage of being easily computable with a calculator where:

r is the average percentage growth rate;
m is the difference in years between the first and the last reading;
X_T is the value of the variable at the start of the series;
X_N is the value of the variable at the last reading.

A computer package will make the calculation automatic once the key figures are provided.

If we wish to compare the growth rates of baptisms and burials [r(baptisms) and r(burials), respectively] shown in Table 5.8 we could use the following calculations:

$$r\text{ (baptisms)} = \left[\left(\frac{84}{44} \right)^{1/28} - 1 \right] \times 100 = 2.3$$

$$r\text{ (burials)} = \left[\left(\frac{150}{56} \right)^{1/29} - 1 \right] \times 100 = 3.5$$

(The baptism growth rate uses the second and the last observation to avoid 1554, which is out of line.) The growth rate of burials is greater than the growth rate of baptisms, though the latter is probably exaggerated more than the former by the high value of the last reading.

Calculation of the trend line

The trend is an alternative and often a better measure of the pace of change than growth rates because it takes account of all readings not just the first and the last. It is formed by calculating and drawing the line of best fit through the series.

We can draw a trend line roughly through a series, after graphing the points as in Figure 5.3, but to get its position exactly right all the distances of observations above the line must be equal to those below.

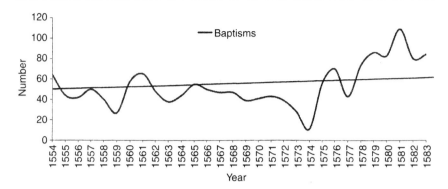

Fig. 5.3 Trend line of baptisms, St Martin in the Fields, London, 1554–83. Source: parish registers, St Martin in the Fields, London, 1554–83.

We can calculate the exact position of the **trend line** by using the general equation for a straight line:

$$Y = a + bX$$

where

Y is the data value;
X is the time unit;
a is the intercept (the value of Y when $X = 0$);
b is the slope.

The intercept a and the slope b of the trend line can be calculated as follows:

$$a = \frac{\Sigma Y}{N}$$

$$b = \frac{\Sigma X Y}{\Sigma X^2}$$

where

Y are the data values;
N is the number of values;
X is the time unit expressed so that $X = 0$ in the middle of the series.

We take the time units expressed so that $X = 0$ in the middle of the series because it makes the calculation much simpler when this is done manually (in particular, it makes the calculation of X and XY less unwieldy, as shown in Table 5.9). Such calculations are normally done using computer software, leaving the time units as in the original observation. In this case the formulae in use are:

$$a = \frac{\Sigma Y - b\Sigma X}{N}$$

$$b = \frac{N\Sigma XY - (\Sigma X)(\Sigma Y)}{N\Sigma X^2 - (\Sigma X)^2}$$

Once we have the trend-line equation we can find all the values of Y which lie on the trend-line by substituting values of X in the equation.

Table 5.9 Calculation of the trend and of the de-trended series of baptisms, St Martin in the Fields, London, 1554–82.

Year	Number of baptisms (Y)	Number of time units from 1568 (X)	X²	XY	Trend values	De-trended series
1554	64	−14	196	−896	37.83	26.17
1555	44	−13	169	−572	38.87	5.13
1556	42	−12	144	−504	39.92	2.08
1557	50	−11	121	−550	40.96	9.04
1558	40	−10	100	−400	42.00	−2.00
1559	27	−9	81	−243	43.05	−16.05
1560	58	−8	64	−464	44.09	1.91
1561	65	−7	49	−455	45.14	19.86
1562	48	−6	36	−288	46.18	1.82
1563	38	−5	25	−190	47.23	−9.23
1564	44	−4	16	−176	48.27	−4.27
1565	55	−3	9	−165	49.32	5.7
1566	50	−2	4	−100	50.36	−0.36
1567	47	−1	1	−47	51.40	−4.40
1568	47	0	0	0	52.45	−5.45
1569	39	1	1	39	53.49	−14.49
1570	41	2	4	82	54.54	−13.54
1571	43	3	9	129	55.58	−12.58
1572	39	4	16	156	56.63	−17.63
1573	28	5	25	140	57.67	−29.67
1574	11	6	36	66	58.71	−47.71
1575	56	7	49	392	59.76	−3.76
1576	70	8	64	560	60.80	9.20
1577	43	9	81	387	61.85	−18.85
1578	74	10	100	740	62.89	11.11
1579	86	11	121	946	63.94	22.06
1580	83	12	144	996	64.98	18.02
1581	109	13	169	1417	66.02	42.98
1582	80	14	196	1120	67.07	12.93
Total	1521[a]		2030[b]	2120[c]		

[a]ΣY [b]ΣX^2 [c]ΣXY
Source: parish registers, St Martin in the Fields, London, 1554–82.

There are three things to note.

- We can now get a much more accurate measure of growth rates by using the first and last value of the trend line instead of the first and last value of the original series (remember that the trend values have taken into account all the values of the series).
- Once we have the linear trend we can subtract the trend value for each time period from the original data value. This will leave us with the **de-trended series** composed of any regular and irregular fluctuations which are present. We can now see these more clearly as a preliminary to possible further analysis.
- We can use the trend line to forecast or to predict what the values of a variable might be in time periods later than that for which data are available. This possibility of extrapolation has many uses in history, in economics and in many other subjects. It has great potential in terms of the insights which can be gained, but it must be remembered that useful forecasting is dependent both upon the accuracy of measuring existing behaviour and upon the unchanging nature of influences which may affect the behaviour of a dependent variable more in one time period than in another.

Following the example in Table 5.8 and Figure 5.3 (the baptism series) we can now create the trend values of baptisms and, by taking each of these trend values from the corresponding data value in turn, we can create the de-trended series of baptisms, as shown in Table 5.9. Spreadsheet or statistical software can, of course, make short work of this sort of calculation even for very long time-series once the data have been inputted.

The formula for the trend line for baptisms is $Y = a + bX$. With respect to the data in Table 5.9, we now know that

$$a = \frac{\Sigma Y}{N} = \frac{1521}{29} = 52.4$$

$$b = \frac{\Sigma XY}{\Sigma X^2} = \frac{2120}{2030} = 1.04$$

The value of b is small because the trend for baptisms is very weak. This may be partly because we have included the years of defective registration which almost certainly significantly underestimate baptisms.

We calculate the trend values from the formula and form the de-trended series by subtracting each trend value from the corresponding data value in turn, as illustrated in Table 5.9.

Given the weakness of the trend in the baptism series, particularly before 1574, one might legitimately question the usefulness of calculating the trend here. The advantages of doing so are much more obvious where time-series have a more notable trend. However, the trend line does allow a more accurate growth rate to be calculated for baptisms over the series as a whole, and the de-trended series does assist in identifying years which are seriously 'out of line'. With such a weak trend and defective data the temptation to extrapolate or predict values for baptisms after 1583 or before 1554 should be firmly ignored.

5.8 Fluctuations

By no means all time-series have regular, periodic fluctuations, but many do. The most common *regular fluctuations* embodied in time-series are *seasonal* and *cyclical*. Seasonal fluctuations are commonly found in temperate parts of the globe and especially in preindustrial data as the rhythm of economic, social and demographic activity was very much underpinned by climatic variations and the agricultural calendar. Seasonal factors continue to influence activity in many areas of economic and social life to the present day. Cycles of booming output and employment followed by years of relative depression are also common in most industrial economies as trade and investment tend to build up in a wave of confidence and optimism to a point at which interest rates rise, markets become overstocked and business confidence lapses. Longer cycles of activity may also be present in long-run output and investment series because economic activity is influenced by the clustering of innovations around new products and/or services which occurs periodically.[9]

Regular cycles occur in all sorts of time-series. For example retail sales can rise and fall in relation to the seasons of the fashion year; food prices may rise and fall in relation to the regular swings of the harvest year; employment levels in jobs affected by seasonal demands rise and fall in relation to peaks of activity at Christmas or Easter; crime figures sometimes rise and fall in relation to the business cycle and the shifts in unemployment and income levels which this creates; profit rates, interest rates and many other series often shadow the regular fluctuations of the business cycle.

Cyclical fluctuations and moving averages

Cyclical fluctuations are regular movements of a time-series which last more than one year. (Cycles which occur within years are called seasonal fluctuations and are considered on pp. 132–4).

It is useful as a first step to check if cyclical fluctuations appear to be present in a time-series by drawing a graph. If important, the cyclical fluctuations will often show up when the series is graphed, and they can then be discussed as part of the analysis of the time-series. If, in the judgement of the historian, cyclical fluctuations of an identifiable periodicity are present, it is possible to use a moving average to eliminate them so that trend and/or irregular fluctuations can be viewed more closely.

A moving average is calculated and applied as follows.

1. It is first necessary to make an informed judgement about the periodicity of the cycle. Does the graph suggest a cycle of seven years (a common business cycle length) or of nine years (sometimes seen in demographic statistics) or of any other clearly identifiable length?
2. Next one must form a new series. The first observation of the new series is taken at the midpoint of the first cycle and is the mean of all observa-

Table 5.10 Mean heights (in inches) and the five-year moving average of mean heights (in inches) of English rural-born female convicts, aged 21–49 years, 1788–1819

Year of birth	Number of convicts	Height	Five-year moving average
1788	7	61.71	
1789	17	61.90	
1790	9	61.53	61.91
1791	15	62.35	61.66
1792	15	62.08	61.56
1793	16	60.47	61.51
1794	11	61.36	61.25
1795	15	61.28	61.17
1796	16	61.06	61.47
1797	18	61.69	61.59
1798	19	61.93	61.68
1799	12	61.98	61.89
1800	16	61.73	61.85
1801	29	62.11	61.67
1802	21	61.48	61.74
1803	29	61.50	61.64
1804	44	61.89	61.61
1805	30	61.24	61.58
1806	30	61.93	61.68
1807	37	61.35	61.65
1808	36	62.00	61.77
1809	33	61.74	61.72
1810	47	61.82	61.67
1811	37	61.68	61.53
1812	47	61.13	61.34
1813	29	61.29	61.19
1814	29	60.78	61.23
1815	28	61.06	61.05
1816	23	61.89	61.12
1817	6	60.21	61.48
1818	10	61.68	
1819	6	62.58	

Source: R. V. Jackson, 'The heights of rural-born English female convicts transported to New South Wales', *Economic History Review*, 59, 3 (1996), p. 586.

tions in the first cycle. Succeeding observations are the means of successive cycle-long groups of observations. The formation of a moving average is illustrated in the example in Table 5.10.

Problems with applying a moving average are as follows.

- Values for several years (half a cycle) at the beginning and end of a series are lost. This is serious if a long cycle is present and if the data only cover a small number of complete cycles.
- The method works to eliminate cycles from the data only if the periodicity of the cycles has been accurately ascertained. A wrong choice of cycle length (illustrated in Figure 5.4) can produce extremely misleading results which invert the appearance of cyclical change in the data. This must be avoided at all costs so use of a moving average to eliminate a regular cycle from a series must be done very carefully and only when there is some certainty that the correct periodicity of the cycle has been identified.

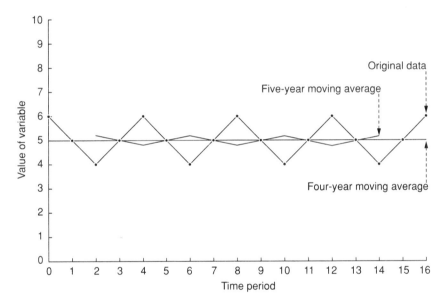

Fig. 5.4 Stylised graph to show the impact of selecting a correct (four-year) and an incorrect (five-year) moving average. Source: R. Floud, *Introduction to quantitative methods for historians* (London, 1973), p. 118.

SMOOTHING THE DATA IN A LONG TIME-SERIES

Moving averages are most often simply used to smooth the data in a graph of a long time-series as is the function of the moving average in Table 5.10. Smoothing data is useful because trends and changes in trends can then be examined. Choosing the wrong periodicity is not so crucial in this case, though a moving average of the most appropriate length should always be the aim. If cycles are not obvious but smoothing is desirable to get rid of exceptional values, a five-year average is commonly chosen.

Seasonal fluctuations

These may be present in any time-series with intervals of less than a year (e.g. quarterly sales figures, monthly unemployment statistics, monthly or weekly food prices). They can be identified by taking the mean value of the variable concerned for each week, month, season or quarter and comparing them. If the original data contain an obvious trend, analysis of seasonality should be undertaken with the de-trended series because trend elements will make the seasonal variations more difficult to observe and to calculate.

Often it is useful to eliminate seasonal variations from a time-series so that irregular fluctuations and/or trends can be viewed more easily. Most official statistics of economic activity (e.g. house prices, unemployment) are 'seasonally adjusted' before they are published.

To separate seasonal fluctuations from a series, one must:

1. calculate trend values;
2. take the mean value of the deviations from trend at each quarter, or season (i.e. the mean of all the first-, second-, third- and fourth-quarter deviations);[10]
3. subtract these means from the original values.

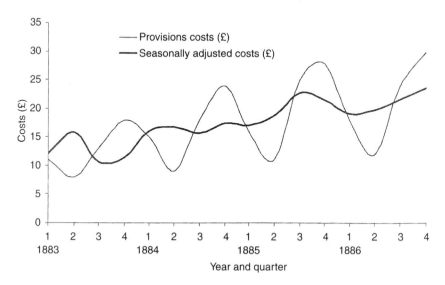

Fig. 5.5 De-seasonalised movement of costs of provisions, Barrow workhouse, 1883–6.
Source: hypothetical data.

It is important to use the deviations from trend series for this exercise rather than the raw data if a linear trend is present. If the de-trended series is not used the estimates of seasonal variation are distorted.

The seasonally adjusted figures leave the trend easier to observe, as in Figure 5.5. The seasonal variations leave the residual non-seasonal, one-off fluctuations easier to observe, as in Table 5.11. These can then become the focus of historical enquiry.

Table 5.11 gives the cost of provisions purchases in the Barrow workhouse in the 1880s. The trend values have been calculated as have the seasonally adjusted costs. These have been calculated by taking the mean deviation from trend for each quarter (−1.05, −7.8, 2.3 and 6.5, respectively) from the original series to create the new series of seasonally adjusted figures (rounded up to one decimal place). The seasonally adjusted costs have been graphed in Figure 5.5. These highlight the trend in the data free from seasonal bias.

In Table 5.11 the trend figures are not derived from the least squares linear calculation but employ a moving average method to avoid imposing a linear trend on the data. (This is why there are no trend figures for the first and second quarters of 1883). The moving average method is often appro-

Table 5.11 Seasonally adjusted costs and residual fluctuations in provisions costs, Barrow workhouse, 1883–6

Year and quarter	Provisions costs (£)	Trend (non-linear)	Seasonally adjusted costs (£)	Seasonal variation	Residual
1883					
1	11		12.1	−1.05	
2	8		15.8	−7.8	
3	13	13	10.7	2.3	−2.3
4	18	13.6	11.5	6.5	−2.1
1884					
1	15	14.3	16.1	−1.05	1.7
2	9	15.8	16.8	−7.8	1
3	18	16.6	15.7	2.3	−0.9
4	24	17	17.5	6.5	0.5
1885					
1	16	18.1	17.1	−1.05	−1.1
2	11	19.5	18.8	−7.8	−0.7
3	25	20.3	22.7	2.3	2.4
4	28	20.6	21.5	6.5	0.9
1886					
1	18	20.6	19.1	−1.05	−1.6
2	12	20.8	19.8	−7.8	−1
3	24		21.7	2.3	
4	30		23.5	6.5	

Source: hypothetical data

priate in establishing trend, and deviation from trend, prior to de-seasonal-ising, but the linear trend figures can also be used. There is a worked example of this in Chapter 6, Table 6.8. It should be noted that there are other more sophisticated methods of isolating seasonal variation some of which are described in the texts listed in the further reading section at the end of this chapter.

Note: if the periodicity of a cycle is known *with some certainty* it is poss-ible to contemplate using the same technique to eliminate the cycle from the series as that used for getting rid of seasonal variations. If a seven-year cycle is present, for example, one could take the mean deviation from trend of each year-one reading, of each year-two reading, etc., and subtract these from the original series. This would have the advantage over a moving average of enabling one to highlight any residual, irregular, short-term fluc-tuations over and above those which one would expect from cyclical activity.

Irregular fluctuations

It follows from the discussion above that if we wish to examine irregular fluctuations more closely we may first de-trend the series. We can then elim-inate seasonal influences, if relevant. If a cycle is present, and we can iden-tify the periodicity, we can also eliminate cyclical influences by using the same technique or by using a moving average. This will leave us with a series of residuals containing irregular variations. We can then concentrate our energy on explaining the extent and the cause of these.

Table 5.11 shows the residual, irregular values which remain after de-trending and de-seasonalising the provisions-cost time-series. These are not large, but the residuals for the third quarters of 1883 (–2.3) and 1885 (+2.4) look sufficiently large to warrant some explanation. Perhaps the number of inmates in the workhouse was the main cause of these variations. This could be checked if complementary sources, such as admissions registers, were available.

5.9 Vital statistics or vital variables

Vital statistics are distributions relating to births, marriages and deaths. They are usually expressed in time-series. Most often these are given as crude birth rates and crude death rates. Crude birth and death rates are the total (live) births or deaths per 1000 of the population during a period of one year.

$$\text{crude birth rate} = \frac{\text{total number of live births} \times 1000}{\text{total population}}$$

$$\text{crude death rate} = \frac{\text{total number of deaths} \times 1000}{\text{total population}}$$

If we wish to compare birth and death rates in two different populations separated in space or time it is necessary to use standardised rather than crude vital rates. Standardised vital rates allow for differing age distributions in the populations concerned. This is done by weighting the crude birth or death rate by the age distribution of a standard population.

Conclusion

Time-series are commonly used by historians who are frequently concerned with identifying and measuring the movement of different variables over time. There are many simple manipulations which assist in the measurement of growth or decline and which enable one to compare the movement of different variables over the same time-period. Indices facilitate the comparison of variables over time and allow the construction of composite variables which incorporate the movement of several components in weighted combination. Real indices can also be produced which reflect the movement of values which have been adjusted to take account of other variables (most often, price movements). The underlying trend in data can be calculated and then removed from the series, enabling regular and irregular fluctuations around the trend to be considered. Time-series can be seasonally adjusted and moving averages can be used to eliminate cyclical fluctuations and to smooth irregularities so that trends can be more easily observed. In all, simple time-series analysis offers a battery of techniques to the historian. Providing these are used with care, with sensitivity to the pitfalls, biases and inaccuracies of the original data, with due regard to the problems inherent in the construction of composite indices and with vigilance in the use of moving averages, they are an invaluable resource for researching the past.

Notes

1 D. C. Coleman, 'History, economic history and the numbers game', *Historical Journal*, 38, 3 (1995), p. 643.
2 R. Price, *British society, 1680–1880* (Cambridge, 1999), p.1
3 In this equation, the number of strikes in 1765 is the numerator and the number of strikes in the base year is in the denominator. (Numerator and denominator are defined in the glossary.) An excellent introduction to very simple calculations of fractions and percentages is given in R. Soloman and C. Winch, *Calculating and computing for social science and arts students* (Buckingham, 1994), chapter 1.
4 C. Feinstein, 'Pessimism perpetuated: real wages and the standard of living in Britain during and after the industrial revolution' *Journal of Economic History* 58, 3 (1998), p. 637.

5 Walther G. Hoffman, *British industry 1700–1950*, trans. W. O. Henderson and W. H. Chaloner (Oxford, 1955).

6 This debate is to some extent covered in P. Hudson, *The industrial revolution* (London, 1992). Revised figures appear in N. F. R. Crafts and C. K. Harley, 'Output growth and the British industrial revolution: a restatement of the Crafts–Harley view', *Economic History Review*, 45, 4, (1992), pp 703–30.

7 T. S. Ashton, 'The standard of life of the workers in England 1790–1830', *Journal of Economic History*, ix, supplement (1949).

8 In the appendix (article 3) you will find questions about a much later study of living standards in the same period by Lindert and Williamson. They discuss the problems of constructing a cost-of-living index in some detail. Their index includes rents (though from a very narrow evidential base) and allowance for the costs of cotton clothing and more varied foodstuffs, but many problems remain.

9 The cycles of regular periodicity in advanced industrial economies usually last around seven years and are called juglar cycles. The longer wave cycles of innovative activity are called Kondratieff cycles after Nikolai Kondratieff, who first identified them.

10 If the sum of these mean deviatons does not add up to 0 the 'error term' (the difference between the sum of the mean deviations and zero) should be divided equally and added to the mean deviation for each quarter.

Further reading

R. Darcy and R. C. Rohrs, *A guide to quantitative history* (Westport, CN, 1995). There is little separate treatment of time-series, and the book is less accessible than Haskins and Jeffrey but includes some useful historical examples.

R. Floud, *An introduction to quantitative methods for historians* (London, 1973; 2nd edn 1979), Chapter 6

L. Haskins and K. Jeffrey, *Understanding quantitative history* (Cambridge, MA, 1991), pp. 60–62, 289–91, 312–14

T. P. Hutchinson, *Essentials of statistical methods*, Version 2: History and Archaeology (Adelaide, 1993)

In most general statistics texts for social sciences, time-series are given little separate treatment.

For more advanced discussion of time-series trends and cycles in relation to economic growth, see T. C. Mills and N. F. R. Crafts, 'Modelling trends in economic history', *The Statistician* 45, 2, 1996, pp. 153–9.

6

Relationships between variables

Q: What effect does going to college have on your chances of remaining unmarried?
A: If you're a woman, it sky rockets your chances of becoming an old maid. But if you're a man, it has the opposite effect – it minimises your chances of staying a bachelor.
  Cornell University made a study of 1,500 typical middle-aged college graduates. Of the men, 93% were married (compared to 83% of the general population).
  But of the middle-aged women graduates only 65% were married. Spinsters were relatively three times as numerous among college graduates as among women of the general population.[1]

The report above appeared in a large-circulation US Sunday newspaper in the 1950s. Fortunately, I was too young to read it or it might have put me off higher education altogether. Even in the 1960s, for a working-class girl a good marriage seemed a less risky way of securing your future than investing in the education necessary for a male-dominated career. Had I read it I would not necessarily have felt that I could challenge such a reputable source of evidence, despite the fact that there is sufficient reassurance in the passage that a woman could attend college without sacrificing her marital prospects.

Looked at closely, the article can be seen to be using a statistical association to support a possibly spurious cause-and-effect relationship. The figures could actually suggest not that college gets in the way of marrying but that women who are less disposed to marry are more likely to choose to go to college, that is, that college attracts feisty progressive girls who want their independence. College might modify these traits and if they had not attended college it may be that even more would have failed to marry! We would really like to know not just the size of the sample of graduates but how it was divided between men and women and how the respondents were selected. Was it justified to call them 'typical', and what middle-age range was covered? Was the general population sampled in the same way to produce the contrasting figures or might we expect the national sample to reflect a different bias?[2] There is another common deception here also: the statistics relate to Cornell, but the conclusions are generalised. Quantitative analysis frequently encourages the temptation to generalise from the particular to all cases, especially where the analysis of relationships between variables is concerned.

A question often asked by historians is: 'Does a relationship exist between two variables?' We might ask this about the relationship between education and nuptiality rates, as above, or about the relationship between other cross-sectional data such as yearly income levels and size of mortgage of suburb dwellers in the 1950s. The same question might also be posed of variables in two or more time-series (e.g. the movement of exports and imports, 1850–75 or of average yearly grain prices and numbers of riots per year in the eighteenth century). Usually, the question is provoked by some hypothesis about the causal connection which may lie behind a relationship (e.g. education affecting nuptiality rates, income affecting mortgage size, exports leading imports, and food prices precipitating riots).[3]

Statistical techniques make it possible to investigate supposed relationships with some precision and also to enquire into the strength and form of relationships. But, as we shall see, identifying and measuring relationships are not primarily matters of statistical technique. Statistical analysis can tell us *nothing* about the reliability of the data in the first place and can indicate only the *statistical probability* of a relationship being present rather than demonstrate the relationship itself. Identifying and assessing relationships between variables in a historical context involves historical judgement and common sense. It cannot be accomplished simply by using statistics. Statistics can serve only as a tool and can never substitute for historical analysis. The historian must choose when to apply statistical techniques and how to interpret the significance of statistical results.

It is important at the outset to form a hypothesis about the possible relationship between variables on the basis of sound historical judgement. Many sets of variables may by chance move or vary in a seemingly related fashion but this does not mean that there is any influence operating between the two or any causal connection. The British birth rate and the world stork population may well have similar variation over time, as may religious observance and the price of cabbages, but we would be foolish to suggest any meaningful connections. *Only if we can think of sound reasons why there might be a relationship between two or more variables should we indulge in the statistical identification and measurement of that relationship.*

6.1 The null hypothesis

Most statistical techniques concerned with the question 'Is there a relationship between two variables?' are based on a comparison between the data set as it is and the data set as it would be if there were no relationship at all. In other words, we pose our hypothesis that there is a relationship against the alternative null hypothesis that there is not. (The null hypothesis is conventionally expressed in shorthand as H_0). We then calculate the statistical probability of the existing distributions occurring by chance in the absence of a relationship. This gives us a measure of the strength of the relationship.

This way of testing a hypothesis, based on probability calculations and the null hypothesis, was developed to deal with situations (as in most social science and, of course, eugenics) where it is impossible to repeat experiments as a test. Being forced to work with the data available and the need to find some standard against which to measure the significance of observations gave rise to probability testing.

There are two commonly used techniques for testing for the possible existence and strength of a relationship between two variables, and each involve use of the null hypothesis:

- the **contingency coefficient**, suitable for nominal, ordinal, interval or ratio data;
- the **correlation coefficient**, suitable only for interval and ratio data, but the most commonly used measure.

The correlation coefficient, as we mentioned in Chapter 2, was devised and promoted by Pearson, who was committed to expressing all variables in the form of continuous numerical data. This arose from the demands of his eugenics research. His critics, including Yule, favoured methods akin to the contingency table, in which discrete nominal and ordinal data could be used.[4]

6.2 The contingency coefficient, C

The contingency coefficient is most frequently used in deciding whether a relationship exists between two variables that have been tabulated in the form of a **contingency table**. *A contingency table is a particular form of data matrix where two variables are plotted against one another.* This is usually called 'cross-tabulation'. The variables may be nominal, ordinal, interval or ratio data. In Table 6.1 sentence lengths (interval data) have been arranged in relation to type of crime (nominal data) by using the information from Table 3.5, page 61.

There are one or two important points to note about the professional layout and presentation of contingency tables:

Table 6.1 Contingency table linking sentence lengths to types of crime, Portland Prison data, 1849

Length of sentence (years)	Type of crime					Total
	Unspecified felony	Larceny, housebreaking, burglary, stealing, theft[a]	Robbery[b]	Horse stealing	Forgery, incendiarism	
7–12	1	4	1			6
14–15		8	3	1	1	13
20					2	2
Total	1	12	4	1	3	21

[a]Theft from property.
[b]Theft from person.
Source: based on Public Record Office, Home Office, 8/102; see also Table 3.5, page 61.

- all categories must be mutually exclusive;
- each column must have a total and each row must have a total;
- the total number of cases should be given in the bottom right-hand cell of the table.

These features are important to aid the reader and as a check that you have included all cases. It almost goes without saying that all contingency tables, like any other tables, should include a note or other reference indicating the source(s) of the data.

If we wish to enquire whether there is a relationship between the variables arranged in a contingency table it is first necessary to form an alternative contingency table based on the null hypothesis. This will give the expected frequencies (those which would occur in the absence of a relationship) to compare with the observed frequencies. In Table 6.2 level of education of men (ordinal data) has been related to family size (interval data) in a contingency table. The expected frequencies for level of education in rela-

Table 6.2 Contingency table linking level of education with family size (expected values given in parentheses).

Level of education	Number of children			Total
	0 or 1	2	3 or more	
Secondary	21 (24.19)	23 (21.16)	21 (19.65)	65
Higher	11 (7.81)	5 (6.84)	5 (6.35)	21
Total	32	28	26	86

Note: examples of how expected values (in parentheses) are calculated are given overleaf.
Source: hypothetical data.

tion to family size have also been calculated and the figures have been placed in brackets in the table.

In Table 6.2 the expected frequencies have been derived from probabilities based on the totals for each variable. For example, the probability of a man selected at random having a secondary education and no children or one child is equal to the probability that he has a secondary education multiplied by the probability that he has no children or one child. Such probabilities are, of course, unknown but they can be estimated from the sample data available. Thus the expected frequency for the above case, E (secondary; 0 or 1), that is, the value in parenthesis in cell $a_{1,1}$ of Table 6.2, is given by:

$$E \text{ (secondary; 0 or 1)} \quad = \quad p(\text{secondary}) \times p \text{ (0 or 1)} \times N$$

$$= \quad \frac{65}{86} \times \frac{32}{86} \times 86$$

$$= \quad 24.19$$

where

$p(\text{secondary})$ is the probability of the man having secondary education;
p (0 or 1) is the probability of the man having no children or one child;
N is the total number of men in the sample.

Similarly, the expected frequency of a man having a higher education and three or more children (cell $a_{2,3}$ of Table 6.2) is:

$$E(\text{higher}; \geq 3) = \frac{21}{86} \times \frac{26}{86} \times 86 = 6.35$$

If level of education plays a strong role in decisions about family size then some of the observed numbers in Table 6.2 are likely to be very different from the expected numbers (in parentheses). On the other hand, if education has no bearing upon family size – if the reality is near to the null hypothesis – the observed numbers should be close to the expected numbers. The **chi-square** (χ^2) technique consists of combining all of the differences between observed and expected counts into a single summary number, called the χ^2 statistic. The χ^2 statistic is a measure of the distribution of divergence between observed and expected results.

If the observed data are identical to the expected values, χ^2 will equal 0. If the value of χ^2 is larger than would be expected by chance, it is possible to reject the null hypothesis. Critical values for χ^2 are available in tables or in software programmes. These convert values for χ^2 into an indication of the probability of a particular χ^2 value occurring purely by chance (i.e. the probability of the distribution of differences between observed and expected frequencies occurring by chance).[5]

The general formula for the χ^2 distribution when applied to a contingency table is:

$$\chi^2 = \sum_{i=1}^{r} \sum_{j=1}^{c} \frac{(O_{ij} - E_{ij})^2}{E_{ij}}$$

where

r is the number of rows in the contingency table;
c is the number of columns in the contingency table;
O_{ij} are the observed values for each cell (row i, column j);
E_{ij} are the expected values for each cell.

The contingency coefficient C is a measure of the probability of obtaining a χ^2 value as large as that found, if it had occurred just by chance, given the null hypothesis of independence.

Example

Let us calculate the contingency coefficient, C, for the data in Table 6.2 by means of the χ^2 distribution. From the equation above, we have:

$$
\begin{aligned}
\chi^2 &= \sum_{i=1}^{2} \sum_{j=1}^{3} \frac{(O_{ij} - E_{ij})^2}{E_{ij}} \\
&= \frac{(21 - 24.19)^2}{24.19} + \frac{(23 - 21.16)^2}{21.16} + \frac{(21 - 19.65)^2}{19.65} + \\
&\quad \frac{(11 - 7.81)^2}{7.81} + \frac{(5 - 6.84)^2}{6.84} + \frac{(5 - 6.35)^2}{6.35} \\
&= 2.76
\end{aligned}
$$

We now find C from the formula:

$$C = \sqrt{\frac{\chi^2}{N + \chi^2}} = 0.18$$

Note: the bigger the value of C, the closer the relationship, but we cannot make comparisons or be precise in predictions because the maximum size of C is affected by the size of the contingency table.

It is important to note that in a contingency table with only two rows and two columns the general formula will produce an inflated result for the χ^2

statistic. An alternative formula is needed, which is also much simpler. To calculate C for a simple 2×2 (2 rows and 2 columns) contingency table with a total of $N \geq 50$ observations, we proceed as follows. Label the cells as below:

A	B	$A+B$
C	D	$C+D$
$A+C$	$B+D$	N

where $N = A + B + C + D$. Then χ^2 will be given by

$$\chi^2 = \frac{N(|AD - BC| - \frac{N}{2})^2}{(A+B)(C+D)(B+D)(A+C)}$$

In this formula $|AD{-}BC|$ indicates the 'absolute value' of $AD - BC$; that is, we ignore the sign and treat the term as positive even if BC is greater than AD. C can then be calculated from the formula:

$$C = \sqrt{\frac{\chi^2}{N + \chi^2}}$$

as before.

6.3 The scatter diagram

The scatter diagram (also referred to as a scatter graph, or scatter plot) is used with interval or ratio data. It is the simplest visual indication of the possible presence of a relationship between two numerical variables. The formation of a scatter graph involves plotting pairs of the variables against one another on a graph. The pairs of variables can be for cross-sectional or time-series data.

Table 6.3 gives time-series data for tea, coffee, sugar and tobacco consumption, and Figure 6.1 shows the pairs of observations of tea and sugar consumption in a scatter graph. If, as in this case, the two variables move roughly together and in the same direction over time the points on the graph will line up (approximately) along a positively sloping line and will be indicative of the presence of a positive relationship.

The reader may like to create more scatter graphs using different vectors from Table 6.3. It is important to have a reasoned hypothesis in mind

Table 6.3 Per capita consumption (in pounds weight) of coffee, tea, sugar and tobacco, and an index of average real wages (1850 = 100), 1850–65

Year	Wage index	Consumption of:			
		coffee	tea	sugar	tobacco
1850	100	1.13	1.86	25.26	1.00
1851	102	1.19	1.97	26.87	1.02
1852	100	1.27	1.99	29.27	1.04
1853	107	1.34	2.14	30.45	1.07
1854	97	1.35	2.24	33.74	1.10
1855	94	1.29	2.28	30.36	1.09
1856	95	1.25	2.26	28.27	1.16
1857	94	1.22	2.45	29.48	1.16
1858	94	1.24	2.58	34.51	1.20
1859	104	1.20	2.67	34.80	1.21
1860	105	1.23	2.67	34.14	1.22
1861	99	1.21	2.69	35.49	1.20
1862	100	1.18	2.69	35.12	1.21
1863	107	1.11	2.89	35.92	1.13
1864	118	1.06	2.99	36.74	1.28
1865	120	1.02	3.27	36.69	1.30

Source: based on B. R. Mitchell and P. Deane, *Abstract of British Historical Statistics* (1962), pp. 343, 356.

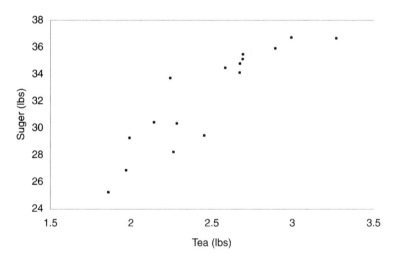

Fig. 6.1 Scatter graph showing tea and sugar consumption, 1850–65. Source: see Table 6.3.

regarding relationships between the variables before drawing the scatter graph.

Figure 6.2 gives data of profit rates for the worsted manufacturing firm of T. and M. Bairstow and the annual average price of the sort of wool which they used (Lincoln half hogs), 1840–58. Wool was by far the most important raw-material cost in the industry. As one might expect, profit rates appear to be associated (negatively) with the price of wool, but the degree of association is not particularly strong (indicating that other variables may have been heavily involved in influencing profitability in this period).[6]

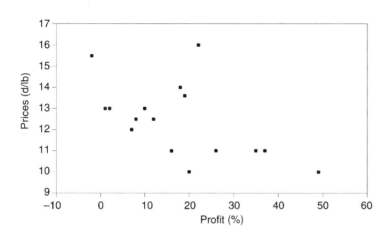

Fig. 6.2 Scatter graph of the profit rate against wool price (pence per pound weight) for T. and M. Bairstow, 1840–58.
Source: P. Hudson, *The genesis of industrial capital: a study of the West Riding wool textile industry, c. 1750–1850* (Cambridge, 1986), chapter 10 and appendix.

In drawing a scatter graph or any other sort of graph involving independent and dependent variables (or variables suspected of being dependent and independent), it is conventional to place the independent variable on the horizontal axis (or *x* axis) and the dependent variable or variables on the vertical axis (*y* axis). Remember: an independent variable is one which is suspected of causing the movement of others without in turn being affected by them; a dependent variable is one whose variation is seen as being causally dependent on the movement of another variable.

Figure 6.3 shows different scatter graph shapes with their different indications. Sometimes it is not clear at a glance whether there is much of a relationship indicated or not. In this case it is sometimes helpful to draw a dotted line through the median point of each variable. If the majority of points fall in quadrants one and three (formed by the dotted lines) a positive relationship may be indicated. If the majority of points fall in quadrants four and two a negative relationship may be indicated. If the points are widely dispersed across all four quadrants there will be no indication of a

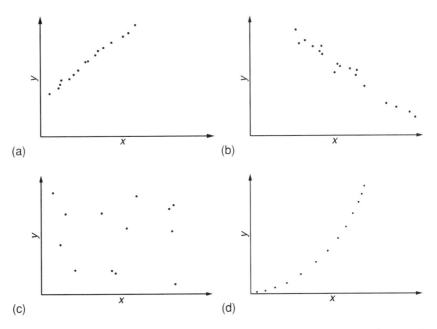

(a)   (b)

(c)   (d)

Fig. 6.3 Scatter graphs with different indications: (a) positive linear correlation indicated (R value near to +1); (b) negative linear correlation indicated (R value around –0.9); (c) no correlation indicated (R value near to 0); (d) no linear correlation indicated but a curvilinear or monotonic increasing relationship is indicated [R value near to 0 but r_s (near to 1). Note: the correlation coefficient, R, and Spearman's rank correlation coefficient, r_s, are discussed in Sections 6.5 and 6.9, respectively.

relationship and this is a signal that it is not worth proceeding with any more sophisticated analysis to measure or test such a relationship.

Scatter graphs sometimes indicate points clustered around a non-linear shape which *may* indicate a non-linear relationship, as in Figure 6.3(d), above.

Spreadsheets and statistical packages can generate scatter graphs with great ease and it is always wise to take this easy first preliminary step in identifying the possible existence of a relationship before attempting any more complex analysis.

If after drawing a scatter graph a linear relationship is suspected it is possible to use statistical techniques to identify that relationship more closely and to measure its strength. The most commonly used tests of statistical association between variables are concerned with linear association and it is these techniques which are the focus of this chapter. It is, however, important to note that there are many other relationships of dependence which need different techniques. If, for example, each increase of 2 units in one variable were matched by an increase of 2^2 (4) units in the other, the plot would be a parabola and not a straight line and any test for linear association would be entirely misleading even though the two variables have a very clear association (see the discussion of Spearman's rank correlation coefficient on pp. 151–3).

6.4 Dummy variables

Before passing to other methods of identifying and assessing relationships between variables, it is necessary briefly to return to our earlier distinction between numeric and categorical variables. We have seen that the contingency table and the contingency coefficient can handle nominal, ordinal, ratio or interval data. Other methods, and most of the techniques of inferential statistics more generally, can cope only with numeric data. To counter this problem categorical variables can in some cases be re-coded as numerical **dummy variables.**

One of the most common uses of dummy variables arises in coding dichotomous variables such as sex. A **dichotomous variable** is one where there can only be two values. For example, instead of 'male' or 'female' one could give a score of 1 to each female, 0 to each male. In a population of 1000 of 600 men and 400 women the 'mean' of the variable 'women' would be 400/1000 (i.e. 0.40). This has an intuitive meaning because 40% of the population is female.

The same strategy can be extended to categorical variables which have more than two values (i.e. which are not dichotomous). In studies of voting behaviour, for example, where voters are Conservative, Labour or Liberal, one would create two new dummy variables, 'Conservative' and 'Labour', each of which would either take the value 0 or take the value 1. There would be no need to create a dummy variable for the Liberal voters because this information would be captured where cases recorded 0 in both the Conservative and the Labour columns. If there were four classes of voter, Conservative, Labour, Liberal and Other, one would create three dummy variables, leaving 'Others' to be captured by the 0 scores under the other three headings. Similarly, with a larger number of categories such as with the occupations found within an enterprise one could create dummy variables to capture the information numerically.

The advantage of dummy variables is that they can be used in statistical techniques such as correlation and regression (see below), whereas the categorical information upon which they are based cannot.

The correlation coefficient, *R*

The correlation coefficient, *R*, is also known as Pearson's product moment coefficient of correlation (after its inventor, Karl Pearson: see Chapter 2).

The correlation coefficient is the most commonly used measure of association between two variables. It is used to test for the possible presence of a linear relationship between two numerical variables. It is wise to plot the data at the outset, in a scatter graph, to make sure a linear rather than a non-linear relationship is suggested. If a non-linear relationship is present, calculation of a correlation coefficient will produce an entirely spurious result. If a linear relationship is suspected we adopt the following line of reasoning and action in calculating R:

1. measure whether a relationship appears to exist between two sets of numerical data by looking at the product of deviations from the mean of each variable for each case;
2. if a relationship exists the products of deviations will be large and positive, if not they will be near to zero;
3. to get more accurate results and to facilitate comparisons, correct for the type of unit and number of cases and also for the spread of values by dividing by
   (a)   the number of cases,
   (b)   the product of the standard deviation of each variable.

These steps are incorporated into the formula for R:

$$R = \frac{\Sigma(X - \overline{X})(Y - \overline{Y})}{N\left[\sqrt{\left(\dfrac{\Sigma(X - \overline{X})^2}{N}\right)}\right]\left[\sqrt{\left(\dfrac{\Sigma(Y - \overline{Y})^2}{N}\right)}\right]}$$

If R is not zero then some sort of relationship may exist.

6.6 How strong is the relationship?

The greater the value of C or R, the closer the relationship. But the drawback of C (contingency coefficient), as we have noted, is that its maximum size (i.e. the indication of a strong and predictable relationship) varies with the size of the contingency table. This limits its use.

R is handier because its value always lies between +1 and −1 and its value is not affected by the number of cases or the spread of the distribution. Values of R from different sets of data can therefore be compared:

- R = +1 if there is a perfect positive correlation,
- R = −1 if there is a perfect negative correlation.

The nearer R is to +1 or −1, the closer the relationship (i.e. one variable is moving in a fixed way proportionately to the other). In a scatter graph this would show up as points clustering around and along a straight line of positive slope if R is near to +1 and of negative slope if R is near to −1 [see

Figures 6.3(a) and 6.3(b), respectively]. An *R* value near to 0 indicates no *linear* relationship, as in Figures 6.3(c) and 6.3(d).

6.7 The form of the relationship

We usually want to know not just that a positive or negative relationship exists between variables but whether one variable is responsible for causing the movement of the other. Statistical tests will never be able to establish this but they can indicate the strength of the association and add weight to a reasoned historical argument about causation. As we have noted, the variable regarded as the dominant or causal variable is usually termed the independent variable whereas the other variable is termed the dependent variable.

It is sometimes obvious which is which, but more usually it is a matter of historical judgement or hypothesis. It is important to remember that judgements and hypotheses about the direction of causality between two variables may be wrong and that the same correlation result would appear whichever direction the causal connection ran. For example, we may be interested in examining the hypothesis that wages are related to prices in a particular locality, but it would be very difficult to disentangle whether high prices caused high wages or vice versa. Similarly, we may be interested in the extent to which unemployment variations in the inter-war period were determined by the level of benefits in relation to locally available wages [i.e. by regional variation in the relative generosity of unemployment benefit indicated by the benefits to wage ratio, B/W (where B is the level of benefits, and W is the index of locally available wages]. Discovery of a statistically suggested relationship between the movement of the two variables, unemployment (U) and B/W could, however, just as easily be a result of the impact of unemployment upon wage or benefit levels.[7]

We should not jump to conclusions about causality on the basis of strong correlation or contingency results without having a good argument, including additional evidence, which will confirm beyond reasonable doubt which is the dependent and which is the independent variable. We must also beware of rushing to conclusions about the causal implications of correlation or contingency results, because the movements of two variables may be dependent upon the movement of a third variable and may not be causally related to one another at all. For example, the rise of both tea and sugar consumption per head of population in the late nineteenth century may be primarily a result of efficiencies in international trade and shipping, or both might result from rising real incomes, rather than one commodity being a major cause of demand for the other. In this context it would be hasty to hypothesise or closely examine the causal effect of tea consumption upon sugar consumption even though the scatter graph and the correlation coefficient between the two variables may be temptingly positive and strong (see Table 6.3 and

Figure 6.1). Sugar was, of course, also used for many other purposes than as an accompaniment for hot beveridges, particularly for preserving.

6.8 Lagged results

An important difficulty which occurs with correlations of time-series data is that an association may appear not to be present either from time-series graphs, scatter graphs or from the correlation calculation. However, if we strongly suspect (on the basis of careful historical judgement) that a causal connection may be in operation it may be worth introducing a lag into the series of the independent variable. Often the causal effect of one factor upon another takes time to work through. The length of the lag which we introduce must have some sound historical reasoning behind it. For example, Wrigley and Schofield's major study of population change in England, 1541 to 1871, suggested that nuptiality was influenced by the movement of real wages, a causal connection which appeared to show up statistically only if a

Table 6.4 Lagged profit rates in the wool textile industry correlated with wage series for four firms (Clough, Bairstow, Foster and Marriner), 1840–58

Variables[a]	Period	N	Correlation coefficient	Significance at 5 per cent level
Money wages on:				
Clough profit rate	1845–56	11	0.40	No
Bairstow profit rate	1840–58	18	0.69	Yes
Foster profit rate	1842–58	16	0.47	Almost
Marriner profit rate	1842–58	16	0.15	No
composite profit rate A	1842–58	16	0.62	Yes
composite profit rate B	1845–56	11	0.67	Yes
Rousseaux real wage index[b] on:				
Clough profit rate	1845–56	11	0.52	No
Bairstow profit rate	1840–58	18	0.76	Yes
Foster profit rate	1842–58	16	0.58	Yes
Marriner profit rate	1842–58	16	0.29	No
composite profit rate A	1842–58	16	0.82	Yes
composite profit rate B	1845–56	11	0.71	Yes
GRS real wage index[c] on:				
Clough profit rate	1844–49	5	0.69	No
Bairstow profit rate	1841–50	10	0.84	Yes
Foster profit rate	1841–49	8	0.51	No
Marriner profit rate	1841–49	8	0.60	No
composite profit rate A	1841–49	8	0.83	Yes

N = Number of observations.
[a]Profit rates lagged by one year.
[b]Real wage index calculated by means of the Rousseaux price series.
[c]Real wage index calculated by means of the Gayer–Rostow–Schwartz price series.
Source: P. Hudson, *The genesis of industrial capital: a study of the West Riding wool textile industry, c. 1750–1850* (Cambridge, 1986), p. 245.

lag of about 30 years was introduced into the real wage series.[8] As this was such a long lag, with little explanation of why real wages may have taken so long to impact upon nuptiality a generation or so later, the causal explanation provoked severe criticism. Joel Mokyr, for example, suggested that 'since no-one controls the fertility of his own children let alone his grandchildren . . . the lag structure Wrigley and Schofield propose is no explanation at all but a description of the data'.[9]

Another example of results to be obtained from lagging data occurs in research on the determinants and impact of profit rates in the Yorkshire textile industry in the early nineteenth century. As wages were the single biggest input cost in the industry my initial hypothesis was that changing wage levels may have had a significant impact upon profit rates, but no significant correlation showed up in the worsted industry between profit rates for various firms and either money wage or real wage movements when the yearly indices were compared without a lag. When the wage series was lagged by a year the correlations were uniformly negative (as one might expect). More surprisingly, lagged profit rates were associated positively with rising real wages but not all of the *R* values were significant, given the short data runs available.[10] Table 6.4 gives the results of the correlation exercises for different wage indices and different profit rate series. For discussion of the significance of correlation results and the impact of small sample sizes see Chapter 7.

6.9 Spearman's rank correlation coefficient

Several correlation coefficients exist other than Pearson's, which is the most commonly used. These are suitable for specific sorts of data, generally where non-linear associations between variables are suspected. One of the most frequently used alternative correlation coefficients in social science research is Spearman's rank correlation coefficient. It was developed for analysing psychology data. Before the advent of computers the Spearman method was used to simplify calculations when estimating Pearsons's correlation coefficient (for linear associations it gives a result quite close to the Pearson coefficient). But Spearman's coefficient can also be used as a measure of the strength of a relationship when variables have a curvilinear association (i.e. when they cluster near a line which is a curve). Such associations are termed 'monotonic'.

Figure 6.3(d) illustrates a monotonic association where the Spearman coefficient would give a score near to +1 whereas the Pearson coefficient would not and would miss the presence of a reasonably clear association simply because it is not linear. Similarly, Spearman's measure would give a better indication of an association between two variables if the monotonic form were negatively sloped.

The Spearman coefficient, r_s, is easy to calculate. Each variable is ranked in size order and then the Pearson correlation coefficient is calculated from the ranks. (Average values are used when the ranking produces tied values.) A scatter graph of the relationships between pairs of rankings can be drawn as a preliminary to further analysis. If this shows that the points line up on a concave or convex curve, the Spearman coefficient can usefully be applied.

Table 6.5 shows the sort of original data which would be used in calculating Pearson's coefficient, alongside the ranking figures which one would employ to calculate Spearman's coefficient. The scatter graph from this exercise is shown in Figure 6.4. This shows a weak positive correlation (r_s is actually 0.59) compared with an R value of 0.50 (on the original data). This suggests the possibility of a monotonic rather than of a linear

Table 6.5 Age at death and value of moveable property of clothiers, with corresponding rankings, 1760s

Age at death (years)	Rank	Value of moveable property £	s	d	Rank
23	1	27	19	4	3
39	2	31	4	3	7
41	3	25	18	10	2
49	4	25	5	0	1
50	5	31	2	4	6
53	6.5	34	12	9	12
53	6.5	42	0	0	14
54	8	29	1	3	4
56	9	32	10	0	8
57	10	30	5	4	5
58	11.5	33	1	6	9
58	11.5	33	17	6	10
60	13	41	2	8	13
61	14	34	10	7	11

Source: hypothetical data of the type which might be derived from matching probate inventory values with family reconstitution evidence on age of death.

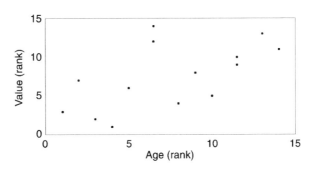

Fig. 6.4 Scatter graph of rank of clothiers' ages at death against rank of value of assets. Source: see Table 6.5.

relationship. The Spearman's coefficient in this case has eased the calculation with little loss of precision in the coefficient.

6.10 The regression line

In addition to deciding about the direction of possible causal connection between variables, we may wish to enquire:

- By how much does X have to alter to produce a change in Y?
- Can we predict by how much Y would change if the value of X were to increase by n units?
- Do changes in variable X explain all changes in variable Y, or are other factors involved?

To answer these questions we need to employ further statistical tools, starting with the regression line. The regression line is a line which represents the closeness of movement between two variables. It can be drawn as the line of best fit through the points in a scatter graph. An example of this is shown in Figure 6.5, which illustrates a hypothesised relationship

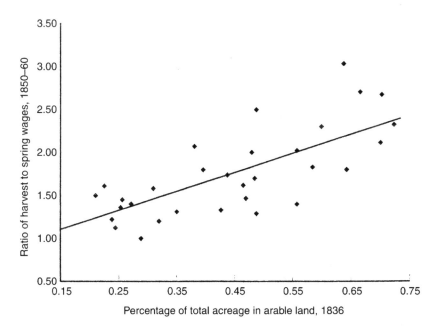

Fig. 6.5 Relationship between ratio of harvest to spring wages and percentage of total acreage arable land, 1836.
Source: K. L. Sokoloff and D. Dollar, 'Agricultural seasonality and the organisation of manufacturing in early industrial economies: the contrast between England and the United States', *Journal of Economic History*, 57, 2 (1997), p. 309.

between the variability of agricultural wages and arable specialisation in different English counties. It is part of an argument by Sokoloff and Dollar about the causes of widespread rural manufacturing in England compared with the United States: that this related to the low off-peak opportunity costs for labour in English agriculture.

The regression line can be plotted and positioned exactly by using the same method we used to find the position of a trend line, or line of best fit, in a time-series (i.e. by the least squares method and by using the same formula; see section 5.7). Remember that the least squares method ensures that the total deviations of observations from the line are minimised. The formula for the regression line is:

$$Y = a + b\,X$$

where

$$a = \frac{\Sigma Y - b\Sigma X}{N}$$

$$b = \frac{N\Sigma XY - (\Sigma X)(\Sigma Y)}{N\Sigma X^2 - (\Sigma X)^2}$$

and where

Y is the dependent variable;
X is the independent variable;
a is the intercept;
b is the slope (or gradient).

The regression line represents the best estimate of the relationship between the two variables on the basis of the available evidence. If the fit is good and there are not too many outlying readings, and if we have accurately identified the dependent and independent variables, our predictive capacity, based on the regression line, will be good. (The fit will be best the nearer R is to +1 or −1.) In other words, we can use the formula for the regression line and knowledge of its slope to predict by how much X has to alter to produce a change in Y and to make suggestions about the likely outcome for Y of values in the independent variable X which lie outside of the available evidence. The equation for the regression line is often called the regression equation.

Since the general form of the regression line is $Y = a + bX$ it has become conventional for researchers to talk about b, B or beta (β) when referring to regressions; these are also known as the slope coefficient. The slope coefficient is the number by which the independent variable is multiplied in the regression equation. Sometimes in discussions of regression the slope coefficient is called a regression coefficient.

A firm relationship with R nearing +1 or –1 can be extrapolated (by using the regression line) beyond the available data set in order to predict the relationship between the variables in earlier or later time periods (in the case of time-series) or across higher or lower ranges of the variables than the information which we have.

An extrapolation is an estimation of missing values of a variable or regression line based on the trend apparent in the known values. A regression equation thus becomes a predictive model.

A regression equation can also be used to test an explanatory model. For example, if it is believed that the explanation for the decline of slavery in the plantation areas of the southern United States came with the rising costs of keeping slaves one could take several sets of plantation or other data indexing costs of upkeep and slave density in different periods or on different plantations and use the regression lines generated to test the model.

6.11 The coefficient of determination

We can get a measure of the 'unexplained' element of change in the dependent variable by using the coefficient of determination. This coefficient represents the degree to which the movement of one variable is associated with variation in another. It is calculated as follows:

coefficient of determination =

$$\frac{(\text{distance between mean and regression estimates})^2}{(\text{distance between mean and data values})^2}$$

In fact, this is always equal to R^2:

$$R^2 = \frac{\Sigma(\hat{Y} - \bar{Y})^2}{\Sigma(Y - \bar{Y})^2}$$

where

Y is the data value;
$\bar{Y}$ is the mean value;
$\hat{Y}$ is the regression estimate.

R tells us exactly what proportion of the variation in Y we have explained by the regression equation (of Y on X) as being due to the influence of X. Note: if, for example, $R = 0.7$, $R^2 = 0.49$ (i.e. only 49% of the variation is attributable to the influence of the relationship). For a dominating influence, we must therefore look for values of R greater than 0.7. $R = 0.8$, for example, means that 64% of the movement of Y can be explained by the movement of X.

6.12 An example of correlation and regression analysis

The sort of analysis we may be faced with in historical work for which correlation and regression techniques are useful is in considering the relationship between social disturbances and the price of wheat. Table 6.6 gives information about the annual number of disturbances, the price of wheat and an index of the business cycle, for the period 1810–21.

The first step in any analysis of data where a linear relationship may be suspected is to hypothesise (on the basis of historical judgement and knowledge) about which of the variables may be dependent and which are independent. Looking at the data in Table 6.6, and knowing the context of discussion in Rostow's book, the major hypotheses might be as follows:

- the number of disturbances may be the dependent variable and be related to wheat prices (an independent variable);
- the number of disturbances (again the dependent variable) may be influenced by the state of the business cycle, the independent variable, which would reflect unemployment and trade levels.

The next step would be to draw the scatter graphs (Figures 6.6(a) and 6.6(b)). These will tell us if it is worth proceeding with causal analysis and what sort of relationship appears to be indicated.

Table 6.6 Economic conditions and social tension in the early nineteenth century

Year	Disturbances (no.)	Price of wheat[a]	Business cycle index
1810	50	105	5
1811	45	95	0
1812	60	125	0
1813	40	105	2
1814	20	75	2
1815	10	65	3
1816	30	75	1
1817	38	95	3
1818	28	85	4
1819	22	75	1
1820	20	65	1
1821	15	55	2

[a]Shillings per quart.
Note: in the business cycle index a value of 0 represents a deep depression, 5 a major peak.
Source: loosely based on W. W. Rostow, 'Trade cycles, harvests and politics, 1790–1950', in *British economy of the nineteenth century* (1948), pp. 123–5.

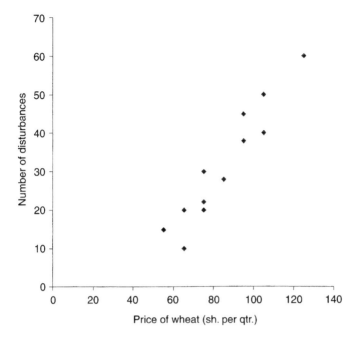

(a)

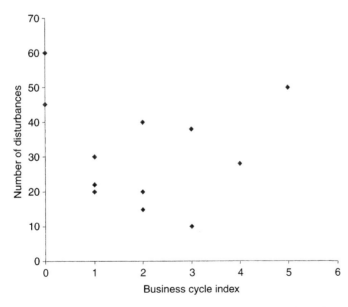

(b)

Fig. 6.6 Scatter graph of (a) wheat prices (shillings per quart) and number of disturbances and (b) business cycle index and number of disturbances, 1810–21.
Source: see Table 6.6.

We can calculate the correlation coefficients by using computer software:

- $R = 0.95$ for number of disturbances against wheat prices;
- $R = -0.11$ for number of disturbances against business cycle.

The associated coefficients of determination are, then, $R^2 = 0.90$ and $R^2 = 0.01$, respectively. In other words it appears that wheat prices *may* account for 90 per cent of the level of disturbances, and business conditions may account for only 1 per cent of the level of disturbances.

The regression equations for the regression lines of best fit through the scatter graph points are

$$Y = -28.7 + 0.71 \ X$$

(where Y = disturbances, X = wheat prices) for the relation between wheat prices and number of disturbances.

$$Y = 33.65 - 1.08 \ X$$

(where Y = disturbances, X = business cycle index) for the relation between the business cycle index and number of disturbances.

The slope coefficients, or regression coefficients, are thus:

$B = 0.71$ for disturbances against wheat prices.
$B = -1.08$ for disturbances against business cycle index.

The significance of the correlation and regression results here is important if we wish to try to generalise from the experience of these few observations. To do this we will need a measure of the probability that the slope coefficients have been thrown up by chance or by error arising from the restricted data available. We consider this in Chapter 7.

We will also find out below that it is possible to run a multiple regression exercise with more than one independent variable instead of considering the importance of the independent variables entirely separately in this way. The multiple regression model would give a more accurate indication of the relative importance of the two influences.

Before leaving the example above, I hope that the data have given some cause for questioning and concern. Even though these are only hypothetical data and have been generated to give a clear example of statistical method, it is important to get into the habit of continuously questioning the reliability, precision and representativeness of figures. How accurate is the measure of number of disturbances and to what extent is this really an index of social tension? Do wheat prices stand as a good proxy for living costs, dearth or economic conditions for the majority of the population? If the subsistence or non-market sector was large people may have been insulated from market prices for food by being able to produce their own; or perhaps oats or potatoes were relatively cheap and could be substituted when prices of wheat were high. In addition, the business cycle index seems a rather contrived and blunt tool, with only five gradations. How has it been created, on what original data was it based and what problems might it give rise to in an exercise of this kind? There are many pitfalls which might arise if we accept this sort of data at face value.

6.13 Multiple regression models

In the real world and in most historical processes a complex web of inter-acting variables is at work. It is often the case that a dependent variable is simultaneously affected by the movement of several independent variables and not just by one independent variable.

Multiple regression models can be used to investigate associations between the movement of variables where there are several causal variables which appear to be operating. Multiple regression enables one to estimate the force of each effect in the presence of other interacting effects. It helps to sort out which explanatory variables appear to be the most important and which are unimportant.

Statistical (and some spreadsheet) programmes enable one to feed in the data for dependent and independent variables and to generate the corresponding regression equations and regression coefficients (together with standard error measures, which may be necessary to take account of the sampling process; see Chapter 7).

When several variables are taken together in a multiple regression model their regression coefficients indicate the effect of each variable, because the other variables in the model are effectively held constant. When each new variable is introduced the coefficient changes. The degree of importance of each independent variable (in impacting upon the dependent variable) can similarly be compared by holding constant the other variables. The coefficient of determination, or R^2, can be assessed for all the major independent variables combined, leaving a measure of the degree of variation which remains unexplained.

Statistical packages make multiple regression manipulations relatively easy, but diminishing returns usually set in after just two or three variables have been included in the model. Very unwieldy, and not always very helpful, models are sometimes created. Use of multiple regression models to make any sort of predictions is a dangerous business. The most important thing that can be achieved with multiple regression models is the ability to sort out which explanatory variables appear to be the most important and which are unimportant.

When encountering research in which multiple regression techniques have been used it is a good idea to beware of what can seem to be a sophisticated battery of almost incontrovertible evidence about the importance of an explanatory model. It is always a good idea to do the following:

- make sure to think about the quality and reliability of the raw data (as with practically all types of quantitative research);
- consider the coefficients of determination, or R^2, and decide whether the model has satisfactorily explained the major causes of change in the dependent variable;
- think about whether any potentially important explanatory variables may have been omitted from the model;
- ask whether some of the independent variables that have been included may be measuring almost the same thing; if the independent variables in the model are themselves highly correlated, this will distort the analysis;
- whether reading historical research which involves multiple regression or whether undertaking such research for yourself, think hard about the explanatory variables which have been included and never just include all the possibilities one can think of, asking the computer to calculate regression equations on every possible combination. As with all statistical work in history the value of the analysis is likely to lie far more in the historical skills applied than in any of the quantitative techniques, which are only valuable when applied with thoughtful historical insight, knowledge of the sources and knowledge of the period and the issues concerned.

An example of the use of multiple regression coefficients is found in the work of Boyar and Hatton on the determinants of rural–urban migration in the southern counties of England and Wales in the late nineteenth and early twentieth centuries.[11] Their regression models incorporate measures of real and expected income incentives, distance, migrant numbers already in the town, the role of live-in service employments (acting as a migration facilitator) as well as change over time. The results of their main exercise are given in Table 7.4 on page 183. We leave further discussion of their findings until Chapter 7 because we there discuss various ways of measuring the significance of their results.

6.14 Non-random error, autocorrelation and multicollinearity

There are various problems to look out for when doing regression analysis. Results can be severely distorted by errors, by misspecifications of relationships and by coincident correlations which may characterise the variables under consideration. These complications tend to be exacerbated when time-series data are used; they are thus particularly problematic in historical applications.[12]

In this section we deal briefly with only three of the complications which can occur. Unfortunately, there are more.

Non-random error

All correlation and regression analysis incorporates errors. These errors will not radically affect the substance of the correlation and regression results providing that the errors are random. For this to be true, however, the omitted variables must be numerous, and each, individually, must be unimportant. They should also change in different directions so that their combined impact upon the dependent variable is unpredictable. The errors should exhibit no systematic pattern in size or direction and they should certainly not increase or decrease over the range. The trouble is that in many regression models derived from economic theory, especially those involving time-series, the error terms do change consistently in their impact. In technical parlance they are not homoscedastic, as in Figure 6.7(a), but change consistently, as in Figure 6.7(b), where they widen at one end of the observations. In production functions for manufacturing concerns (such as the Cobb–Douglas production function) causal factors not included in the model (such as organisational efficiency, technological differences between plants and entrepreneurship) would vary consistently: it is likely that their influence would be greater in large firms than in small firms. If the observations in a scatter graph were to show increasing variation from the regression line as the values of X and Y increase, estimates for values of Y derived from values of X would be subject to unacceptable error.

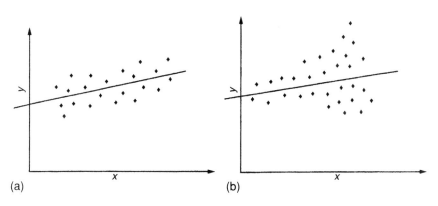

(a)   (b)

Fig. 6.7 (a) Homoscedastic errors; (b) non-homoscedastic errors.
Source: hypothetical data.

Autocorrelation

A second problem is that the error term may be influenced by its value in an earlier period. This is called autocorrelation. It is generally caused by the omission of an important explanatory variable from a regression model or by misspecifying the model (e.g. by fitting a linear trend to a curve) or if the effects of random factors such as wars or bad harvests carry over from one period into another. If autocorrelation is present the regression results will not be robust, and prediction based upon the results will not be 'efficient'. The errors can be corrected by including the omitted variable, or by re-specifying the model.

Historians frequently make use of a test for autocorrelation called the Durbin–Watson test, named after its inventors. This involves the calculation of d^*, calculated from the following formula:

$$d^* = \frac{\sum_{t=2}^{n} (e_t - e_{t-1})^2}{\sum_{t=1}^{n} e_t^2}$$

In this formula e are the residuals (i.e. the differences between the regression line estimates and the mean, and the data values and the mean, for each pair of observations) and t is the time period.

Interpretation of the importance of d^* involves use of a set of conversion tables, but as a rough guide a d^* value of 2 indicates no autocorrelation, and a d^* value nearing either 0 or 4 indicates that there is positive or negative autocorrelation, respectively. When using the test both the value of d^* and the interpretation placed upon it should be clearly stated.

Von Tunzelmann's correlation and regression analysis of British imports and exports in the mid-nineteenth century was accompanied by the calculation of d^*.[13] Similarly, Boyar and Hatton's analysis of the determinants of agricultural wages, 1866–1912, was accompanied by the Durbin–Watson statistic (see Table 7.3, page 183).

6.14.3 Multicollinearity

Multicollinearity can also be a major problem. Multicollinearity occurs when variables are already correlated for reasons other then their association with each other. This is frequently the case in correlation and regression analysis of time-series which embody linear trends. Correlation will always show up as strong in such cases (R near to ±1) and regression will seem significant. This is because of the trends in the series and not necessarily as an indication that the two variables may, in any other sense, be associated:

- if both the variables are rising on a linear trend then R will be near to +1;
- if one variable is declining and the other rising on a linear-trend *R* will be near to −1.

If we wish to enquire, for example, about the degree of association between exports and imports in the eighteenth century we would not want our correlation and regression estimates to be influenced by linear trends in the data. The relationship between exports and imports over time is normally very difficult to measure because general growth in the economy (or decline) will effect both and will contribute to a common trend.

There is a strong tendency for economic variables to move together in prosperity and recession, and the increasing use of lagged variables in models (which allow for the delayed impact of a variable) has increased the probability of errors caused by multicollinearity. Sometimes the trend elements are clearly visible when the data are graphed, but if not the Durbin–Watson statistic will again give a measure of the disturbing effects of time. If multicollinearity is suspected there are ways to deal with it.

6.15 Dealing with autocorrelation and multicollinearity

If autocorrelation or multicollinearity are identified or suspected there are several ways of minimising their impact upon correlation or regression analysis. The different methods are appropriate for different sorts of distributions and the underlying nature of stochastic, cyclical and trend elements in the time-series. These must be identified by careful attention to historical context and complementary historical evidence as well as by analysis of the statistics themselves. Many of the methods are beyond the scope of this volume, though it helps to be aware of them in understanding research which you might read.[14]

- The simplest method, which has limited use and is only appropriate for linear data, is to use the 'series of first differences' instead of the original time-series. Series of first differences are formed by subtracting each value from its predecessor. In Table 6.7 the original series, an index of money wages, has been converted to the series of first differences. A version of this method was used by Von Tunzelmann to remove the effects of autocorrelation from his analysis of import and export variation in the nineteenth century.[15]
- An alternative method of eliminating the impact of autocorrelation upon correlation and regression analysis is to use the de-trended rather than

Table 6.7 Conversion of a wage index to a
series of first differences, 1790–1850

Year	Money wage index (1840 = 100)	Series of first differences
1790	70	
1795	82	–12
1800	95	–13
1805	109	–14
1810	124	–15
1816	117	7
1820	110	7
1824	105	5
1831	101	4
1840	100	1
1845	98	2
1850	100	–2

Source: index derived from P. K. O'Brien and S. L.
Engerman, 'Changes in income and its distribution
during the industrial revolution', in R. Floud, and D.
N. McCloskey, (eds), *The economic history of
Britain since 1700* (Cambridge, 1981), vol. 1,
p. 169.

the original series for the analysis. As was shown in Chapter 5, the trend
line for each variable can be calculated and the de-trended series is
formed by subtracting the trend values from the data values for each variable. A good example of this is given in Table 6.8, which calculates the
trend and seasonal components in wheat prices for Winchester College in
the early eighteenth century. This leaves the de-trended, de-seasonalised
series available for analysis. (The methods used for de-seasonalising as
well as de-trending were discussed in Chapter 5, section 5.8, together
with other examples.)

If it is thought that seasonal or cyclical components are causing multicollinearity they can also be 'removed' by using various filters calculated
for different periodicities. Crafts, Leybourne and Mills used the Kalman
filter on their series of British industrial production which exposed an
identifiable acceleration in the trend rate of growth during the decades of
industrialisation.[16]

Other methods of dealing with autocorrelation and multicollinearity are
available, depending upon the sort of data involved and their distribution
over time.[17] The aim of all is the same: to transform the series into one
which is stationary (i.e. not distorted by the impact of particular chronological influences).

Table 6.8 Separation of trend and cyclical components from wheat prices (in shillings per quart) for Winchester College, 1713–18

Year and quarter	Wheat price	Trend value[a]	Deviation from trend	Seasonal component[b]	De-trended, de-seasonalised series	De-seasonalised series
1713						
1st	42.67	46.71	−4.04	−0.09	−3.95	42.76
2nd	56.88	45.86	11.02	1.55	9.47	47.41
3rd	49.78	45.01	4.77	0.73	4.04	49.05
4th	46.21	44.16	2.05	−2.19	4.24	48.40
1714						
1st	32.00	43.31	−11.31	−0.09	−11.22	32.09
2nd	32.00	42.46	−10.46	1.55	−12.01	30.45
3rd	32.00	41.61	−9.61	0.73	−10.34	31.27
4th	28.44	40.76	−12.32	−2.19	−10.13	30.63
1715						
1st	46.21	39.91	6.30	−0.09	6.39	46.30
2nd	49.78	39.06	10.72	1.55	9.17	48.23
3rd	42.67	38.21	4.46	0.73	3.73	41.94
4th	35.56	37.36	−1.80	−2.19	0.39	37.75
1716						
1st	39.10	36.51	2.59	−0.09	2.68	39.19
2nd	39.10	35.66	3.44	1.55	1.89	37.55
3rd	40.29	34.81	5.48	0.73	4.75	39.56
4th	33.77	33.96	−0.19	−2.19	2.00	35.96
1717						
1st	43.84	33.11	10.73	−0.09	10.82	43.93
2nd	32.00	32.26	−0.26	1.55	−1.81	30.45
3rd	32.00	31.41	0.59	0.7	−0.14	31.27
4th	32.00	30.56	1.44	−2.19	3.63	34.19
1718						
1st	24.89	29.71	−4.82	−0.09	−4.73	24.98
2nd	23.70	28.86	−5.16	1.55	−6.71	22.15
3rd	26.67	28.01	−1.34	0.73	−2.07	25.94
4th	24.89	27.16	−2.27	−2.19	−0.08	27.08

[a]The trend values were calculated from the estimated linear trend equation.
[b]The seasonal component was calculated by taking the mean of the deviations from trend for the first quarter of the year, then the mean of deviations for the second quarter, etc. This gave values of −0.08, 1.56, 0.74, −2.17; summing these values gave 0.05, but by definition the seasonal variation should have a neutral or zero effect over the whole year. The seasonal means were therefore adjusted by approximatley −(0.05/4) in each case, taking them as −0.09, 1.55, 0.73 and −2.19, which sum to zero, and these were used as the estimate of seasonal variation. Source: R. Floud, *An introduction to quantitative methods for historians* (2nd edn, 1979), p. 114; figures derived from W. H. Beveridge, *Prices and wages in England from the twelfth to the nineteenth century* vol. I (London, 1939), p. 82.

Conclusion

This chapter has dealt entirely with inferential statistics. These are techniques of statistical analysis which go beyond a description or display of

data. Inferential statistics involve making predictions or estimates and testing hypotheses concerning causality. There are many more pitfalls here for
the unwary researcher or reader than there are in relation to descriptive statistics but, providing care is taken to be a good historian first, and a 'number cruncher' only second, these techniques can be both powerful and useful.

Notes

1 Darrell Huff, *How to lie with statistics* (London, 1973), p. 90.
2 For more on sampling and sampling bias see Chapter 7.
3 It is not always clear which way a causal connection might run, especially with
   something such as exports and imports, education and nuptiality, so historians
   must be prepared for the possibility that the direction of causality might be
   different from what they expect. It is also, of course, possible, as we shall see,
   that a close relationship between variables has no causal basis whatsoever. If this
   is suspected there is no point in exploring it.
4 The 'politics of the contingency table' and the conflicts between Pearson and
   others are discussed in D. A. MacKenzie, *Statistics in Britain 1865–1930: the
   social construction of scientific knowledge* (Edinburgh, 1981), especially pp.
   153–82.
5 There are many uses for the χ^2 distribution. Application to contingency problems
   is only one of the most common uses.
6 For the raw data and information about other variables see P. Hudson, *The
   genesis of industrial capital: a study of the West Riding wool textile industry, c.
   1750-1850* (Cambridge, 1986), chapter 10 and appendix.
7 Benjamin and Kochin's work on modelling and testing the relationship between
   unemployment and benefits payments in inter-war Britain started a lengthy
   debate in the 1970s and 1980s about regional versus national level correlations
   and about the degree to which the causal connections could run in the opposite
   direction to that posed. The debate had big exposure both inside and outside
   academia because it appeared to support the contemporary Thatcherite policy of
   'pricing people back into jobs' (i.e. bringing down wages but bringing down
   benefits even more so that the lack of attraction of benefits would force people
   back to work). This, of course, supposed that there were jobs available and no
   demand deficiency in the economy. See D. Benjamin and L. Kochin, 'Searching
   for an explanation for interwar unemployment', *Journal of Political Economy*,
   87 (1979), which is included as an exercise in the Appendix, article 10. For
   critiques, including one by M. Collins, using regional figures, see issues of
   Journal of Political Economy (1980).
8 E. A. Wrigley and R. S. Schofield, *The population history of England,
   1541–1871* (Cambridge, 1981).
9 J. Mokyr, 'Three centuries of population change' *Economic Development and
   Cultural Change*, 32 (1983), p. 190.
10 P. Hudson, *The genesis of industrial capital: a study of the West Riding wool
   textile industry, c. 1750-1850* (Cambridge, 1986), pp. 244–5.
11 G. R. Boyar and T. J. Hatton, 'Migration and labour market integration in late
   nineteenth-century England and Wales', *Economic History Review*, 50, 4 (1997).
12 Only a brief survey of these problems is given here. More detail is available in R.
   Floud, *An introduction to quantitative methods for historians*, second edition,
   (1979), pp. 156–63, and C. H. Lee, *The quantitative approach to economic
   history* (London, 1977), Chapter 3. See also note 14. .

13 N. Von Tunzelmann, 'On a thesis by Matthews', *Economic History Review*, 20 (1967), pp. 548–54; quoted by Floud, *An introduction to quantitative methods for historians*, p. 160.
14 For more detail on these issues in the context of historical research, see N. F. R. Crafts and T. C. Mills, 'Modelling trends in economic history', *The Statistician*, 45, 2 (1996), pp. 153–9, a recent contribution to a long-running debate on time-series analysis which followed the publication of N. F. R. Crafts, S. J. Leybourne and T. C. Mills, 'Trends and cycles in British industrial production 1700–1913', *Journal of the Royal Statistical Society*, 152 (1989), pp. 43–60.
15 See note 13.
16 Crafts, Leybourne and Mills, 'Trends and cycles' *Journal of the Royal Statistical Society*, 152 (1989), pp. 43–60.
17 In statistical parlance, one needs to identify in what order the series is integrated.

Further reading

A. Aron and E. N. Aron, *Statistics for the behavioural and social sciences* (New Jersey, CN, 1997), Chapters 11 and 12.

F. Clegg, *Simple statistics: a coursebook for the social sciences* (Cambridge, 1982), pp. 173–86

F. Daly, D. J. Hand, M. C. Jones, A. D. Lunn, K. J. McConway, *Elements of statistics* (Harlow, 1995), Chapters 11, 13, 14

R. Darcy and R. C. Rohrs, *A guide to quantitative history* (Westport, CN, 1995), Chapters 6, 8 and 9

R. Floud, *An introduction to quantitative methods for historians* (London, 1973; 2nd edn 1979), Chapter 7

T. Hannagan, *Mastering statistics* (London, 1982; 3rd edn 1997), Chapter 10

L. Haskins and K. Jeffrey, *Understanding quantitative history* (Cambridge, MA, 1991), Chapter 6

C. H. Lee, *The quantitative approach to economic history* (London, 1977), especially, Chapters 2 and 3

C. Marsh, *Exploring data: an introduction to data analysis for social scientists* (Cambridge, 1988), Chapters 8, 10, 12 and 13

R. Soloman and C. Winch, *Calculating and computing for social science and arts students* (Buckingham, 1994), Chapters 4 and 6

|7|

Sampling and significance testing

There was once man who did not believe in sampling, and who campaigned against it up and down the country. He emphasised all the dangers ... pointing out in particular that sampling was necessarily based on probabilities rather than certainties, so that you could never be sure that you conclusions were correct. One day he was due to give a lecture on the evils of sampling in a nearby town. He got up, and went down to breakfast. His egg did not look too good, so he tasted a bit of it, found that it seemed all right, and finished the lot. He put his hand outside the door, felt that it was raining, and decided to take an umbrella. He looked in the rack for a magazine to read in the train, thumbed through one or two, found one that looked interesting, and put it in his pocket. When the train pulled into the station he chose the carriage that looked the cleanest and travelled to the nearby town. He went to the lecture hall, and gave his anti-sampling lecture, which was received with rapturous applause by an audience of about a hundred people. 'How did it go?', his wife asked him when he got home again. 'Wonderful, wonderful', the man repled, 'it's obvious that there's a strong feeling in the country against sampling'.[1]

Sampling is an everyday occurrence and we all do it. You have probably sampled this book by looking at only one or two chapters. It is sometimes done with great care, sometimes rather sloppily, without much thought about the selection of the sample or the significance of its character as a guide to wider understanding (as in the example above). The same is the case with social science and historical research which uses samples.

Often the historian is presented with a massive **population** of cases and it becomes necessary to take a sample for analysis rather than attempt to look at the whole lot. The word 'population' is used here in a statistical, rather than a demographic, sense and means those cases which constitute the full data set under consideration.

The most common reason for using samples, and for applying sampling theory, is to reduce the amount of work to manageable proportions with as little reduction in the accuracy and reliability of research results as possible.

7.1 The purpose and procedures of sampling

The sorts of historical research where sampling will be necessary include the following. In each example the time, cost and/or practicality of studying the full data set (or population) make this prohibitive:

- Study of the households of England and Wales as listed in the 1851 Census. Professor Michael Anderson of the University of Edinburgh studied such households by using a 2 per cent sample.[2] He selected the total population in 1 in every 15 enumeration districts (945 in all), which included information about 415,000 individuals.
- Analysis of transactions recorded in business ledgers over many years: here the sheer volume of material and its repetitiveness suggest the need for sampling. Much business history involves sampling from this sort of data. My work on the West Yorkshire woollen and worsted industries in the early nineteenth century and on the accounting techniques used by textile business firms in the later nineteenth century used samples of business ledgers to look at the sorts of transactions made and the ways in which they were recorded. For this I selected records from a wide variety of firms whose archives had survived and considered ledgers for sales and purchases from successive five-year periods.[3]
- Interviews with persons working in car factories in the 1960s: here it would be impossible to trace and interview all cases or even a majority of cases. Huw Beynon's classic study *Working for Ford* was based upon interviews at the Speke factory in Liverpool in the late 1960s. His sample of interviewees was a cluster of contacts amongst shop stewards and rank-and-file workers made largely through the Transport and General Workers Union. The aim of the study was to 'extend beyond its specific context – one assembly plant in Liverpool in the 1960s – to say something about the wider fluency of working lives in general'.[4]
- Study of early modern probate inventories: these are detailed lists of movable possessions at death and were made in connection with the administration of wills. They are an important source for studying the layout and contents of homes, the balance of industrial and agricultural tools and equipment, debts and credit, and the dissemination of new or more varied consumer goods. Many thousands of inventories have survived across the regions and localities of England, in different record offices. They date largely from the mid-seventeenth to the late eighteenth centuries and are sometimes stored in date order, sometimes by name and sometimes rather haphazardly. Some collections are indexed and some indexes include names and occupations. It would be impossible to look at

them all but it is quite feasible to take a sample. Lorna Weatherill's study of consumption goods and consumer culture took, roughly, a 10 per cent sample from selected repositories to reflect a good geographical spread and to cover the main locations.[5] But in practice it was not always possible to take every 10th document from each box, and some compromise had to be made in selecting a sample (as free from bias as possible) without trespassing on the patience and strength of archivists needing to haul around the boxes. One of the biggest current studies of the probate inventories of Cornwall and Kent, by a team of researchers at the University of Exeter, has also decided to take a 10 per cent sample and to stick to every 10th record where possible. As the Kent and Cornwall archives have reasonably detailed catalogues it was possible to contemplate choosing a sample which would reflect a good spread of occupations, social classes and gender, but this was rejected in favour of more systematic methods which would give all types of inventories a chance of being chosen as part of the sample.

The purpose of sampling in all these cases was to create a manageable research project with minimum reduction in the accuracy and reliability with which the research results would represent wider features of the populations concerned.

A historian who uses a sample should always make clear that it is just that – a sample. He or she should not argue that the sample results necessarily reflect wider experience or practice in the whole population. The only context in which it is justified to suggest wider implications of the sample results is where it can be demonstrated convincingly that the sample is fully representative of the population as a whole.

Statistical procedures can assist both in sampling (to ensure a representative and unbiased sample is selected) and in analysing the wider significance of sample results. Such procedures are designed to allow us to make measurably accurate predictions about the nature of the total population simply from analysis of a much smaller sample.

When a historian studies a body of data deliberately obtained by sampling from a larger population, the sampling method should always be discussed and justified in terms of commitment to the goal of representativeness. The size of the sample should also be mentioned and justified because with some sampling methods and in some situations a larger sample may be required to ensure the minimisation of bias. The most representative sample possible is an *independent random sample*, and it is this type of sample upon which the foundation of further statistical analysis rests.

7.2 Independent random sample

An independent random sample is a sample of cases taken from the total population so that each case has an equal chance of being chosen as part of the sample. The Electronic Random Number Indicator (ERNI) is a good example of machinery introduced to ensure the choice of a random sample, in this case winners in the regular prizes for premium bonds (savings certificates issued by the British government since the 1950s). The various ball machines used by the National Lottery are similarly designed to yield a random group of 7 numbers from the 49 available.

Statistical software usually includes a random number indicator, but where no computer is available random number tables can be used to dictate the sample. Random number tables and random number software create a stream of numbers (up to a maximum dictated by the population size) which occur entirely at random, i.e. each number in the population has an equal chance of being chosen as part of the sample. Both the random number indicator and random number tables select cases at random from the number available until the required sample size is reached.

Only by selecting a sample in this random way can analysis of the sample be heavily relied upon accurately to predict the nature of the population as a whole, and for this to be so the random sample must also contain at least 100 cases.

Experience has shown, and statistical theory confirms, that a well-chosen sample (i.e. a sample chosen to avoid bias, but especially one which is independent and random) can reveal a full range of experience and can generate predictably accurate measures for the population as a whole providing there are 100 or more cases in the sample. The historian's urge to collect evidence from as many cases as possible may thus be misplaced. The 101st observation gives much less additional precision than the 100th. Statistical theory shows that the proportion does not matter to the accuracy of the sample, what matters most is the selection of an unbiased sample. To be precise the accuracy of a random sample varies inversely with the square root of the absolute number in the sample. We can say this because of our knowledge of the properties of the normal distribution, to which we turn in Section 7.6.

Obviously, any method of selecting or sampling cases which can be justified as being representative will provide a basis for some sort of estimate of the nature of the total population, but only independent random sampling gives us a means of judging exactly how close our sample results are to those which would be obtained from the population as a whole.

Sampling theory and method are based on the assumption that an independent random sample is obtainable, but, in reality, a true random sample is seldom used in historical research. What tends to happen is that a random sample is impossible to obtain, so another sort of sample is used as if it were random. This must involve some discussion of whether the researcher believes the sample to be similar to a random one. In other words, biases need to be discussed. If the researcher goes on to use statistical procedures appropriate only for a truly random sample, it must be made explicit that a departure has been made from strict statistical practice. This must be justified by explaining the nature of the sample and by explaining how one can be confident that it is representative of the population and near to random.

Where a population is large and the historian decides to take a sample, it is often not practical or not possible to take a true independent random sample. In fact, the only circumstance where a true independent random sample is usually taken from a very large data set is when the data set as a whole has been fed into a computer and is machine readable. That way random number software can be applied to extract the random sample. With large data sets, scattered in separate boxes in archives or on many reels of microfilm, such as the 1851 Census of households or the probate inventories of Cornwall, it would be entirely impractical to extract random cases from the thousands available.

7.3 Systematic and stratified samples

Most often, instead of a random sample a systematic sample is taken of a proportion of the population. Alternatively, a stratified sample is selected. A systematic, proportional sample is formed where the historian takes a certain proportion of cases to represent the whole and where these are selected systematically as a way of avoiding bias. Usually, every 10th or 10th case is selected, but this depends on the size of the population, the required sample size and the nature of the research. Where such a sample is selected the historian must be careful that the method of selection has not predisposed the sample to bias, especially where, for practical reasons (such as illegible or missing documents), it is not possible to stick strictly to every 10th or every 100th case. Bias may also occur simply from sticking to a fixed periodicity within the sample. If records exist in date order, for example, the researcher must be careful that any sort of cyclical or seasonal variation in the cases does not coincide with the periodicity of selection of the sample.

To assist in avoiding bias a system of regularity is often introduced from an initially random choice. For example, if a 2 per cent sample is required from 100 000 names, the first is selected at random from the first 50 names [50 because the population is 50 times greater than the sample size (i.e. 50 $\times$ 2000 = 100 000]. If the 23rd name is picked the names are then selected at regular intervals until the sample is complete (e.g. 23rd, 73rd, 133rd, etc.). The initially random starting point is what is generally regarded as characterising a systematic sample, though the term is used more loosely to denote any proportional sample with a regular periodicity which has been justified in terms of its probable lack of bias.

A stratified sample is one which is deliberately selected so that the various groups or strata in the population are represented – as nearly as possible in proportion to their distribution in the population as a whole. The assumption behind stratified sampling is that the strata are quite different with respect to the variable being studied. This often occurs with mixed urban and rural samples or with a population which has clear divisions along status or class lines. Stratified sampling may appear attractive to the researcher at first sight but is rarely easy to achieve as one needs to know reasonably accurately the distribution of the whole population between strata. If this knowledge is subject to error then so too will be the sample. In addition, the imposition of fixed criteria for the selection of cases can be problematic if the population changes character over time or if the strata have greater fluidity of classification, meaning or character (with respect to the variable being studied) than the historian has assumed. In his oral history of the Edwardian period Paul Thompson tried to include respondents from different occupations and social strata. As no further statistical analysis was hanging on the accuracy of the sample, it was not vital whether the range of respondents reflected the overall distribution of the population.[6] Sometimes, stratified samples are preferred because the researcher wishes deliberately to bias the results in favour of the strata in the population which is judged to exhibit more variation. This can occur with, for example, urban populations in relation to variables such as housing type. As long as the rationale is explained and the results are not then used to infer anything about the population as a whole this is perfectly acceptable.

The characteristic of random, systematic and stratified sampling is that every individual has a known probability of being included in the sample, providing the rules governing the selection of such samples are followed to the letter.

7.4 Other sorts of samples

Other samples frequently used in historical research come about not through the selection of cases from a large data set but because the historian has to work with the sample that is most easily available to him or her.

A *cluster sample* is formed when a sample is selected on the basis of the ease of access to a particular group within the population. Street-corner interviews are usually given as the most obvious example of a cluster sample in social science research. These can be justified in terms of their representative nature providing it can be argued that the variable being studied has no relationship to the likelihood of someone being on a street corner at a particular time of day. Cluster samples are often preferred by researchers when they believe that most of the variation in the factor being studied takes place within rather than between clusters. In this context, the cluster can be justified by both ease of access and representativeness. In oral history interviews are sometimes conducted in one or two old people's homes, or amongst a network of friends or neighbours. Documentary sources may also provide a cluster sample where papers survive only in, or for, one location or social group or for a limited number of locations or social groups. Surveys very commonly are forced to use cluster samples of various kinds because, even if the net is cast wide, those who agree to take part in an interview or written survey are self-selecting and may be a particular sort of person with a particular sort of experience which is different from the mass of the population who have no interest in participating in research. Sometimes the researcher takes the self-selected cluster sample and re-weights it to reflect the stratification of the population as a whole, but this has the danger of introducing additional biases rather than eliminating the problems and should generally be avoided in favour of a full exploration of the biases inherent in the cluster.

A cluster sample may be regarded as one of a number of types of samples of convenience. In historical work, such samples are very common. Other samples of convenience, used by historians, include surviving samples and those which are better documented than others.

A *surviving sample* is used where the bulk of records have not survived but where the historian wishes to say something about the nature of the population as a whole on the basis of information from the surviving cases only. For example, with the use of business records, diaries, autobiographies, settlement certificates, wills, household budgets the researcher is at the mercy of what has survived. With such research it is necessary carefully to explore the ways in which the surviving sample may be biased. Autobiographies might survive for the more literate and successful individuals in society or because they were written for publication (and therefore got printed and preserved) rather than for private use. In the case of business records the larger more successful firms are often better represented in documentary sources than are smaller more ephemeral businesses whose stories end in bankruptcy rather than expansion. The wave of business histories of the 1950s and 1960s gave heroic accounts of large and successful firms which for a time may have biased our understanding of British business-people and their efficiency and of the commercial climate within which they functioned.

A *better-documented sample* is often used where the records relating to a sample of cases contain the information required for the research (or fuller details) but where the majority do not. Use of a better-documented sample can result in a richer history being written but it is necessary to contemplate the distortion which may have been introduced by using such a sample if one's concern is to describe and analyse the population as a whole. Better-documented samples often give undue prominence to notorious or exceptional cases. It is often tempting when researching court cases, for example, to spend much longer on those with fuller evidence in depositions. This can yield interesting histories of such cases but these must be qualified by suggesting how well-documented cases may have differed from those, for the same or different crimes, where the records are shorter and less informative.

7.5 Sampling error

All samples introduce elements of bias and distortion which should be discussed by the researcher as openly as discussion of the pitfalls and biases of the sources themselves. We must be careful to think about and allow for these, particularly if our concern is to use the sample in order to say something about the population as a whole. An independent random sample of over 100 cases reduces distortions to a minimum, but even an independent random sample is subject to 'random sampling error': error in representativeness caused by chance or the 'luck of the draw'. Other sorts of samples have their own peculiarities and difficulties. Most are not suitable for further statistical analysis and the results of research upon such samples must be evaluated solely upon the evidence which they reveal about the sample itself. In these circumstances it is possible only to generalise, impressionistically, about the population as a whole. Other samples, especially independent random samples and certain proportional samples (which can be argued to be little removed from random), make further statistical analysis possible in order to calculate the certainty with which we can rely on sample results to give us an accurate picture of the character of the population as whole.

Further statistical analysis of samples involves the use of probability theory (sometimes termed 'error theory') and the properties of the normal distribution (sometimes known as the 'error distribution').

The analysis revolves around estimating the sampling error arising from an independent random sample and deciding if it is tolerable for one's purposes. A sampling error is the difference between the 'true' value of a characteristic within a population and the value estimated from a sample of that population. 'Error' occurs because *no* sample can be expected exactly to represent the population from which it was drawn.

7.6 The normal distribution

The **normal distribution** is a particular kind of frequency distribution: an ideal type. We encountered the normal distribution in Chapter 4, Section 4.3. It has two properties:

- the mean, the median and the mode are all the same;
- a constant proportion of cases lie between the mean and multipliers of the standard deviation from the mean:
  - 68.26% fall between one standard deviation above and below,
  - 95.46% fall between 2 standard deviations above and below,
  - 99% fall between 3 standard deviations above and below.

For an illustration of a normal distribution, see Figure 4.4, page 104.

Where does this concept of the normal distribution fit into sampling theory and technique?

7.7 The distribution of sample means

Let us assume that we repeatedly take random samples of N cases from a population where

- the mean of the population is μ (pronounced mu),
- the standard deviation is σ (pronounced sigma).

Provided that the number in the sample, N, is greater than or equal to 100 ($N \geq 100$):

- the frequency distribution formed by the sample means will be a normal distribution (known as the sampling distribution). It will always be normal, no matter what sort of frequency distribution was formed by the population itself.

We can then say:

- the mean of the sample distribution will be the same as the population mean (i.e. μ);
- the standard deviation of the sample distribution (the 'standard error') will always be $\dfrac{\sigma}{\sqrt{N}}$

Bearing in mind the properties of the normal distribution:

- there is a 68.26 per cent chance that the mean of a random sample will be in the range $\mu \pm \dfrac{\sigma}{\sqrt{N}}$
- there is a 95.46 per cent chance that the mean of a random sample will be in the range $\mu \pm \dfrac{2\sigma}{\sqrt{N}}$

7.8 Estimation of the population mean and standard deviation from a sample

We can use the facts outlined in Section 7.7 above to estimate the population mean, μ, and standard deviation, σ, from the random sample. This is possible as it can be shown that a good estimate for $\dfrac{\sigma}{\sqrt{N}}$ is

$$\frac{s}{\sqrt{N-1}}$$

(where s is the standard deviation of the sample). Thus in 95.46 per cent of all samples the population mean will lie in the range

$$\overline{X} \pm 2 \left[\frac{s}{\sqrt{(N-1)}} \right]$$

where $\overline{X}$ is the sample mean.

7.9 Samples and populations: some examples

A seemingly straightforward example of the use of sampling to provide estimates of population characteristics is given by Floud.[7] His example concerns the use of a random sample of 100 female marriage ages to estimate the mean age of marriage in a town. 'We gather the information on marriage ages from the parish registers and then take a random sample of 100 women'. The mean age of first marriage, $\overline{X}$, is found to be 27 years, with standard deviation 2.2 years.

Applying what we know about sampling theory, probability and the properties of the normal distribution, we know that in 95.46 samples out of 100 the sample mean will lie in the range $\mu \pm 2\sigma/\sqrt{N}$, which is equivalent to saying that in 95.46 samples out of 100 the population mean will be somewhere in the range $\overline{X} \pm (2\sigma/\sqrt{N})$. Since we do not know σ we use $s/\sqrt{N-1}$ as an estimate of $\sigma/\sqrt{N}$. We therefore know that, for this example, in 95.46 samples out of 100 the population mean will be in the following range:

$$\mu = \overline{X} \pm 2 \frac{s}{\sqrt{(N-1)}} \text{ years}$$

$$= 27 \pm 2 \frac{2.2}{\sqrt{100-1}} \text{ years}$$

$$= 27 \pm 0.44 \text{ years}$$

The population mean will therefore be between 27.44 and 26.56. The range around the mean, ± 0.44 years, is known as the 95 per cent confidence interval because we can have approximately 95 per cent confidence that the population mean will lie in that range.

From the statistical point of view there is little wrong with this example. From a historian's point of view it does, however, raise some useful questions such as how were the marriage ages of the women in the sample calculated from the parish registers? And over what period of time is the study located and how was the random sample selected? Most parish registers for periods pre-1800 give no direct evidence of age of bride. This can be calculated only from linking marriage to baptism entries, being certain of the correct match and then allowing an estimated time for the birth–baptism interval. The baptism evidence for all brides is unlikely to be found, so that it would almost certainly be impossible to get a true independent random sample of female marriage ages. Floud's example might have been less questionable had he suggested that the female marriage ages were randomly drawn from Civil Registration evidence, which is available in Britain from 1837 and which includes date of birth of the bride. There is, however, no indication in Floud's example of the period of the study, which would need to be finite to allow a random sample of entries to be collected.

Another sort of example of the use of sample results to infer wider characteristics in a population might be the selection of over 100 households from the census enumerators books (CEBs) for a large city for 1881. Statistics from the sample such as average size of household, average age of head of household, average age of household resident, proportion in household not born in the city, etc., could all be considered in relation to the confidence intervals which we might accept for the population as a whole.

Of course, in practice, even in using random number tables or random number software (if one is lucky enough to have access to computerised CEB transcripts),[8] a researcher might need to diverge from strict random selection. This might occur if the random cases included non-households such as hotels, lodging houses, hospitals, prisons or other institutions. If the research concerns households these selections would need to be rejected in favour of the next random number or the household nearest to the random number of the institution; in either case a departure from strict random selection would have been made and would need to be explained and justified in relation to the maintenance of a representative sample.

7.10 Difference-of-means test

The difference-of-means test is used where we want to compare two samples, sample 1 and sample 2, taken from the same population at different time periods. Our two samples may have different means and standard deviations, but we will want to make sure that this difference really does reflect change in the population as a whole rather than just the result of the sampling process. Again, we make use of the properties of the normal distribution. *The difference of means test makes use of the fact that if we take a large number, N, of samples, where $N \geq 100$, from two populations and calculate the difference between the means of each pair of samples, the sample distribution of the differences will itself be a normal distribution.*

The sample distribution will have a mean equal to the difference between the two population means. Its standard deviation or standard error will be:

$$\sqrt{\left(\frac{\sigma_1^2}{N_1} + \frac{\sigma_2^2}{N_2}\right)}$$

where subscripts 1 and 2 indicate the sample in question. From the normal distribution we know that there is a 95.46 per cent chance that the difference between the means of the two samples will be in the range

$$\pm 2 \sqrt{\left(\frac{\sigma_1^2}{N_1} + \frac{\sigma_2^2}{N_2}\right)}$$

of the difference between the means of the population. We thus know that only in 4.54 per cent (100 − 95.46) of samples would we be likely to have a difference of means greater than two population standard deviations from zero.

These facts allow us to calculate a measure, z, of the extent to which the differences between the sample means exist only by chance; z is the difference of means divided by the number of pooled standard errors. Since the population standard deviation is unknown, the sample standard deviations are used as proxies.

The formula for z is thus:

$$z = \frac{\overline{X}_1 - \overline{X}_2}{\sqrt{\left(\frac{s_1^2}{N_1 - 1} + \frac{s_2^2}{N_2 - 1}\right)}}$$

In Floud's example of marriage ages he suggests that a mean age of 27 years and a standard deviation of 2.2 years might be compared with measures a century later of 26.5 years and 1.6 years for the same variables, for a repeated sample of 100 cases. On the surface, such a comparison might suggest that the average age of marriage in the wider population had declined by 6 months over the century. But such a 'shift' is small enough to have been the result purely of the errors produced by sampling. The first sample may have overestimated the average age of marriage and the second may have underestimated it. In this hypothetical example:

$$z = \frac{27 - 26.5}{\sqrt{\left(\frac{2.2^2}{99} + \frac{1.6^2}{99}\right)}} \text{ years } = 1.83 \text{ years}$$

Since z is 1.83 years we know that there is a greater than 4.54 per cent chance that the difference between the sample means (6 months) is a result of using the samples. Using tables which reflect the shape of the normal distribution we can be exact in saying that there is a 6.73 per cent chance that the difference between the samples were the result of sampling and not the result of the two populations being any different. Whether we think this a too large a risk is a question of historical as well as statistical judgement, however. Statistical convention suggests that anything greater than a 5 per cent chance should not be dismissed, but the researcher is in charge and must make the decisions on the basis of these figures and not just relate them as a statistical fact.

The difference-of-means test generates the percentage probability that the different sample results were thrown up purely by the sampling process. If the result is small (e.g. 5 per cent or less) one can have more confidence that the population as a whole has changed over the period, but it is up to the researcher to decide whether a 5 per cent chance is small or large, tolerable or intolerable, depending upon his or her purposes.

7.11 The significance of sample results

The decision on whether to accept that sample results are an accurate estimate of population characteristics depends on how certain one wants to be. It is a historical not a statistical decision or judgement. If the central thesis of a research project rests heavily on such an estimate one would need to be very confident, accept only a small sampling error and seek further complementary and supporting evidence. If only a subsidiary part of the research rests on this evidence one might accept a larger sampling error.

Statistical significance merely tells one the probability that the sample results will be an accurate reflection of the population as a whole. The chance taken in accepting sample results is usually expressed as statistical significance at the 10 per cent, 5 per cent, or 1 per cent levels. For example, if a result is said the be significant at the 5 per cent level it simply means that there is a 5 per cent or less chance that it was produced by the sampling process.

The measure of significance is done by the so-called *t*-test which, like much in probability theory, also takes advantage of the properties of the normal distribution, this time in estimating what proportion of sample results will lie at the outer limits of the error distribution. Only 5 per cent of the sampling distribution will lie more than 2 standard deviations away from the population distribution itself.

The *t*-test is a hypothesis-testing procedure in which the population variance is unknown; it compares *t* scores from a sample to a comparison distribution called a *t* distribution to give levels of statistical significance for sample results. It is useful for dealing with small samples and was pioneered by William Sealy Gosset (1876–1937) for testing the quality of small samples of beer at Guiness, where he was employed.[9]

7.12 The significance of correlation and regression results

It is possible to test the significance of correlation and regression results in a similar way in order to allow for the probability that results derive only by chance. With small data runs a higher correlation coefficient is required for statistical significance than if the data runs are long. Table 7.1 shows the results of running correlations between profit rates in the West Yorkshire wool textile industry during the industrial revolution and export levels. Table 7.2 gives the correlation results for profit rates against wool prices. In this early research of mine, I had suspected that export levels and wool prices may have been important determinants of profitability. Because of the availability of the evidence some of the data runs are very short, and although some high correlation figures have been produced this is not always sufficient, given the short data run, to produce a statistically significant result. Were I to live my life again I would almost certainly not bother to calculate correlations on such short and 'blunt' data sets. At the time it seemed better than nothing as a commentary on the fortunes of the industry in the period. Fortunately, my entire thesis and my academic career did not depend on these results!

From the data in Tables 7.1 and 7.2 I was able to suggest that profitability in the woollen industry may have been significantly influenced by export variation and by raw wool prices. The data runs were too short and the data itself insufficiently robust to engage in regression or multiple regression analysis.

Tables 7.3 to 7.5 give further examples of the ways in which historical work incorporates measures of the statistical significance of correlation and modelling results. Table 7.3 indicates the determinants of changes in agricultural wages in England and Wales, 1866–1912, under three possible sets of conditions, which are modelled in columns 1, 2, and 3.[10] The t statistics are given in parentheses, which is a common way of displaying them. Some confusion might arise from the use of the letter t in the specification of the variables in the left-hand column, but here t stands for time. One time period is indicated by t, and $t - 1$ indicates that the series has been lagged by one time period (in this case one year).

On the basis of the results in Table 7.3 Boyar and Hatton argued that economic conditions in urban areas had a strong influence on short-run wage changes in agriculture. In the same article they also considered the determinants of rural–urban migration in southern counties, and Table 7.4 gives results for five variables, over three different decades, as incorporated into models to produce the figures in numerical columns (1)–(3). From this they were able to suggest that economic incentives, especially the expected income gap between countryside and towns, were important in migration, but an even more important factor was prior migration (measured as

Table 7.1 Correlation of profit rates with export levels in the West Yorkshire wool textile industry for seven firms (Hague, Cook & Wormald; Illingworth; T. & M. Bairstow; Foster; Marriner; Broadbent; Clough), 1822–58

Variables	Period	N	Correlation coefficient	Significant at 5 per cent level?
Blanket exports from UK, by volume, on:				
Hague, Cook & Wormald profit rate	1822–55	34	0.55	Yes
Hague, Cook & Wormald profit rate	1840–55	16	0.83	Yes
Illingworth profit rate	1828–33	6	0.87	Yes
Export of wool goods from Great Britain, at current prices, on:				
Hague, Cook & Wormald profit rate	1822–29	8	0.55	No
T & M Bairstow profit rate	1825–29	5	0.86	No
Export of wool goods from United Kingdom, at current prices, on:				
Hague, Cook & Wormald profit rate	1826–58	33	0.44	Yes
Illingworth profit rate	1828–33	6	0.68	No
Yarn exports, by volume, on:				
Foster profit rate	1842–50	9	0.76	Yes
Marriner profit rate	1842–50	9	0.70	Yes
Total cloth exports, by volume, on:				
Broadbent profit rate	1840–50	11	0.60	Yes
Foster profit rate	1842–50	9	0.67	Yes
Marriner profit rate	1842–50	9	0.70	Yes
Clough profit rate	1845–56	12	0.51	No

N = Number of observations.
Source: P. Hudson, *The genesis of industrial capital* (Cambridge, 1986), p. 242.

Table 7.2 Correlation of profitability and wool prices in the West Yorkshire wool textile industry for the company T. & M. Bairstow, 1840–58

Variables	Period	N	Correlation coefficient	Significant at 5 per cent level?
Price of Lincoln half-hogs, on:				
T & M Bairstow profit rate	1840–58	19	−0.61	Yes
Composite profit rate	1842–58	17	−0.56	Yes
T & M Bairstow profit rate	1845–50	11	−0.66	Yes
Composite profit rate	1842–50	9	−0.67	Yes

N = Number of observations.
Composite profit rate = average rate in worsted branch based on three other firms.
Source: see P. Hudson, *The genesis of industrial capital* (Cambridge, 1986), p. 243.

Table 7.3 The determinants of change in the agricultural wage in England and Wales, 1866–1912

	(1)		(2)		(3)	
Constant	−0.075	(3.07)	−0.084	(2.99)	−0.058	(3.71)
Change in price (t)	0.166	(4.59)	0.159	(4.22)	0.167	(4.61)
Change in price ($t - 1$)	0.097	(2.47)	0.091	(2.26)	0.092	(2.42)
Urban/rural wage ($t - 1$)	0.291	(3.53)	0.308	(3.62)		
Urban employment rate ($t - 1$)	0.214	(2.79	0.215	(2.80)		
Urban or rural wage × employment rate ($t - 1$)					0.242	(3.95)
Union dummy, 1872–6	0.017	(2.89)	0.019	(2.85)	0.015	(2.83)
Time			0.0001	(0.54)		
ρ	0.509	(3.26)	0.542	(3.55)	0.456	(2.87)
R^2	0.745		0.747		0.742	
RSS	0.0028		0.0028		0.0028	
Durbin–Watson statistic	1.859		1.904		1.871	

Note: t statistics are given in parentheses; in the left-hand column, t = time; $t - 1$ indicates the series has been lagged by one time period (one year).
Source: G. R. Boyar and T. J. Hatton, 'Migration and labour market integration in late nineteenth-century England and Wales', *Economic History Review*, 50, 4 (1997), p. 722. © Economic History Society

Table 7.4 The determinants of male migration rates from southern counties in Great Britain to six urban destinations, 1870s–1890s

	Dependent variable: log migration rate					
	(1)		(2)		(3)	
Constant	2.19	(4.68)	2.25	(4.82)	0.71	(0.40)
Distance	−1.02	(7.37)	−1.01	(7.38)	−1.04	(7.41)
Wage gap	0.51	(3.88)			0.46	(3.29)
Expected income gap			0.48	(4.38)		
Migrant stock	0.49	(7.63)	0.49	(7.72)	0.47	(7.32)
Service employment					0.51	(0.85)
D^{1870s}	0.13	(1.75)	0.08	(0.95)	0.13	(1.64)
D^{1880s}	−0.40	(4.87)	−0.44	(5.19)	−0.51	(3.40)
D^{1890s}	−0.62	(6.56)	−0.64	(6.84)	−0.74	(4.42)
Origin-county dummies	yes		yes		yes	
Destination-county dummies	yes		yes		yes	
R^2 statistic	0.880		0.881		0.880	
N	452		452		452	

Note: t statistics are given in parentheses; the dependent variable and all explanatory variables except the dummy variables are defined in logarithms; N = number of observations. D^{1870s} = decade of 1870s, etc.
Source: G. R. Boyar and T. J. Hatton, 'Migration and labour market integration in late nineteenth-century England and Wales', *Economic History Review*, 50, 4 (1997), p. 712. © Economic History Society

migration stock in the models), which reflected human networks of communication and assistance. These are very interesting results but the pitfalls of carrying out such exercises given the available data are numerous and the degree of error which may be introduced by the modelling process is great. The pitfalls are thoroughly discussed by the authors themselves, which is good professional practice. The Boyar and Hatton article is the subject of an exercise in the appendix (article 13).

Table 7.5 is from Botticini's article on Tuscan dowries, which is also included as an exercise in the appendix to this book (article 12). Note the mix of dummy and interval variables in the model and the asterisks which flag up those t statistics which are statistically significant at the different levels. The table includes two different specifications of the model. Column 1 places more weight upon the difference between the bride's and groom's ages and has a more significant regression result for the importance of the bride's age in determining dowry size. The second specification allows for the groom's age, which gives a much less significant coefficient for the impact of the bride's age on dowry size. As with most exercises of this type, much historical acumen and energy must go into the specification of the model and in discussing the advantages and disavantages of using different combinations of causal factors. Even more important is the need for wise discretion in discussing the real significance of a variable which has shown up as statistically significant. The F statistic, referred to in Table 7.5, is the ratio of the between-group estimate of the population variance to the within-group estimate of the population variance. In other words, it is a further indication of the comparison between sample and population variance. Botticini uses these results to argue that dowry values were positively correlated with the age of brides and that the parents of girls who married down the social scale gave bigger dowries than those who married up.[11]

Conclusion

Sampling and the analysis of samples are frequently used in the social sciences. In fact, much of the modern apparatus of sampling theory and significance testing, building upon the work of R. A. Fisher, was developed in sociological research. For the historian, sampling theory and significance tests can be very useful where there are large data sets and where it is possible to take a random or near random sample. Most often, however, samples are forced upon historians because of the non-random survival of evidence or by the practical exigencies of collecting a data set. In all circumstances the best practice to adopt is to examine the sample closely and openly to discuss the degree to which the sample is representative of the population as a whole. Finally, and most importantly, one must always consider the relia-

Table 7.5 Estimates of the dowry function (dowry is the dependent variable), Cortona, 1415–36

	1		2	
	coefficient	t statistic	coefficient	t statistic
CONSTANT	18.51	0.32	5.87	0.09
YEAR dummy	15.46	1.46	15.67	1.48
GROOM REMARRIED dummy	−14.33	−0.71	−15.14	−0.73
BRIDE REMARRIED dummy	86.75	3.28***	86.52	3.26***
GROOM'S AGE			4.01	1.3
GROOM'S AGE squared			−0.03	−0.87
AGE OF THE GROOM'S FATHER	−0.68	−1.25	−0.69	−1.27
BRIDE'S AGE	8.59	2.33**	5.57	1.39
BRIDE'S AGE squared	−0.19	−2.45**	−0.16	−1.93*
AGE OF THE BRIDE'S FATHER	−0.09	−0.2	−0.05	−0.12
AGE DIFFERENCE	3.29	2.02**		
AGE DIFFERENCE squared	−0.06	−1.46		
GROOM'S HOUSEHOLD'S WEALTH	0.01	4.72***	0.01	4.71***
BRIDE'S HOUSEHOLD'S WEALTH	0.01	6.14***	0.02	6.19***
AGRAGRUP dummy	−0.53	−0.04	−0.14	−0.01
AGRUPDOWN dummy	33.3	1.51	33.1	1.5
AGRUPUP dummy	98.25	5.26***	95.7	5.14***
NONAGRNONAGRDOWN dummy	109.43	6.12***	109.59	6.1***
NONAGRNONAGRUP dummy	75.89	3.26***	76.25	3.25***
NONAGRDOWNDOWN dummy	98.3	4.9***	98.51	4.89***
NONAGRDOWNUP dummy	63.21	3.69***	63.78	3.71***
NUMBER OF CHILDREN IN GROOM'S HOUSEHOLD	−4.5	−1.27	−4.35	−1.23
PERCENTAGE OF DAUGHTERS IN GROOM'S HOUSEHOLD	45.32	1.4	44.48	1.37
NUMBER OF CHILDREN IN BRIDE'S HOUSEHOLD	−8.28	−2.91***	−8.43	−2.95***
PERCENTAGE OF DAUGHTERS IN BRIDE'S HOUSEHOLD	−11.05	−0.59	−11.72	−0.62
RESIDENCE dummy	26.36	2.19**	25.55	2.11**
R^2 statistic	0.68		0.68	
Adjusted R^2 statistic	0.65		0.65	
F statistic	19.18		18.99	
Number of observations, N			224	

*Significant at the 10 per cent level.
**Significant at the 5 per cent level.
***Significant at the 1 per cent level.
Note: YEAR dummy is equal to 1 for marriages after 1427; AGE DIFFERENCE is the groom's age minus the bride's age; the omitted dummy is AGRAGRDOWN; AGRUPDOWN is equal to 1 when a bride from a peasant household (AGR) marries a non-peasant groom (UP) with lower wealth (DOWN). Analogously, AGRUPUP equals one when a bride from a peasant household (AGR) marries a non-peasant groom (UP) with higher wealth (UP); NONAGRDOWNDOWN (NONAGRDOWNUP) are similarly defined for non-peasant brides marrying peasant grooms; NONAGRNONAGRDOWN (NONAGRNONAGRUP) are similarly defined for non-peasant brides marrying non-peasant grooms; RESIDENCE dummy is equal to one if the bride's and/or the groom's households lived in the town of Cortona, and is equal to O if both households lived in the countryside.
Source: M. Botticini, 'A loveless economy? Intergenerational altruism and the marriage market in a Tuscan town, 1415–1436', Journal of Economic History, 59, 1 (1999), p. 115.

bility of the sample results not only in relation to tests of statistical significance but also in relation to the nature of the research project, its aims and the centrality of the sample to the overall results.

Notes

1 R. L. Meek, *Figuring out society* (London, 1971), p. 72.
2 M. Anderson *et al.*, 'The national sample from the 1851 census of Great Britain', *Urban History Newsletter* (1977), pp. 55–9.
3 P. Hudson, *The genesis of industrial capital* (Cambridge, 1986). It is difficult to estimate what proportion of the industry the archival evidence covers or exactly how representative it is. Some idea of the total amount of Yorkshire textile business records which have survived for the period can be gauged from P. Hudson, *The West Riding wool textile industry: a catalogue of business records* (Edington, 1974).
4 Huw Beynon, *Working for Ford* (London, 1973), p. 14.
5 L. Weatherill, *Consumer behaviour and material culture in Britain, 1660–1760* (London, 1988).
6 Paul Thompson, *The Edwardians* (St Albans, 1977).
7 R. Floud, *An introduction to quantitative methods for historians* (London, 1973), p. 176.
8 Census enumerators' transcripts for the 1881 Census are in fact currently being converted to machine readable form. Details are available from http://hds.essex.ac.uk/. See, Matthew Woollard, 'Creating a machine-readable version of the 1881 Census of England and Wales', in C. Harvey and J. Press, *Databases in historical research* (Basingstoke, 1996), pp. 98–101.
9 The Guinness Company prohibited employees from publishing their work, so Gossett published under the pseudonym 'Student'. The *t* distribution test is thus sometimes called the Student's *t* test.
10 G. R. Boyar and T. J. Hatton, 'Migration and labour market integration in late nineteenth century England and Wales', *Economic History Review*, 50, 4 (1997), pp. 697–734.
11 M. Botticini, 'A loveless economy? Intergenerational altruism and the marriage market in a Tuscan town, 1415–1436', *Journal of Economic History*, 59,1 (1999), pp. 104–21.

Further reading

A. Aron and E. N. Aron, *Statistics for the behavioural and social sciences* (New Jersey, CN, 1997), especially Chapters 4–9

F. Clegg, *Simple statistics: a coursebook for the social sciences* (Cambridge, 1982), pp. 31–123

F. Daly, D. J. Hand, M. C. Jones, A. D. Lunn, K. J. McConway, *Elements of statistics* (Harlow, 1995), Chapters 2–5, 7, 8, 10

R. Darcy and R. C. Rohrs, *A guide to quantitative history* (Westport, CN, 1995), Chapters 2, 4 and 5

R. Floud, *An introduction to quantitative methods for historians* (London, 1973; 2nd edn 1979), Chapter 8

T. Hannagan, *Mastering statistics* (3rd edn, 1997), Chapters 3, 4 and 8

L. Haskins and K. Jeffrey, *Understanding quantitative history* (Cambridge, MA, 1991), Chapter 4

C. Marsh, *Exploring historical data: an introduction to data analysis for social scientists* (Cambridge, 1988), *passim*

R. Soloman ad C. Winch, *Calculating and computing for social science and arts students* (Buckingham, 1994), Chapter 5

P A R T

III

MODELS AND COMPUTERS

|8|

Econometric history

*It is a truth perpetually, that accumulated facts, lying in disorder begin
to assume some order when a hypothesis is thrown among them.*[1]

Interest in economic change has always necessarily involved an interest in
quantities and measurements – of population growth, agricultural and
industrial outputs, raw material inputs, exports, imports, prices, wages,
productivity. This interest gave rise to major collections of historical statistics in the early part of this century – building, in Britain, upon earlier traditions of political economy (see Chapter 2). Such collections were the
inspiration and necessary foundation for the rise of quantitative analysis.
Once statistics relating to the economy are collected, and even in the
collecting of them, ideas derived from economic theory are inevitably
brought into play. As McCloskey has argued, 'little of what historical economists do by way of collecting statistics escapes the touch of economic
theory'.[2]

Basic first principles of economic theory, particularly supply and demand,
form the bedrock of much seminal economic history which is often
primarily qualitative rather than quantitative. But we here concentrate upon
the combination of modern economic theory with quantitative historical
data, an approach which became increasingly prominent in the second half
of the twentieth century and which has made a big difference to the way in
which research in economic history is carried out.[3] In this approach statistical techniques are often allied to the testing of models derived from
economic theory and expressed in algebraic equations and graphs. This
experienced a boom in the late 1960s, 1970s and early 1980s, spawning a
great deal of controversy and debate. Economic history thus provides a key
to understanding some of the most fundamental issues concerning 'history
by numbers', especially where this is wedded to economic (or other) quantitative modelling. Economic historians will no doubt find this chapter a good
deal more interesting and useful than other historians, but many of the

debates raised by economic history have a wider resonance and relevance to users of quantitative methods in history as a whole.

8.1 Some definitions

- **Econometrics**: econometrics is the application of mathematical statistics to economics. During the past three decades academic economics has come to be dominated by this approach, which generally involves the building of formal economic models and their statistical testing.[4] Econometrics is now the core component in the training of an economist, certainly in Britain and North America, and econometric analysis is regarded as the high-status, cutting edge of virtually all applied research in economics.[5] Some 30 or 40 years ago this was much less the case.
- **Econometric history**: econometric history is the application of modern economic theory and method (including the centrally important statistical methods) to history. Most of the statistical methods used are simple and have already been covered in this volume. Descriptive tools such as graphs, frequency distributions, indices, growth rates and trends are joined by inferential statistics involving correlation and regression analysis, sampling and significance testing. In econometric history these are used in combination with economic theory and model building, particularly in supply-and-demand arguments, general and partial equilibrium theory, business-cycle analysis, national accounts (input–output) research and work on comparative advantage.[6] These models are usually informed by and expressed in graphs or in algebra, forming difference equations or functional equations.[7] Econometric history has been described as being 'born of the marriage contracted between historical problems and advanced statistical analysis, with economic theory as bridesmaid and the computer as best man!'[8]

Peter Temin described econometric history in its heyday in 1973 as 'a form of applied neo-classical economics':

> Examples … typically start with a formal model of some aspect of economic behaviour, assemble data for use in the model, and draw conclusions by joining the data and the model. The last step can be done in many ways: by constructing hypothetical answers to questions under varying assumptions, by estimating parameters to specified equations, by using facts in the context of a deductive argument to reject alternatives. The common element is the use of a specific model with explicit assumptions.[9]

Since 1973, as we shall see, the scope of modern economic analysis has widened and basic assumptions of neoclassical economics have become more flexible and more complex, allowing more sophisticated theories to be applied to both past and present.

- **Model building:** economic 'model building' in history refers to the construction of models of historical economies or sectors. Like most econometrics these have been almost exclusively based upon the ideas and assumptions of neoclassical economics, and to a lesser extent upon new and older forms of classical economics. Occasionally, Marxist models or other alternative models have also been employed. Usually, data are incorporated into a model of the interaction of variables in an economy or sector. The model is then used to simulate (in a simplified way) the operation of the major influences so that unknown elements in the model can be estimated or the model can be employed to understand events and circumstances in the past. Many models employ regression analysis, including multiple regression techniques, in investigations of cause and effect. Most models employ inferential statistics of some kind because their aim is to manipulate the data available in order to infer a great deal more about missing variables or about the functioning of the economy than would otherwise be possible.

- **Extrapolation:** extrapolation is often used to estimate values outside the existing data set. This is often done by adding hypothetical additional figures to data which display a definite linear trend or curve in time-series, introducing predictive power into a regression line. The technique of 'back projection' is a form of extrapolation used to infer or estimate figures for periods where the data is unavailable on the basis of later periods where figures do exist. Extrapolation and back projection are part of an armoury of quantitative techniques used by historians whether or not they are simultaneously engaged in more complex modelling. They are commonly used in economic analysis but also in conjunction with demographic models. For example Wrigley and Schofield, with the assistance of the demographer R. D. Lee, projected population data from the 1851 Census back into the eighteenth century in order to calculate the shortfall of vital events, and hence population, recorded in parish registers. In this case the back projection is based on a simulation of demographic increase based on known or estimated facts about family size, marriage ages and life expectancy.[10]

- **Counterfactual history:** a strong current in econometric history especially in the 1960s and 1970s was counterfactual history. This is the calculation of costs and benefits of a particular innovation or institution in the past compared with the costs and benefits that would have obtained in the absence of that innovation and using a 'second-best' system. The difference in total net cost to society is the 'social savings' gained or lost. The social savings gained by having a railway system, for example, is the cost of the economic resources that would have been required in the second-best transport system and which can then be released for alternative uses. Counterfactual history is based on the notion that we cannot tell how much an event or innovation matters in the past without calculating what would have happened without it. This idea is certainly not unique to econometric history: historians have commonly asked 'What if?' sorts of questions, and there has been something of a flowering of largely qualitative counterfactual history in recent years with the appearance of articles on hypothetical history or **virtual history**.[11]

8.2 The history of econometric history

Econometric analysis has an interesting history in the context of different national traditions and through the activities of particular exponents. Thanks to Morgan we know a great deal about this history up to the 1950s.[12] The development of econometrics was delayed until the twentieth century partly because most economists of the nineteenth century believed that mathematics and statistics worked in different ways: maths they regarded as a tool of deduction, statistics as a tool of induction. Statistical thinking had been incorporated into economic writings in Britain since the eighteenth century, particularly in measurements of economic variables, as we have seen. Such descriptive uses of statistics remained strong amongst economists of the historical and institutional traditions in Europe, and the inductive approach was strengthened by a conscious rejection of what was seen as the increasingly deductive, abstract, unrealistic and unhistorical neoclassicism of the marginal school of economics in the late nineteenth century.[13] The adoption of statistical tools in the *analysis* of large bodies of data had to wait until statistical theory had become a more sophisticated tool of deductive reasoning. Even then it was often the case that economists who used statistical evidence were often those who most strongly rejected mathematical models and methods.[14]

In the 1930s the International Econometric Society grew in influence, and the journal *Econometrica* was founded, which included papers by economists from many different schools of thought. What supporters of econometrics in this period had in common was not so much adherence to just one sort of theory but the desire to conjoin mathematical economics and statistical economics.[15] By the 1940s this project had become firmly established and econometrics has been the most important form of applied economics ever since. This was endorsed by a growing formalism (mathematical model building and testing) in the 1950s and 1960s, and since that time econometrics grew more prominent in historical research, particularly in the United States. In the United States and Canada, economic history in universities had always been closely tied to economics departments. It was thus natural that when econometric techniques became more prominent in economics they would also feed through into historical work in those countries in particular.

During the late 1960s and 1970s the early econometric studies in history came to be referred to and seen as the 'new economic history'. The term **cliometrics** was also coined, again meaning the application of economic theory to historical facts in the interest of history. Famous studies appeared on European manorialism, transport (especially railway innovation), the economics of slavery, open-field agriculture in England, the quality of nineteenth-century entrepreneurs, British industrial competitiveness, and the causes of the Great Depression in the United States in the 1930s.[16] During this period econometric history gained in reputation, and its most vigorous exponents claimed it would eventually provide definitive answers to many of the most fundamental questions asked by economic historians. The implication was that this approach could restore objectivity and dispassionate scientific precision to history.[17] In short, the econometric movement was underpinned by a renewed positivism which was to create much critical reaction.

The econometric tools which historians of the 1960s and 1970s were using were relatively unsophisticated compared with those of today, yet little effort was made to address the technical limits to economic theorising. The underlying assumptions of the models were oversimplified and insufficiently related to the context in which they were being applied. Little attention was paid to institutions or to cultural or social variables which lay outside the models and could not be easily quantified. Enthusiasm for modelling and the testing of models often displaced critical discussion of the reliability or detail of the historical sources themselves. For all these reasons, but also because of the deep conservatism of historians, only a restricted number became converts to the 'new economic history', and initial enthusiasm tended to die away in the late 1980s and 1990s, hastened by the criticisms not just of historians but of economists themselves, such as Solow:

As I inspect some current work in economic history, I have the sinking feeling that a lot of it looks exactly the kind of economic analysis I have just finished caricaturing: the same integrals, the same regressions the same substitution of *t*-ratios for thought.[18]

During the past two decades, econometric history (as opposed to other sorts of quantitative and qualitative approaches) has formed an important but minor field in Britain but has remained significantly stronger in the United States and Canada. On the European continent it has always tended to be less prominent than it has in Britain. During this period, however, economic theory has become enormously more sophisticated, as has the power of computer-aided multivariate modelling. Since the 1950s and 1960s econometrics has also moved much closer to statistical modelling and statistical method and is less tied to the use of mathematical models. Mathematical economics was a prerequisite for certain applications of statistics in economics, but there is no necessity for the two approaches to go together. Increasingly, they have not been taken together, and the cutting edge of econometrics and econometric history today relies much more on statistical methods. It remains to be seen whether increasingly sophisticated techniques of econometric and statistical analysis will provide a new springboard for the application of economics to history, but below we highlight some new developments and make some speculations (see Section 8.6).

8.3 Neoclassical model building

As the dominant form of economic theorising in the 1960s and 1970s was neoclassical, the cliometrics of the period almost always employed the methodology and assumptions of neoclassical theory. The nature of this theorising and the sorts of economic relationships and models arising from it are important in understanding much of the criticism of econometric history. Most criticism revolves around rejection of the ideological underpinnings of free-market, *laissez-faire* theorising. What is often at stake between neoclassical theorists and their critics is optimism or pessimism about the functioning of markets. In addition there is fundamental disquiet over the applicability of neoclassical theory, especially in the context of economies and markets in the past.

At the heart of the neoclassical model is the view of the economy as a competitive regime of production and exchange where the price system allocates resources in a semi-automatic way. Study of the price system and the formation of models based on it can be done only with the aid of a range of assumptions (sometimes called stylised facts). These assumptions, though recognised as false or exaggerated, are regarded as being sufficiently close to reality when large numbers of economic actors are involved.[19] The stylised facts enable certain features of the environment and of human motivation, such as tastes and preferences, to be taken for granted (or held to be constant). This enables one to abstract the economy or economic activity from the wider context of society and social relationships so that models can be constructed with a manageable number of variables.

What are the most important assumptions, and are they affected when we apply neoclassical analysis to the past? There are two main postulates:

- The market postulate and market clearing: much neoclassical theory assumes that markets will achieve equilibrium and clear in the short or medium term, which assumes a competitive environment, near perfect mobility of factors of production and hence good communications and information flows.
- The rationality postulate: this states that if an individual is presented with a situation of choice in an economic setting he or she will act to optimise his or her economic position.

Institutions which protect private property and enforce contracts are seen as important in providing the conditions for the market and rationality postulates to be fully developed. In short, then, most neoclassical theory is based on a logical analysis of the maximising behaviour of large numbers of well-informed and independent individuals active in markets which are governed by legal systems which enforce property rights and contracts. These conditions have in mind an advanced capitalist economy rather than the sort of economy and economic environment prevalent in the past. The further back in time we go the less applicable the basic assumptions of neoclassical economics are likely to be. As the anthropologists Douglas and Isherwood argued many years ago, 'the view of the world organised as a competitive power-seeking game between individuals exhibits a cultural and temporal bias'.[20] In other words, what is often presented in economics as a general rule of behaviour in the mass and as the tendency of 'human nature' at all times and places (where large numbers are involved) is in fact only approaching a reality in certain times and for certain cultures. Even in modern advanced capitalist societies, 'Considering that most of us wander in a fog of indecision and emotion the bright sunlight in which the rational man strides toward his goal is difficult to credit'.[21]

Most historians and anthropologists would argue that economic rationality should be regarded as a variable and not as a fixed postulate.[22] In past societies and in different cultures it often appears more rational for individuals to act to maximise the economic position of the village, the estate or the extended family than that of the individual or the nuclear family. Alternatively, the most 'rational' behaviour in some past societies may not have been to maximise material welfare at all: sufficiency may be more important than maximisation. Where mortality is high and disease rife and/or where there are few consumer goods available, leisure rather than wealth might be a prized possession. Thus the problem, as Coleman has argued, is that 'For the historian, rationality in the choice between alternatives is not a necessary assumption of human behaviour . . . [whereas] for the economist, it is crucial to the proper functioning of models of that behaviour'.[23]

Sahlins's study of various hunter–gatherer groups in Africa, Australia and the Pacific demonstrates that these peoples would be regarded as both poor and lazy from the point of view of Western economic science but in reality they were working to a different set of priorities and goals from those of the West, goals which were more rational to them in their circumstances. They were relatively affluent with regard to their needs and wants, with varied diet and plenty of leisure time. Sahlins takes to task the dominant definition of economics, defined by Lionel Robbins in the 1930s as 'the logic of choice . . . the study of how scarce resources are allocated among competing ends'. Sahlins stresses that ends should not be taken for granted as insatiable or unvarying and that scarcity is understandable only in relation to a society's wants and desires. He states, 'it is not that hunters and gatherers have curbed their materialistic "impulses"; they simply never made an institution of them'.[24]

In addition, market clearing is unlikely to be smooth or efficient and may not even be a tendency in markets of a pre-industrial economy. Even in advanced economies, markets with 'sticky' factors of production, such as labour, fail to clear efficiently or at all.[25] Thus an economic historian needs to be open to alternative ways of conceptualising and thinking about economic behaviour in the past. The tools and assumptions of neoclassical economics can be very helpful in some circumstances, but in others, and especially in pre-industrial societies, the historian must try to understand the 'cultural otherness' that lies behind motivations and behaviour with respect to material life which do not fit into our contemporary experience. Karl Polanyi argued that historians should adopt a substantivist approach to understanding the economies of earlier times. By this he means that they should, like an anthropologist, try to understand past societies and economies on their own terms and not through the lens of our own time and culture. In a remarkably prescient passage, given the importance now attached by historians to language, Polanyi argued:

> Terms like supply, demand and price should be replaced by wider terms such as resources, requirements, equivalences. The historian would then be able to compare the economic institutions of different periods and regions without foisting on the bare facts, the market shape of things.[26]

Polanyi suggested that there are many types of economic action other than market interaction in earlier societies, all of which need to be understood and theorised as much as we have theorised market behaviour. He cites the importance of householding in the past: exchange and the husbanding of resources at the level of the household. He also emphasises reciprocity as an action which should be seen as much more than just exchange without money. Reciprocity is driven by different motivations and relationships from those of the market, and it certainly does not disappear with the growth of markets, as the size and importance of gift-giving sectors in advanced economies testifies.[27] The redistribution of wealth and well-being both through charities and through state-organised taxation is another undertheorised area emphasised by Polanyi.

Finally, the dominant paradigm in economics – neoclassical optimisation – is not a source of deep insight into discontinuity or change over time. It has always been more concerned with function, balance and equilibrium:

> For the economist time is a troublesome intruder, bringing disorder to the symmetry of theory, threatening the exactitude of the short term, conveniently defined by the *ceteris paribus* assumption that other things indeed will remain equal. The historian's interest however is almost always with the long run when things will not remain equal but will change in indefinable ways. So the precision of the models is secured by the drastic device of omitting any attempt to evaluate the effect upon economic change of non-economic influences, be they technological or political, cultural or demographic: a very high price to pay for a particular achievement.[28]

It is important to understand these criticisms of neoclassical theory as they are often confused with criticism of the quantitative methods associated with the theory. This was particularly the case in what is coming to be known as the 'first wave' of econometric history.

8.4 Econometric history: the first wave

The boom in econometric history in the 1960s and 1970s is often seen today as representing a 'first wave' whose achievements came far from matching their ambitions and whose work provoked a negative reaction from which cliometrics is struggling to recover, particularly in Britain. The energy and enthusiasm which went into this first wave, the results which it produced and the criticisms which it sustained are important for anyone hoping to understand the nature of 'history by numbers'.

Railway history

A very significant cluster of studies in the 1960s and 1970s was concerned with railway innovation. These studies form a major experiment in quantitative counterfactual history. They took the form of cost–benefit analyses applied to the past. They were concerned to calculate social savings (i.e. the extra cost of the economic resources which would have been required in using the second-best transport system). The path-breaking work here was R. W. Fogel's *Railways and American economic growth: essays in econometric history*.[29] In this, Fogel constructed a model of what the US economy might have looked like in 1890 if railways had never existed. He chose 1890 as a year by which many of the benefits of the railways would have been apparent, but otherwise the choice is arbitrary. He justified the need for such a benchmark because it was easier to calculate social savings at a finite point in time and because there was less scope for error than would have been the case if social savings had been calculated over a longer time period. The major problem with Fogel's study and with that of all similar calculations is that the construction of the hypothetical or counterfactual economy involves many arbitrary and subjective decisions. Fogel, for example, allowed his hypothetical US economy to respond to the absence of railways, and he created an imaginary canal system and road system designed to carry the same volume of goods between the same destinations as did the rail system.

Fishlow's study of the same subject not only took an earlier benchmark of 1859 but did not allow the hypothetical economy to react to the absence of railways because of the risk of introducing too many additional errors into the calculation.[30] The trouble is that the counterfactual world must necessarily involve adjustments, otherwise it is of limited use to social savings calculations. But in creating a hypothetical world the door is open to a multitude of alternatives. A close look at Fogel's work highlights some wider problems in constructing the counterfactual model. He can, for example, be criticised because goods in this hypothetical scenario would not necessarily travel between the same destinations in the absence of railways. He also assumes that railways do not create traffic and that higher-cost transport does not lower demand (in economists' parlance he assumes that the price elasticity of demand for transport is low). He also assumes that railways and alternative forms of transport are perfect substitutes, whereas for many goods they clearly would not be. Fogel defends his approach to some extent by saying that he does not have to create an entirely accurate counterfactual model in order to show that the social savings of railways were relatively small. His aim from the outset was not accurately to calculate social savings but to question the long-held assumption (based largely on impressionistic evidence) that railways were indispensable for the US economy. To do this, all that was necessary, he argued, was to make sure that his hypothetical world was one which would allow social savings estimates for railways to be maximised. Where a range of estimates was possible in his calculation he always erred toward biasing the case against himself and in favour of the impact of the railroads. Thus he showed that even with the most generous of his estimates, the role of railways in US economic growth had been previously overstated to a considerable degree.

Emulatory studies of the railways in other national contexts came to similar conclusions: that railways speeded up economic growth but that the same growth could have been achieved by alternative forms of transport. Several studies also attempted to place a precise figure upon gross national product (GNP) savings to the economy of rail development. G. R. Hawke's study of England and Wales, for example, suggested that there had been a saving of 4 per cent GNP (£28 million), and Metzer's study of Russia placed the figure in that country at 4.6 per cent. Hawke and Metzer used the same approach as Fogel: they both took a benchmark year for measurement (1865 and 1904, respectively) and both allowed their hypothetical economies to adjust to the absence of railways. But in attributing a figure to social savings and making this the centre point of their research they drew more criticism than did Fogel because of the difficulties involved in making the counterfactual model accurate.[31] Calculations for the United States, Russia and other large, relatively landlocked and agrarian economies were criticised, in particular, because of the difficulties in estimating the wider benefits brought about by such innovation. In relatively undeveloped economies where alternative forms of transport are not viable, railway innovation considerably effects costs and prices throughout the economy, opens up huge new areas to trade and makes it impossible to estimate any road or canal alternatives.[32]

All such studies, of course, suffer from those problems which dog the technique of cost–benefit analysis as an aid to economic decision-making in the present. As everything has to be costed in monetary terms decisions have to be made about the value to be placed on relatively intangible factors such as health, pollution, wider travel and economic horizons, if these are to be included. The problem of where to draw the line with such analyses, what to include and what to omit, is also crucial. When does one decide that all significant costs and benefits have been estimated and accounted for? How does one decide what is significant? Do we include indirect costs and benefits, such as the effects of railways not just on the cheaper and more efficient supply of perishable foodstuffs but, through this, on nutrition and efficiency of the workforce? A third difficulty concerns uncertainties. How do we decide what will be the price of coal or other important commodities under different hypothetical economic circumstances? In any case, do market prices represent the value placed upon commodities by society?

Construction of the counterfactual world without railways is obviously highly subjective, with the difficulty in particular being in deciding how economic activity responds to the absence of railways. Do the same goods pass between the same destinations using roads, sea or canals or must the model allow for the development of different sectors and different sales and freight flow patterns? How would other forms of transport have developed in the absence of railways? There is much scope for ignorance and 'guesstimation'.[33] With the benefit of hindsight provided by our increased knowledge of growth models and the long-term impacts of links between major innovations and the rest of the economy it has recently been suggested that Fogel's social savings should be multipled by about 5 to capture the present value of the dynamic benefits of the railways![34]

Slavery

Conrad and Meyer's work on slavery is often regarded as marking the beginnings of the 'new economic history'.[35] They postulated that black slavery in the United States was characterised by two production functions and that an efficient system developed whereby those regions best suited to the production of cotton specialised in agriculture whereas less productive areas produced slaves to be exported to the staple crop areas. The model applied was a neoclassical two-region, two-commodity trade system. The data required for this path-breaking exercise were slave prices, cotton prices, average outputs of field hands and field 'wenches', the life expectancy of negroes born in slavery, the cost of maintaining slaves during infancy and other non-productive periods, and the net reproduction rate and demographic composition of the slave population in the breeding and

Table 8.1 Annual returns on a prime field wench investment (working on land which yielded 3.75 bales per prime male field hand, assuming a 7.5 cent net farm price for cotton and 10 'saleable' children born to every wench)

Year from purchase date	Personal field returns ($)	Child field returns ($)	Child sale returns ($)	Personal upkeep ($)	Child upkeep ($)	Net Returns ($)
1	56			20		36
2	40			20	50	−30
3	56			20	10	26
4	40			20	60	−40
5	56			20	20	16
6	40			20	70	−50
7	56			20	30	6
8	40	3.75		20	80	−56.25
9	56	7.50		20	45	−1.50
10	40	15.00		20	95	−50.00
11	56	22.50		20	60	−1.50
12	40	37.50		20	110	−52.50
13	56	52.50		20	75	13.50
14	40	75.00		20	130	−35.00
15	56	97.50		20	95	47.50
16	40	127.50		20	150	−2.50
17	56	157.50		20	115	78.50
18	40	195.00		20	165	55.00
19	56	232.00		20	130	134.30
20	40	195.00		20	170	920.00
21	56	232.50		20	130	138.00
22	56	195.00	875	20	120	986.00
23	56	232.50		20	120	148.50
24	56	195.00	875	20	110	996.00
25	56	232.50		20	110	158.00
26	56	195.00	875	20	110	1,006.00
27	56	232.50		20	100	168.00
28	56	187.50	875	20	90	1,008.50
29	56	225.00		20	90	171.00
30	56	180.00	875	20	80	1,011.00
31		210.00			80	130.00
32		157.00	875		60	972.50
33		180.00			60	120.00
34		120.00	875		40	955.00
35		135.00			40	95.00
36		67.50	875		20	922.50
37		75.00			20	55.00
38			875			875.00

Source: A. H. Conrad and J. R. Meyer, 'The economies of slavery in the antebellum south', p. 63 in A. H. Conrad and J. R. Meyer, *Studies in Economic History* (London, 1965), pp. 43–72; article first published in *Journal of Political Economy* (April, 1958).

using areas. Table 8.1, one of many produced by their research, gives a flavour their work: the quantification detail and at the same time the cold and inhuman language used, which is partly what drew the fire of critics. Conrad and Meyer concluded, in the face of other opinions, that slavery was profitable for all the Southern States at the time of the Civil War and that political forces were required if it were to end.

Robert Fogel and Stanley Engerman developed this sort of approach with their landmark study of the profitability of American slavery: *Time on the cross: the economics of American negro slavery*.[36] This used statistics from plantation records and censuses to demonstrate that planters in the mid-nineteenth century were a rational and humane group and that slaves were prosperous and well-treated. They also confirmed that slavery had not ceased to be profitable to owners at the time of the Civil War. This work led to a most acrimonious debate with historians who suggested that *a priori* prejudices had led to selective use of evidence and a rosy view of both slavery and the motives of slave owners. A major criticism was that Fogel and Engerman had misinterpreted slavery because of a desire to make everything fit into a neoclassical model in which 'each and every slave owner regarded slaves solely as productive instruments and used them for a single transcendent purpose: the maximisation of pecuniary gain'.[37]

Economic growth and entrepreneurship

Econometric debate about the performance of the British economy and of British entrepreneurs in the late nineteenth century was ignited by McCloskey's article of 1970, 'Did Victorian Britain fail?'[38] This followed a considerable traditionally researched literature which had blamed Britain's retardation and relative economic decline upon the inefficiencies of factor and product markets, low rates of investment and the conservative behaviour and attitudes of British entrepreneurs of the period. McCloskey applied a very crude neoclassical model to argue that markets were working well and that the late Victorian economy was growing as fast as was possible. Formalising the problem of British entrepreneurship in terms of neoclassical profit-maximising models also showed that generalisations about the conservatism and incompetence of entrepreneurs was exaggerated. Slow adoption of the basic process in steel-making and the retention of mule spinning in cotton were, for example, correct (i.e. 'rational') choices given relative factor costs.[39] These arguments have not been accepted without criticism and are now seen to be based on a very crude neoclassical model of growth in which the competitive market environment was seen as precluding entrepreneurial failure and where productivity growth was seen as dependent almost entirely upon external rather than internal factors.[40]

Growth rates for the British economy in the earlier period of the industrial revolution have also been considerably revised by quantitative and econometric analysis. Thanks to output figures based upon weighted sectoral index numbers, the classic industrial revolution now appears much more gradual than was previously thought. Although there is much debate about the data extrapolations, proxy figures and the 'index number problem' (the sectoral weights which are largely based on the distribution of male occupations drawn from parish register figures), there is no doubt that our ideas about the overall pace of industrialisation have been permanently revised by this work.[41] We also have much more idea about the impact of the Napoleonic war period upon investment and growth thanks to the debates between Williamson and others who have argued over neoclassical models of factor markets of the period and over the extent to which the markets for labour and capital failed and therefore slowed down growth.[42] Williamson's later work on nineteenth-century urbanisation in Britain has also been important in highlighting models of rural–urban migration, the efficiency of the labour market and the fact that underinvestment in city infrastructure had a negative impact the migration of labour.[43] Boyar made a similar detailed analysis of the operation of the English poor law during the same period by using multiple regression models to consider the impact of the poor relief system upon migration and economic growth.[44]

Research on British economic developments in the twentieth century have also received attention from econometric analysis. Prominent in this has been debate over the so-called Phillips curve – the theorised trade-off between controlling inflation and minimising unemployment, particularly since 1945. Attempts have been made to estimate the non-accelerating inflation rate of unemployment (NAIRU). This is the balancing point in the labour market at which the level of unemployment is just consistent with a stable rate of inflation. Applications of the theory to data for the inter-war period have, however, floundered, indicating to Crafts, at least, that 'a satisfactory macro model of the 1920s and 1930s is virtually impossible to construct'.[45] Middleton's recent book covers the 'profoundly ideological' quantitative and econometric debates about Britain's post-war economic policy very well.[46]

Finally, in the first wave was an early attempt to compute a general equilibrium model. A general equilibrium model is one in which the various markets of the economy are seen to be simultaneously in equilibrium. This is, of course, an entirely theoretical concept but it can be useful as a model in suggesting what would happen to the equilibrium if certain factors shift while others remain the same. Williamson combined some counterfactual exercises with a general equilibrium framework to model the entire US economy. He used 72 equations in the model, but even this number in Williamson's own view did not capture much detail. To keep the calculations viable Williamson confined his analysis to the markets for labour, capital, part of the land, all manufactured goods taken together and all agricultural production. Services were not included; thus three factors of production and two goods are made to stand for all US assets. But all models need to simplify, and the test for Williamson and others is whether their particular simplification appears to yield a useful addition to knowledge. Amongst other things, Williamson was able to test the validity of traditional positive interpretations of the impact of the open frontier by means of two counterfactual models: first, with the frontier closed in 1870, and, second, with a boundless frontier as had been the case earlier in the century.[47] He suggested that the closed frontier would have had the effect of raising the output per acre of eastern agriculture by 120 per cent instead of the 19 per cent which it experienced, and that the open frontier slowed the shift of labour into secondary and tertiary employments. In a review of Williamson, Lee has argued that:

> Whether the mathematics and estimates in such models are completely accurate is of secondary importance (compared with . . . the possibility of eliminating) . . . a wide range of erroneous relationships, patterns of growth, assumptions about cause and effect, and even entire explanatory constructions.[48]

This comment highlights the main, very valuable, contribution of econometric studies of the first wave.

8.5 The models, the evidence, the reality

At the heart of general methodological criticisms in economics and hence in econometric history has been the problem of instrumentalism, in other words, judging theories on the basis of their predictive ability:

> Given that economists are often concerned with prediction rather than explanation up to a point this may be an acceptable criterion and, for example, firms may be regarded *as if* they maximise profits if their actions are not inconsistent with profit maximisation. For an economic historian this may be a dangerous oversimplification leading to an erroneous belief that motives have been understood or that all decisions are based simply on profit maximisation.[49]

A further methodological problem is that the hypotheses derived from economic theory are rarely subjected to tests which can falsify them.[50] Because there are so many stylised facts and *ceteris paribus* elements, failure of a model to line up with the evidence is always easy to explain away in terms of the need to adjust the parameters of the model, or an auxiliary hypothesis in some way. Prior subjective belief in models is almost always present. Chicago School economists are, for example, readier to accept empirical results consistent with standard price theory and less willing to believe in market failure than those trained elsewhere.[51] In addition, most historians believe that historical statements of causation are always necessarily weaker and more complex than those of economists and that they are unsuitable for testing by the economists' method of isolating just one cause and assessing the outcome *ceteris paribus*. The concept of causation and the closed and deterministic nature of economic models are therefore both regarded with extreme scepticism:

> As Sir John Habakkuk put it, 'one man cannot think in two ways'; the economist's search for clearly specified models of collective behaviour, susceptible to test by quantitative methods, leads him to approach history in a way which differs fundamentally from the search for the sources of individual behaviour which is characteristic of the work of many historians.[52]

One of the main difficulties with all forms of quantitative history is that the original data may be too unreliable, biased or incomplete to allow any meaningful manipulation of the figures. When the statistical testing of economic or other models is the central point of the research such data problems need to be particularly carefully considered. Any unreliability or bias may become magnified if variables in a model are relied upon heavily for predictive or extrapolative purposes. In the enthusiasm for modelling it is especially easy to give too little consideration to how the original evidence was gathered and categorised, what elements may be missing from it, what other forms of distortion it may contain. The problems are compounded where, as is often the case, proxy variables are used because the information which the historians would ideally like to have is not available. Sometimes proxies are sought which may have too tangential a relationship to the variables under consideration:

> Lacking output data we use trade figures which are themselves based upon customs returns or other tax statistics; parish register and hearth taxes stand for vital statistics; excise figures for industrial output. The figures once gathered in, invite processing. So they are put into time series, tested, correlated, made to yield growth rates, or coefficients of one sort or another, find their way into equations and end up in computer programs. Some assumptions of economic rationality are made; and out come the results to two places of decimals. Scientific history gets a boost; positivism is reborn. The cautious stress that it is all probabilistic, a mere step towards truth via the formulation and testing of models.[53]

8.6 Econometric tools for future history

Perhaps the first wave of econometric history did suffer from the excesses of its pioneers and enthusiasts and from too heavy a reliance upon basic neoclassical theorising and assumptions. The majority reaction of the historical profession was highly critical. The techniques were largely rejected by development economists and there was little emphasis upon micro-economic applications. Surviving practitioners in this country and in the United States have continued to produce valuable and thought-provoking work, highlighting new lines of enquiry and disturbing old impressionistically-based assumptions. However, the majority of historians, certainly in Britain, remain unsympathetic to econometric history. Some of the antipathy is based upon ignorance and misunderstanding: ignorance of the techniques involved and the terminology applied and consequent misunderstanding of the degree to which the statistical testing of economic propositions can contribute to knowledge. Further antipathy has been created by the legacy of the first wave and particularly by its often careless and inflated evaluation of the reliability of the data used in calculations. The first wave was insufficiently self-critical and too ambitious to recognise the technical limits to the economic and statistical tools and theorising of the day.

The most successful quantification in Britain following the first wave of econometrics avoided theory to a large extent in favour of creating new data sets, national income accounting and estimations of the growth of output, national income and population change. Many such studies were synthesised by Maddison to create international comparative data of growth indices.[54] There has been a continuing important thread of econometrics in the economic history of Britain but nothing quite so ambitious as in the first wave. Some of the most productive and convincing developments have been in micro-economic applications, particularly in relation to single firms or sectors.[55] US economic history by contrast has remained dominated by econometric approaches, both micro and macro, and much technical progress has been made which is not always apparent to the wider body of historians in Britain. The range of application of economic theory has also expanded to include much broader areas of human interaction: marriage and family decisions, crime, politics, drugs, corruption. This micro-economic 'imperialism' (as critics have called it), associated particularly with the work of Gary Becker and his followers, offers new opportunities to apply an economic approach in any circumstances where optimising behaviour, market equilibrium and stable preferences might be assumed.[56]

Crafts has surveyed those areas of economic theory where ideas are much more sophisticated now than they were in previous decades.[57] He rightly argues that contemporary economic and political theory are pushing out the boundaries of what can and should be incorporated in modelling the economy. The development of economic theory has resulted in the ability to create models which are much closer to simulating the variety and complexity of real-world situations and which are much less hedged in by stylised facts than were models in the past. The technical limits of economics have been greatly extended. Crafts sees these advances particularly in time-series analysis and general equilibrium modelling where package programmes have been developed. He also stresses the growing ability of economics to formalise 'previously intractable aspects' of the real world such as imperfect competition and economies of scale.[58] New developments in growth theory, new industrial economics, new international economics, multiple equilibria theorising and new theories about invention have all developed in the past 15 years or so together with a much greater use of game theory in economics. The greater sophistication of rationality assumptions and the ability to allow for changing tastes and conventions might also be stressed, and developments in economic geography and in economic sociology are also helping to create ideas for economic models which can be applied to a larger variety of circumstances.[59] All of these developments have served further to highlight the crude nature of the first wave of econometric history and to suggest that the future might be brighter.

Economic history itself has had a role in the general undermining of neoclassical growth economics by emphasising the importance of factors internal to economies in furthering or hindering the growth process, such as 'social capability', the quality of 'human capital', market size, institutions, tax regimes and capital accumulation strategies.[60] Not all countries or cultures respond in the same way to international market forces or the global availability of new technologies: catch-up and convergence are not automatic; divergence and overtaking are more likely. Thus endogenous growth models have developed which are more attuned to the circumstances and nuances of different cultures and countries in different historical circumstances and over the longer term.[61] Another area where quantitative economic history is influencing and working alongside growth economics is in developing more sophisticated measures of living standards which incorporate life expectancy, infant mortality, literacy levels, political and civil rights as well as real income per head. Although there are problems with weighting and quantifying these components of the Human Development Index (HDI), their contribution to twentieth-century comparative economic history and to standard-of-living debates is very valuable.[62]

Economic theory today is seldom based upon models of perfect competition. Neither is supply-and-demand analysis based on unquestioned marginal equivalences or on unproblematic information flows. The neoclassical stress upon the importance and computability of shifts in supply, demand or price at the margin has been replaced in historical work in particular by acknowledgement of customary and inflexible elements on wages and prices. More attention is also now paid to asymmetric information where one party in a transaction knows more than the other.[63] This asymmetry is likely to have been more important in the past, especially in areas of long-distance trade.[64] It also occurred between lenders and borrowers in regions and cities in the eighteenth century where it was mitigated by notaries and attorneys. In an example from more recent economic history Olney's article on consumer credit in black and white households in early twentieth century US cities uses the theory of asymmetric information to sophisticate her supply-and-demand model. Lenders faced 'moral hazard' risks as the debtor could always behave imprudently and default. The pool of applicants for credit may have also had proportionately more bad credit risks than the population as a whole, so lenders also faced 'adverse selection'. Creditors thus screened applicants partly on the basis of race but were less worried regarding instalment credit than shop credit because risk was reduced by the ability to repossess consumer durables (see appendix, article 11, and the bar chart in Figure 3.1, page 68).[65]

Reinforcing theories of asymmetric information is the acknowledgement of agency problems. Agency theory is concerned with how people get others to do what they want in situations where there is asymmetric information and where incentives and monitoring will be required. Insight from the economic literature on efficient contracts enabled Ann Carlos to reconsider the level of opportunism among Royal Africa Company agents in the seventeenth century and to research in a similar way the agency problems of the Hudson's Bay Company with Nicholas.[66] The related concepts of adverse selection and moral hazard in decision-making by economic actors go some way towards creating a more realistic set of assumptions for the application of economic theory to the past as well as to the present.[67]

Economists are also much more concerned now than they were in the past with considering how people bargain and cooperate 'on the ground'. What role do institutions play and how do transaction costs shift to impact upon human economic interaction?[68] The importance and overlap of economic, social, familial and communal networks have been stressed by historians, economic sociologists and geographers, and the importance of local cultures and understandings in underpinning the dynamism of localities within a wider framework of global change is now firmly recognised. Finally, economic theory is slowly being influenced by gender perspectives which are set to undermine it more radically. In particular, the application of standard neoclassical tools to the 'new household economics' of Becker and his followers has come under attack for ignoring intrahousehold bargaining games and for endorsing existing family structures as 'efficient'. As Humphries has argued 'despite the changes neoclassical economics has been undergoing, so long as it continues to privilege the individual over the social in the hierarchy of causation, then it must assume that whatever exists must be optimal, otherwise it would already have been changed'.[69] Gender and other critiques of neoclassical assumptions, often deriving from broader social science and historical research, have made some impact upon economic theory, so that economic theory is now potentially better equipped for analysing a variety of complex influences affecting economic agents and exchange relations.[70]

Rational choice has been the dominant paradigm in neoclassical theory and has strongly influenced other social sciences, but empirical investigation more recently has increasingly shown that choice is biased and that rationality is bounded.[71] Choice is naturally myopic: biased towards the present and against the future. It is oriented towards the aversion of risk, regret and loss and in favour of fairness. This implies that preferences will often be reversed over time and that choice is likely to be time-inconsistent. The concept of time inconsistency is most often used where a rational private sector is aware that a policy-maker has an incentive to renege on a policy and takes this discovery into account by changing behaviour.[72] But, as Kenneth Arrow has argued.

the very concept of rationality becomes threatened . . . [when] perceptions of others, and in particular of their rationality become part of one's own rationality. Even if there is a consistent meaning it will involve computational and informational demands totally at variance with the traditional economic theorist's view of the decentralised economy.[73]

Rational action is affected by many circumstances: by power relationships as well as by the degree of information to which economic agents have access (hence their expectations) and by their cognitive ability in processing such information. It is also influenced by an array of more complex psychological factors which are essentially 'irrational' and are only beginning to be explored in this context.[74] The assumption of rational behaviour will always therefore be prone to challenge, particularly in analyses of societies with poorer information flows, more devolved power structures, more forceful customary arrangements and lower levels of literacy and education.[75]

Future relationships between economics and history look potentially more fruitful than at any other time since the 1970s. This is because the preoccupations of some economists are changing and are more in line with the central concerns which economic historians have had for many years. Such concerns include the varieties of market and other forms of exchange behaviour and practice; gender relations in the formation of household decisions; 'irrational' behaviour and the variation of performance of firms under similar sets of conditions; the structure of trade; the role of trust and reputation, custom and habit; economic horizons in risk-taking and decision-making, backward and forward linkages, economic and financial crises and quality of life. Whether this will flower into a new, second wave, of econometric analysis is debatable but new potential for relationships between economic theory and history is boosted by the development of more varied and more sophisticated techniques of computer-aided statistical analysis.[76] The real challenge for econometric history is how to incorporate new variables into meaningful, formal computable models with the attendant problem of deciding in which circumstances it is no longer very useful to do so (given the growing complexity of the model and problems of source materials). It is interesting to note that most of the historical work incorporating efficient contracts theory, asymmetrical information, institutional arrangements, gender and other factors has so far relied very little on quantification or on the statistical manipulation or testing of models.

Conclusion

We have seen that many advantages can be derived from applying quantification to history but that additional vigilance is required in marrying quantification with the construction and testing of models based on specific theoretical constructs. We have considered the nature of neoclassical analysis and the potential problems of applying simplified neoclassical assumptions to historical contexts. New developments in theory have been outlined which may assist in rejuvenating the econometric cause and which certainly point to a healthy future for economic history. But, in order to create a new momentum in econometric history, it will be important for historians to avoid the mistakes of the past: carelessness with sources and with questioning the data, preoccupation with oversimplified neoclassical and macro-level theorising, anachronistic application of present-centred assumptions, orientation towards production or the supply side of the economy and towards equilibrating markets and optimising behaviour. We might add the problems of studying men not women, nations not regions or localities, England and West Europe and not the rest of the world. We need to continue to shift the focus from production to consumption, from macro-economic generalisation to micro-level problems of choice and decision-making in the management of home, family and work; from optimisation to bounded rationality and imperfect information; from costless adaptation to the role of transaction costs; from harmony and stability to conflict and change; combining simulation with storytelling.[77] If this happens, economic theory, numbers and history may have an increasingly fruitful relationship in the coming century.

Notes

1 Herbert Spencer, quoted by Alfred H. Conrad and John R. Meyer, *Studies in econometric history* (London 1965), p. 3.
2 D. N. McCloskey, *Econometric History* (1987), p. 44.
3 One only has to look at articles published in the American journal *Explorations in Economic History* or even in the more broadly based *Journal of Economic History* and the *Economic History Review* to see how important statistical techniques have become in the past 35 years or so. The former journal ran from 1949 to 1958 as *Explorations in Entrepreneurial History*, 1st series, vols 1–10, and second series, 1963–9, vols 1–6. Since 1969 it has been called *Explorations in Economic History*, starting vol. 7. Entrepreneurial history experienced considerable early application of econometric techniques, and the journal now specialises in the publication of econometric history. The *Journal of Economic History* and the *Economic History Review* are the major journals in the United States and Britain, respectively, which cover economic history more generally, so it is instructive to analyse the changing proportion of articles which use statistical method as an index of first the growth and then the subsequent established importance of econometric techniques during recent decades.

4 By 'formal economic models' one here means the construction of a set of inter-locking economic relationships which can be hypothesised to exist on the basis of the first principles of economic theory, generally neoclassical economic theory (see section 8.3). From such models, which are often constructed using dedicated computer software, the theoretical impact of change in any one variable can be calculated.

5 At first, econometrics was based on fairly simple supply–demand and market-clearing models derived from the first principles of neoclassical economics. These models contained a very limited number of variables. This narrowed the scope of academic economics as a social science whilst broadening it as a field of mathe-matical or statistical enquiry. For a critique of this development, see Benjamin Ward, *What's wrong with economics?* (London, 1972). Ward gives a cynical view of how the narrowing of the subject of economics developed and was perpetuated. For an amusing account of the intellectual college of economics and of the mind set and habits of economists as a tribe, see Axel Leijonhufud, 'Life among the Econ', *Western Economic Journal* (1973), pp. 327–37. This account remains as amusing now, because of its accurate insights, as when it was written. On the positivism of the narrowing of economics as a discipline, and for a defence of that approach, see B. Caldwell, *Beyond positivism: economic method-ology in the twentieth century* (Boston, MA, 1982).

6 If any of these terms are new to you and you wish to learn more about them, an introductory economics textbook is recommended.

7 Difference equations and functional equations describe patterns of change in ways which permit predictions. Difference equations relate a future data value to the immediately preceding data values. If the pattern is applied again and again, future predictions can be made. Functional equations describe patterns of change in a way that permits predictions without applying the pattern repeatedly. Social and demographic phenomena often defy models of this kind because the kind of regularity which permits future predictions is only one kind of order. Situations which cannot be modelled in this way are called **chaotic systems** but progress is continuously being made in efforts to model chaos.

8 R. W. Fogel and G. R. Elton, *Which road to the past? Two views of history* (London, 1983), p. 2.

9 P. Temin (ed.), *New economic history* (Harmondsworth, 1973), p. 8.

10 E. A. Wrigley and R. S. Schofield, *The population history of England: a recon-struction, 1541–1871* (London, 1981).

11 N. Ferguson (ed.), *Virtual history* (London, 1998). R. Cowley (ed.), *What if? The world's foremost military historians imagine what might have been* (London, 2000).

12 This history is admirably traced and documented by Mary Morgan, *The history of econometric ideas* (Cambridge, 1990). For summary accounts, see C. H. Lee, *The quantitative approach to history* (London, 1977), and D. N. McCloskey, *Econometric history* (London, 1987). For an earlier survey which includes atten-tion to national accounts and input–output analysis, see G. R. Hawke, *Economics for historians* (Cambridge, 1980).

13 C. H. Lee, *The quantitative approach to economic history* (London, 1977), p. 5. See essays 17–19 in Lorenz Kruger, Lorraine Daston, Michael Heidelberger (eds), *The probabilistic revolution* (Cambridge, MA, 1987).

14 Morgan, *The history of econometric ideas* (1990), p. 6.

15 Morgan, *The history of econometric ideas* (1990), introductory chapter.

16 These are all briefly described in McCloskey, *Econometric history* (1987).

17 The flavour of this confidence can be gained from R. Fogel and S. Engerman (eds), *The reinterpretation of American economic history* (New York, 1971).

18 R. Solow, 'Economics: is something missing?', in W. N. Parker (ed.), *Economic history and the modern economist* (Oxford, 1986), p. 26; quoted by N. F. R.

Crafts, 'Economic history', in J. Eatwell, M. Milgate and P. Newman (eds), *The new Palgrave: a dictionary of economics*, vol. 2 (London, 1987), p. 38.

19 In this sense, economics has a natural affinity with statistics. This is no accident, because like biometrics and the other disciplines of social science, it evolved alongside the development of statistical theory geared to ideas about the regularities of large numbers.

20 M. Douglas and B. Isherwood, 'Why people want goods', in *The world of goods: towards an anthropology of consumption* (Harmondsworth, 1980), chapter 1, remains the best simple text to read on the shortcomings of utility theory.

21 D. N. McCloskey, 'The economics of choice', in T. G. Rawski (ed.), *Economics and the historian* (London, 1996), p. 143. McCloskey also mentions that it has been reported that 10 per cent of French companies currently make use of astrologers.

22 It is interesting that demographic transition from high to low fertility which occurred in many 'advanced' countries between 1870 and the 1930s has been seen as evidence that it is at least arguable that the neoclassical optimisation model is appropriate in demographic analysis only for the past 100 years of West European fertility. Earlier, group rules appear to have predominated: E. A. Wrigley, 'Fertility strategy for the individual and the group', in Tilly, C., ed., *Historical studies in changing fertility* (Princeton, NJ, 1978), pp. 135–54.

23 D. C. Coleman, 'History, economic history and the numbers game', *Historical Journal*, 38, 3 (1995), p. 643.

24 Marshall Sahlins, *Stone Age economics* (London, 1974), p. 14.

25 Neoclassical economics has itself, of course, been concerned with the implications of markets not clearing, but such situations are treated as exceptions requiring explanation rather than as norms.

26 Harry W. Pearson (ed.), *The Livelihood of Man: Karl Polanyi* (New York, 1977), p. x.

27 For more on the difficulties which economists have in theorising gift giving and reciprocity, see Avner Offer, 'Between the gift and the market: the economy of regard', *Economic History Review* 50, 3 (1997), pp. 450–76.

28 Coleman, 'History, economic history and the numbers game', p. 643.

29 R. W. Fogel, *Railways and American economic growth: essays in econometric history* (Baltimore, MD, 1964).

30 A. Fishlow, *American railroads and the transformation of the antebellum economy* (Cambridge, MA, 1965).

31 G. R. Hawke, *Railways and economic growth in England and Wales* (Oxford, 1970); J. Metzer, 'Railroads in Tsarist Russia: direct gains and implications', *Explorations in Economic History*, 13, 1 (1976), pp. 85–111.

32 Such problems are summarised well by P. K. O'Brien, *The new economic history of the railways* (London, 1977), and in C. H. Lee, *The quantitative approach to economic history* (London, 1977), chapter 4. See also C. M. White, 'The concept of social saving in theory and practice', *Economic History Review*, 29, 1 (1976), 82–100.

33 Some of these issues are discussed in C. H. Lee, *The quantitative approach to economic history* (London, 1977). Outside of the railways the only major counterfactual study of innovation in Britain was von Tunzelmann's research on the steam engine, which came to similar conclusions about the continued productiveness of the older technologies; G. N. von Tunzelmann, *Steam power and British industrialisation to 1860* (Oxford, 1978). Similar, but less complex, innovation models were applied to other innovations, for example, coke smelting, the mechanical reaper and the coal-cutting machine. In each case the neoclassical model proved capable of sharpening the questions for discussion or highlighting the importance of comparative costs in innovation decisions: D. Greasley, 'The

diffusion of machine cutting in the British coal industry, 1902–1938', *Explorations in Economic History*, 19, 3 (1982), pp. 246–68; Paul A. David, *Technical choice, innovation and economic growth* (Cambridge, 1975); C. K. Hyde, 'Technological change in the British wrought iron industry 1756–1815: a reinterpretation', *Economic History Review*, 27, 2 (1974), pp. 190–206.

34 N. F. R. Crafts, 'Quantitative economic history', working paper 48/9, Department of Economic History, London School of Economics, London (1999), p. 9.

35 A. H. Conrad and J. R. Meyer, 'The economics of slavery in the antebellum South', in A. H. Conrad and J. R. Meyer (eds), *Studies in econometric history* (London, 1965).

36 Robert Fogel and Stanley Engerman, *Time on the cross: the economics of American negro slavery* (Boston, MA, 1974). The second volume was entirely devoted to the statistical appendices, giving critics the research material which they needed to establish their careers.

37 Paul A. David, H. Gutman, R. Sutch, P. Temin and G. Wright, *Reckoning with slavery: a critical study of the quantitative history of American negro slavery* (New York, 1976), p. 341.

38 D. N. McCloskey, 'Did Victorian Britain fail?', *Economic History Review*, 23, 3 (1970), pp. 446–59.

39 The key research here was D. N. McCloskey, *Economic maturity and entrepreneurial decline: British iron and steel, 1870–1913* (Cambridge, MA, 1973) and L. G. Sandberg, *Lancashire in decline* (Columbus, OH, 1974).

40 For example, Kennedy has shown that market failures reduced the check on inefficient management, whilst Crafts and Thomas argued that comparative advantage may have been confined to low-wage, labour-intensive export industries and the investment in human capital was also suboptimal: N. F. R. Crafts, and M. F. Thomas, 'Comparative advantage in UK manufacturing trade, 1910–1935', *Economic Journal*, 96 (1986), pp. 629–45; W. P. Kennedy, 'Foreign investment, trade and growth in the United Kingdom, 1870–1913', *Explorations in Economic History*, 11 (1974), pp. 415–44. More fundamental is the problem of the exogenous growth model implied by McCloskey's argument: see N. F. R. Crafts, 'Exogenous or endogenous growth: the industrial revolution reconsidered', *Journal of Economic History*, 55, 4 (1995), pp. 745–72.

41 The new figures are principally associated with the research of N. F. R. Crafts, and can be found in his *British economic growth during the industrial revolution* (Oxford, 1985), and in N. F. R. Crafts and C. K. Harley, 'Output growth and the British industrial revolution: a restatement of the Crafts–Harley view', *Economic History Review* 45, 4 (1992), pp. 703–30, though some of the figures have been adjusted in subsequent journal articles. For a critique of such estimations, see J. Hoppit, 'Counting the industrial revolution', *Economic History Review*, 43 (1990), pp. 173–93, and P. Hudson, *The industrial revolution* (London, 1992), chapter 2.

42 For summary coverage of this debate and all the relevant references see Hudson, *The industrial revolution* (1992), chapter 2.

43 J. G. Williamson, *Coping with city growth during the industrial revolution* (Cambridge, 1990).

44 G. R. Boyar, *An economic history of the English Poor Law, 1750–1850* (Cambridge, 1990). A follow up to the work of Williamson and Boyar, using similar techniques, is found in the Boyar and Hatton article in the Appendix (article 13).

45 N. F. R. Crafts, 'Economic history', in *The new Palgrave* (1987), p. 38. But, on estimates of NAIRU post 1945, see R. Middleton, *The British economy since 1945: engaging with the debate* (London, 2000).

46 R. Middleton, *The British economy since 1945* (London, 2000).

47 J. G. Williamson, *Late nineteenth-century American development: a general equilibrium history* (Cambridge, 1974).

48 C. H. Lee, *The Quantitative approach to economic history* (London, 1977), pp. 91–2.

49 N. F. R. Crafts 'Economic history', in *The new Palgrave* (1987), p. 39. The key statement on instrumentality is found in M. Friedman, 'The methodology of positive economics', in M. Friedman (ed.), *Essays in positive economics* (Chicago, IL, 1953) pp. 21–2.

50 This has been regarded as important in the hypothetico deductive methodology of the sciences and social sciences and was stressed as such by Karl Popper, *Conjectures and refutations* (London, 1972).

51 Crafts, 'Economic history', in *The new Palgrave* (1987), p. 39.

52 Quoted in R. Floud, 'Cliometrics' in J. Eatwell, M. Milgate and P. Newman (eds), *The new Palgrave* (1987), p. 253.

53 D. C. Coleman, 'History, economic history and the numbers game', *Historical Journal*, 38, 3 (1995), p. 641.

54 Work by Feinstein, and by Crafts, Harley and their critics (see note 41) has been central here. C. Feinstein, *National income, expenditure and output of the United Kingdom, 1855–1965* (Cambridge, 1972); also E. A. Wrigley and R. S. Schofield, *The population history of England, 1541–1871* (London, 1981). For comparative data see A. Maddison, *Monitoring the world economy, 1820–1992* (Paris, 1995).

55 A new journal, *European Review of Economic History*, reflects this growing emphasis in research on the British side of the Atlantic.

56 For an introduction to the ideas of Becker, and to the variety of possibilities which they raise, see G. S. Becker, *The economic approach to human behaviour* (Chicago, 1976); A. Sandmo, 'Gary Becker's contributions to economics', *Scandinavian Journal of Economics* 95, 1 (1993), pp. 7–23 and M. Tomasi and K. Lerulli, *The new economics of human behaviour* (Cambridge, 1995).

57 Crafts, 'Quantitative economic history' (1999), see note 34. Most of these areas of theory are introduced in a highly accessible manner in John Maloney (ed.), *What's new in economics?* (Manchester, 1992).

58 Crafts, 'Quantitative economic history', (1999), p. 4.

59 For a flavour of the contributions from sociologists and geographers which are not easy to incorporate into formal economic theorising, see R. Swedberg (ed.), *Economic sociology* (1996), part 2, and R. Lee and J. Wills (eds), *Geographies of economies* (London, 1997).

60 N. F. R. Crafts, 'Exogenous or endogeous growth: the industrial revolution reconsidered', *Journal of Economic History*, 55, 4 (1995), pp. 745–72.

61 Though undermining traditional neoclassical growth theory, these models remain premised on the assumptions of rational expectations and profit maximisation by actors who use available information efficiently.

62 See N. F. R. Crafts, 'Some dimensions of the "quality of life" during the British industrial revolution', *Economic History Review*, 50, 4 (1997), pp. 617–39.

63 The key text on this currently appears to be B. Hillier, *The economics of asymmetric information* (Basingstoke, 1997).

64 Research on the trading problems of the big chartered companies of the seventeenth century has highlighted this. See note 66 below. See also, A. Greif, 'Reputation and coalition in medieval trade: evidence on the Maghribi traders', *Journal of Economic History*, 49, 4 (1989), pp. 857–82.

65 M. J. Olney, 'When your word is not enough: race, collateral and household credit', *Journal of Economic History*, 58, 2 (1998), pp. 408–31.

66 Carlos concluded that the Royal Africa Company contracts, which included a bond and high pay, were well-designed to mitigate moral hazard and that the

failure of the company cannot be attributed to inefficiencies in this respect: A. M. Carlos, 'Bonding and the agency problem: evidence from the Royal African company, 1672–1691', *Explorations in Economic History* 31 (1994), pp. 313–35. The Hudson's Bay Company understood the agency problem and had strategies in place to minimise opportunistic behaviour: A. Carlos and S. Nicholas, 'Agency problems in early chartered companies: the case of the Hudson's Bay Company', *Journal of Economic History*, 50, 4 (1990), pp. 853–75.

67 Insights from this area of theory are especially important in providing tools for analysis of the growth and operation of long-distance trade and relationships within and between firms. For a further historical application of principal-agency theory, see D. Sunderland, 'Principals and agents: the activities of the Crown agents for the colonies, 1880–1914', *Economic History Review*, 52, 2 (1999), pp. 284–306. For an introduction to the theory, see Maloney, *What's new in economics?* (1992), pp. 61–5, 116–17.

68 The path-breaking historical work here was by D. C. North and R. P. Thomas, *The rise of the Western world: a new economic history* (Cambridge, 1973); more recently D. C. North, *Institutional change and economic performance* (Cambridge, 1990). More importantly for economic theory, see O. E. Williamson, *The economic institutions of capitalism* (New York, 1985). For a survey, see Avner Greif, 'Microtheory and recent developments in the study of economic institutions through economic history', in D. M. Kreps and K. F. Wallis (eds), *Advances in economics and econometrics: theory and applications*, vol. 2 (Cambridge, 1997), pp. 79–113.

69 J. Humphries, 'Towards a family-friendly economics', *New Political Economy*, 3, 2 (1998), p. 237. There is a large and growing literature of feminist economics and feminist critiques of neoclassical economics. For early developments, see J. Humphries (ed.), *Gender and economics* (Aldershot, 1995). For more recent work, see E. Kuiper and J. Sap (eds), *Out of the margin: feminist perspectives on economics* (London, 1995). For Becker's work see note 56.

70 G. Grabher (ed.), *The embedded firm: on the socio-economics of industrial networks* (London, 1993).

71 R. Nozick, *The nature of rationality* (Princeton, NJ, 1993).

72 As an economist would express it: discounting in economic decision-making is not exponential but hyperbolic. The path-breaking work in developing the theory of myopic choice is found in G. Ainslie, *Picoeconomics* (Cambridge, 1992). See Maloney, *What's new in economics?* (1992), pp. 264–6, 302–4.

73 K. J. Arrow, 'Economic theory and the hypothesis of rationality', in J. Eatwell, M. Milgate and P. Newman (eds), *The new Palgrave: a dictionary of economics* vol. 2 (London, 1987), pp. 69–74.

74 Some of these are discussed in Daniel Kahneman and Amos Tversky (eds), *Choices, values and frames* (Cambridge, forthcoming), and are briefly surveyed in 'Rethinking rethinking', *The Economist*, 18 December 1999, pp. 77–9.

75 For an accessible introductory discussion of time inconsistency, rationality and the force of rational expectations, see Maloney, *What's new in economics?* (1992).

76 Just to give one example, the use of Bayesian alternatives to the Pearson probability paradigm has only recently become possible in many applications because of the degree to which computer software can assist in the discounting of chance. Bayesian approaches appear to be taking off across a range of academic subjects.

77 Avner Offer stressed several of these shifts in a paper to the Standing Conference of Economic Historians, Institute of Historical Research, London, 1998.

Further Reading

D. C. Coleman, 'History, economic history and the numbers game', *Historical Journal*, 38, 3 (1995), pp. 635–46

N. F. R. Crafts, *British economic growth during the industrial revolution* (Oxford, 1985)

N. F. R. Crafts, 'Cliometrics, 1971–1986: a survey', *Journal of Applied Econometrics* 2, 2 (1987), pp. 171–92

N. F. R. Crafts, 'Quantitative economic history', LSE working papers in economic history, 48 (January 1999)

Paul A. David, Herbert Gutman, Richard Sutch, Peter Temin and Gavin Wright, *Reckoning with slavery; a critical study of the quantitative history of American negro slavery* (Oxford, 1972)

R. W. Fogel, *Railroads and American economic growth:essays in econometric history* (Baltimore, 1964)

R. W. Fogel and S. L. Engerman (eds), *The reinterpretation of American economic history* (New York, 1971)

R. W. Fogel and S. L. Engerman, *Time on the cross: the economics of American negro slavery* (Boston, 1974)

Bo Gustaffson, *Power and economic institutions: reinterpretations of economic history* (Aldershot, 1991)

G. R. Hawke, *Economics for historians* (Cambridge, 1980)

Lorenz Kruger *et al* (eds), *The probabilistic revolution* (Cambridge, MA, 1987)

E. Kuiper and J. Sap (eds), *Out of the margin: feminist perspectives on economics* (London, 1995)

C. H. Lee, *The quantitative approach to economic history* (London, 1977)

J. Maloney, *Whats new in economics* (Manchester, 1992)

D. N. McCloskey (ed.), *Essays on a mature economy: Britain after 1840* (London, 1971)

D. N. McCloskey, *Econometric history* (London, 1987)

Mary Morgan, *A history of econometric ideas* (Cambridge, 1990)

P. K. O'Brien (ed.), *The new economic history of the railways* (New York, 1977)

Karl Polanyi, *The great transformation* (London, 1948)

Thomas G. Rawski (ed.), *Economics and the historian* (London, 1996)

Marshall Sahlins, *Stone age economics* (London, 1974)

Peter Temin (ed.), *New economic history* (London, 1973)

M. Tommasi and K. Lerulli, *The new economics of human behaviour* (Cambridge, 1995)

J. G. Williamson, *Late nineteenth-century American development: a general equilibrium history* (Cambridge, 1974)

9

Computers and history

An image of my early days as a graduate student sticks in my mind after almost 30 years. Half a dozen of us are standing around a clanking, whirring machine in a harshly lighted basement room. There in the middle stirs sociologist Samuel Stouffer, talking fast, cigarette swinging from his mouth, ashes showering his vest. Stouffer grabs a deck of punched cards, shoves them into the hopper at one end of the machine, pushes a button, and watches the cards sort themselves into glass-topped bins. He peers at the size of the various piles. Then he says 'OK. Now let's try breaking on religion'.[1]

A lot has changed since Charles Tilly's introduction to computer use in the early 1960s. The speed and ease of operation and the range of queries and manipulations of data of all kinds which can now be attempted could hardly have been foreseen at that time. Yet some of the most fundamental problems of computer use remain exactly the same as in those days, especially problems caused by rigid categorisation of data prior to inputting and the ease with which 'breaking on religion' and other manipulations for sorting, retrieving and measuring can be accomplished casually and without sufficient historical justification. No book on history by numbers at the beginning of the twenty-first century could fail to include discussion of the impact which computers have had and continue to have on the practices of research and writing.

The aim of this chapter is not to give an up-to-date survey of new hardware and software developments useful for historians. Such a survey would quickly become dated and is best dealt with in periodic reviews in journals or 'on-line'. Excellent texts have also appeared in the past few years which look in detail at computer techniques and programmes useful for historical work. The best of these are listed in the further reading section at the end of this chapter and in the notes. The aim here is to provide a more general introduction to broad types of computer-aided analysis in historical research, to consider computer-aided analysis as an aspect of 'history by numbers' and to look at the pitfalls as well as the advantages which have arisen from the major extension of computer use in history in the past two decades or so. There is also a practical section which you can turn to immediately for advice with spreadsheet, database or other software in historical research or project work (Section 9.4). This will help you to get started and advise you where to look for more detailed, specialist help and for worked examples.

9.1 Historical background

Early computers were slow and cumbersome and could deal only with numbers, so all historical information had to be coded, usually onto punched cards, before it could be fed into the machine. Data input was slow, laborious and expensive, involving the employment of small armies of clerical assistants even on modest projects. Usually, these assistants were women and the majority of project leaders were men, which had the unfortunate side-effect of endorsing existing gender hierarchies, and gender attitudes, in the profession. In addition, few software programmes existed which were of any use to historians. Thus all historical and social science researchers had to be prepared to write their own programmes in a computer language (e.g. FORTRAN, COBOL, ALGOL) which they first had to learn. There were only a few mainframe terminals in each university, so access was poor and delays common. For all these reasons most historians were either discouraged from using computer techniques or had a set of ready excuses for ignoring them.

This situation changed, particularly from the early 1970s, with the widespread introduction of the microchip which made possible the development of cheap, personal microcomputers. This was accompanied by a big increase in the availability of software packages which were easy to use without much prior knowledge of computer languages or programming. Now historians commonly have their own personal machinery with constant access and an array of easily available software covering a variety of analytical techniques. The development of laptop models has also meant that computers can be taken into archive repositories and information can be fed in directly, thus avoiding some of the time-consuming and error-prone process of transcription of primary sources, or the cost of photocopying or microfilming. This use of portable machines has been a major stimulus to increased computer use in the study of history.

Furthermore, by the late 1980s it was no longer the case that mainframes were better from the point of view of storage potential (memory and disk space) and software sophistication than personal computers (PCs). PCs have thus come to be most widely used by academics as there are no problems of access, and the capacity of machines is sufficiently expanded to take the software packages and the data involved in big projects without becoming too slow with processing.

9.2 The slow advent of computer use in the study of history

These days, virtually all historians use computers in one way or another. At minimum they are used for word processing, storage and retrieval of research notes, drafts and bibliographies and to examine archive, bibliographic and abstracts lists produced by libraries and repositories worldwide. In addition they are increasingly employed to access on-line journals, website discussions and electronic bulletin boards. Computers are often used also for much more fundamental tasks of research and analysis from the use of scanners to transcribe documents to the use of sophisticated software for both quantitative and qualitative analysis of evidence. This widespread use of computers by historians is a phenomenon new to the last two decades or so of the twentieth century. Not all historians have taken enthusiastically to computer use in the period, however, despite technological and commercial changes which have made computers both easier and cheaper to use. Why?

One reason for the slow advent of computer use in history in Britain has been the strength of the British empirical tradition. This tradition has always regarded the primary task of historians to be the direct collection of evidence from archives. This places emphasis upon sensitive treatment of documents in their archival context. Close direct involvement between the historian and his or her sources is seen as paramount. The distancing of historians from their evidence, which computers often entail (particularly where machine-readable data sets become the main source material), runs counter to this empirical tradition.

Perhaps the most important delaying factor, however, has been the association of early computer use solely with quantitative work (sometimes of mixed quality) and the promotion of quantitative history (possibly at the expense of other approaches) which the computer has encouraged. Computers were at first associated with what contemporaries saw as the advent of cliometric history. This included quantitative history of all kinds but especially econometric history where economic modelling and the statistical testing of economic models was involved. This created a backlash against computer use. Many historians objected to the promotion of quantification and modelling, pointing out that historical data were rarely sufficiently robust for the sort of rigorous statistical manipulation which was being encouraged by computer software. It was argued that preoccupation with numbers and their uses was too often a substitute for properly conceived historical questions. Richard Cobb warned of obsession with numbers in and of themselves with no, or even an antihistorical, purpose:

> the computerisation of 516 urban riots . . . in France for the whole period 1815–1914. The end product will no doubt reveal some highly interesting patterns: that, for instance, market riots occurred on market days, on or near the market, that marriage riots take place after weddings, that funeral riots take place either outside the church or near the cemetery, that Saturday riots take place on Saturday evenings after the wineshops and bals have closed . . . that rent riots occur on rent days . . . that religious riots, especially in towns or bourgs in which there exist two or more religious communities, favour Sundays, Catholic feast days, St. Bartholomew's Day or the Passover. Perhaps we thought we knew already; but now we *really* know; we have a model. Riot has been tamed, dehumanized and scientificated.[2]

Charles Tilly, whose work was the object of Cobb's derision, felt forced to admit in an ensuing discussion that the scale and complexity of historical computer projects produce periods when the researcher is so preoccupied with problems of coding, file construction, statistical procedure, computer techniques and coordination of the whole effort that they practically lose contact with the people, events, places and times they are studying.[3] He warned that:

> In these days of the computer it is easy, tempting and relatively cheap to run large statistical analyses that are appropriate neither for the data at hand nor for the arguments that the investigator is really prepared to make . . . The ease with which historical social scientists can run a hundred multiple regressions, carry out a large factor analysis, or compare every vote in a given legislature to every other one makes it easy to coax striking pseudo-results from almost any substantial collection of data.[4]

This not unjustified and widespread outlook had the effect, amongst historians, of encouraging the unhelpful bifurcation in the profession between those who did and those who did not use computers and a high element of quantification in their work. This was aggravated by a lack of interest in anything before about 1750 on the part of the quantifiers because of the easier availability of quantitative data after that date. There were those who talked in huddled groups at conferences of nothing but their latest hardware and software acquisitions, excitedly using the new jargon of computer-speak. And there were those who rejected the use of computers entirely. Disenchanted by their colleagues, encouraged by the methodological short-comings of computer-aided quantitative analysis, but sometimes just deeply conservative, many historians suggested that the relationship between computing and history was not quite respectable. This slowed down the rate of acceptance of computer use in historical research, and even word processing was met with suspicion in many quarters. It made more sense to give 'typing' to female secretaries who, after all, had the expertise and nimble fingers!

Thanks largely to developments in computer software and hardware, and the spread of computer ownership, which have occurred independently of historians' needs, those historians who were critics of computer use in the 1970s and early 1980s have generally been converted to the computer as an indispensable tool of the trade. The computer is no longer used largely with quantification, model building and cliometrics, although deep suspicion of computers does linger because of its earlier associations. In addition, research in archive repositories (which critics saw as being undermined by the new technology in the 1970s) is currently being promoted and reinvigorated by computerised methods of archive administration, the use of laptop and notebook machines, scanners and new types of software. Where computers were once employed mainly in the study of easily available, mostly national, highly structured statistical series and the formation and testing of quantitative models, their historical use is now growing fastest in relation to very different sorts of empirical investigations, including those which use regional and local data and involve the analysis of qualitative as well as quantitative evidence.[5]

9.3 Software

The types of software used by historians in research fall into five broad types, though some types, together with interfaces, cover more than one of the following areas:

- statistics and graphics packages,
- spreadsheets,
- databases and database management systems,
- software for textual processing and analysis,
- software for qualitative data analysis.

We will consider each, briefly, in turn.

Statistics and graphics packages

Statistical and graphics packages designed for general or social science applications have been widely used in history for several decades. Dominant in many quarters from the late 1970s to the mid-1990s was SPSS (Statistical Package for the Social Sciences) with its variants SPSSx, for more powerful machines, and SPSS-PC, for personal computers. The big attraction was that it was geared to social science applications and to projects which collected similar data and asked similar questions to those posed in much historical research. The disadvantage was that a lot of coding of information was required prior to processing. The same problem applied to Statistical Analysis System (SAS), a similar package. For most simple statistical exercises smaller and less complicated software was often preferred even though it did not have a specific social science purpose or any academic connection. One such was MINITAB, popular in the 1980s and early 1990s. This package was used by students studying the course upon which this book has been based.

In the past 10 or 15 years researchers have turned away from dedicated statistical packages, for social science or academic use, regarding them as generally too wide-ranging and complicated for the relatively simple descriptive and summary statistics in which most historians are engaged. For this reason spreadsheet software is now used for most of the statistical processing of historical data covered in this book. Spreadsheets are easily available (being included with most PC packages) and are quick and simple to run. They are to be preferred where information is easily tabulated in a data matrix.

The construction of cartograms and other mapping tasks have been revolutionised in the past 15 years by the introduction and spread of cartography packages and of Geographical Information Systems (GIS) in particular. GIS enables vast amounts of statistical data to be stored, assembled and viewed in relation to its spatial distribution. Several sets of data can be simultaneously mapped according to their geographical coordinates. This enables theories concerning growth poles and geographical concepts such as central places to be put to the test.[6] Computers may no longer be associated exclusively with statistical analysis, but the sophistication of software for this purpose and the simplification of its use have encouraged the widespread and increasing employment of such packages in historical research.

Spreadsheets

A spreadsheet is a computer application for the processing and display of statistical information. It allows the storage of numerical and textual data in matrix format and enables a variety of statistical and graphical manipulations to be performed. The use of spreadsheets in academic studies has been growing rapidly in the past decade, although they were first developed for business and commercial applications. In historical research they combine some of the functions of statistics packages and of database software but are usually much simpler than either of these to use (though more limited). Excel is perhaps the most popular spreadsheet software currently available as it is part of the 'monopoly' created by Microsoft Office. Other examples currently are Quattro Pro and Lotus.

Spreadsheets enable information to be tabulated under a variety of headings and subheadings and they are particularly useful for large data sets, to show and examine change in data over time, and for comparative study of different sets of data. In elementary statistical processing spreadsheets have the big advantage of speed and accuracy over manual techniques. They can be used easily to produce measures of central tendency and dispersion, frequency distributions, scatter graphs, bar charts, pie charts and line graphs. Many spreadsheets can now incorporate statistical add-ins and can perform simple correlation and regression analysis and operate random sampling techniques and tests. If more sophisticated graphs or figures are required it is usually possible to use a graphical user interface (GUI). The main problem with spreadsheets is that as virtually all were developed for business or home accounts, not for historical use, the default settings are often inappropriate for historical work, and adjustments are frequently necessary.

Databases and database management systems

A database is a collection of related data, organised in a predetermined manner and according to a set of logical rules. Such data can be stored in a computer in machine-readable form. A database management system (DBMS) is a computer programme which allows one to organise and manage the information stored in the database. DBMSs are used for storage, sorting, retrieving and interrogating numerical and other information which is inputted and arranged in a series of tables in the database. As with spreadsheets the data are arranged in electronic tables, but databases differ from spreadsheets in performing complex tasks of selective reordering and retrieval of information (like a sophisticated filing system) and in being able to handle, process and retrieve non-numeric data in the cells of the matrix more easily than can a spreadsheet. Currently available database programmes can handle several pages of text in each record and can use these texts in searches. They can now also include images and live links to documents and files outside the DBMS. Examples of these are Access, Paradox, Foxbase and Dbase 3. These have been continuously updated over the years, are easier to use than their forerunners were in the past, can be customised for views, browsing and reporting and are more 'intelligent' in detecting inconsistencies, defective structures and illogical queries than were their predecessors. The new wave of DBMSs also facilitate movement of data and results across systems, to statistical analysis and graphical packages, and to spreadsheets.

Each row of a database table is a unique record relating to a case. Each column contains one 'field' of information relating to the cases. This is illustrated in Figure 9.1. Using a DBMS enables selective information about all cases or just some particular cases to be called up and analysed. This includes the ability to call up information from more than one table. Thus the researcher is able to create units of analysis geared to the research question being posed, usually by breaking down the information and joining them in an order different from that occurring in the original sources. The most common interrogation format used with DBMS is ISQL

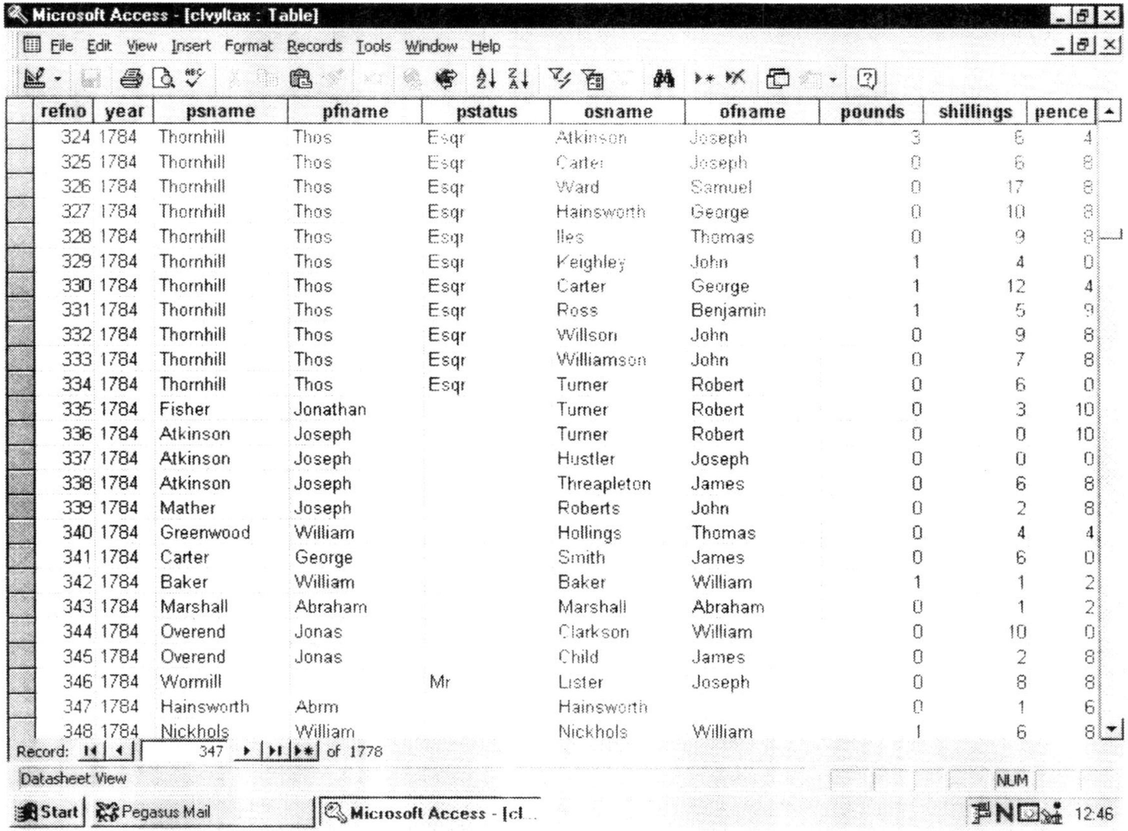

Microsoft Access - [clvyltax : Table]
File Edit View Insert Format Records Tools Window Help

refno	year	psname	pfname	pstatus	osname	ofname	pounds	shillings	pence
324	1784	Thornhill	Thos	Esqr	Atkinson	Joseph	3	6	4
325	1784	Thornhill	Thos	Esqr	Carter	Joseph	0	6	8
326	1784	Thornhill	Thos	Esqr	Ward	Samuel	0	17	8
327	1784	Thornhill	Thos	Esqr	Hainsworth	George	0	10	8
328	1784	Thornhill	Thos	Esqr	Iles	Thomas	0	9	8
329	1784	Thornhill	Thos	Esqr	Keighley	John	1	4	0
330	1784	Thornhill	Thos	Esqr	Carter	George	1	12	4
331	1784	Thornhill	Thos	Esqr	Ross	Benjamin	1	5	9
332	1784	Thornhill	Thos	Esqr	Willson	John	0	9	8
333	1784	Thornhill	Thos	Esqr	Williamson	John	0	7	8
334	1784	Thornhill	Thos	Esqr	Turner	Robert	0	6	0
335	1784	Fisher	Jonathan		Turner	Robert	0	3	10
336	1784	Atkinson	Joseph		Turner	Robert	0	0	10
337	1784	Atkinson	Joseph		Hustler	Joseph	0	0	0
338	1784	Atkinson	Joseph		Threapleton	James	0	6	8
339	1784	Mather	Joseph		Roberts	John	0	2	8
340	1784	Greenwood	William		Hollings	Thomas	0	4	4
341	1784	Carter	George		Smith	James	0	6	0
342	1784	Baker	William		Baker	William	1	1	2
343	1784	Marshall	Abraham		Marshall	Abraham	0	1	2
344	1784	Overend	Jonas		Clarkson	William	0	10	0
345	1784	Overend	Jonas		Child	James	0	2	8
346	1784	Wormill		Mr	Lister	Joseph	0	8	8
347	1784	Hainsworth	Abrm		Hainsworth		0	1	6
348	1784	Nickhols	William		Nickhols	William	1	6	8

Record: 347 of 1778
Datasheet View
NUM
Start
Pegasus Mail
Microsoft Access - [cl...
12:46

Fig. 9.1 Screen from Calverley Land Tax return, 1784
Source: P. Hudson and S. A. King, research project on two textile townships

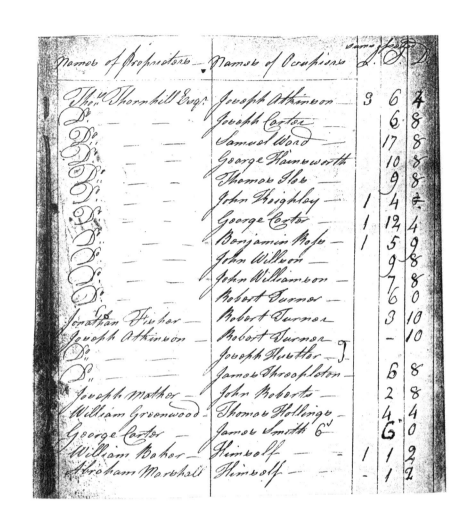

Fig. 9.2 Page from the Land Tax return for Calverley with Farsley, West Yorkshire, 1784.
Source: West Yorkshire Archive Service, Wakefield.

(interactive structured query language), which enables the calling up of certain vectors of information relating to particular cases in the table or tables, the ordering and summing of such vectors and other more complicated commands involving highly selective cells of information and the linking of one record with another, sometimes across different data sets within the database.

Figure 9.1 is a screen from the file created from eighteenth century Land Tax returns for Yorkshire villages. It is part of a much bigger relational database which can link Land Tax payers and occupiers to other records. (See Table 9.1 for details of the other sorts of files in the database). Figure 9.2 gives a page from the corresponding primary source, for comparison.

Table 9.1 Details of a selection of computer files on Sowerby township in a relational database

Document	Filename	Fields (no.)	Entries (no.)
Poor rate assets, assessments 1738–1855	ARRP	10	5 539
Parish register baptisms, 1668–1825	BAPTISMS	19	13 874
Bonds of indemnity, 1755–1781	BONDS2	24	27
Parish register burials, 1699–1837	BURIALS	23	11 211
Rate Assessment, Blackwood, 1804	BWOODRA	14	1 178
Hearth Tax 1664, 1666, 1672, 1674	HEARTHTAX	8	1 822
Independent baptism register, 1740–1837	INDBAPS	19	1 205
Land Tax assessments, 1750–81	LANDTAX1	11	1 392
Land Tax assessments, 1782–98	LANDTAX2	14	3 540
Land Tax assessments, 1799–1800	LANDTAX3	17	612
Parish register marriages	MARRIAGE	17	90
Methodist baptism register, 1790–1837	MBAPS	18	337
Militia Tax, 1716	MILITIA	11	287
Settlement exams, 1744–1808	SETEXAMS,	15	52
	NEWEXAMS	16	52
Pauper Apprentice records, 1720–1801	PAUPERAPS	17	551
Household Census, 1764	POPBOOK1	17	597
List of proprietors and occupiers, 1827	PROPLIST	13	335
Removals, 1712–1751	REMOVALS	9	5
1811 Census	SCENSUS	11	461
Settlement certificates, 1688–1749	SETTLEMENT	13	170
Apprentice indents, 1721–1801	TRADAPS,	20	78
	TRADEAPS	21	80
Window Tax, 1759	WINDOWTAX	8	135
Probate inventories, 1689–1785	SPROBATE	14	111
Wills, 1689, 1785	SWILLS	20	111

Source: P. Hudson and S. A. King, research project on two textile townships.

Databases can be flatfile (simple, and usually composed of just one table) or relational (involving many tables with the possibility of linking data across files and interrogating several tables simultaneously). Table 9.1 lists the different major files for Sowerby township, contained in a relational database concerning two Yorkshire townships in the eighteenth century. The aim of the project here was to use nominal record linkage to work outwards from family reconstitution to a more detailed reconstruction of the circumstances and life courses of ordinary people. Where a relational database is employed, dedicated software can be added which specifies the linkage criteria to be used in various searches or analysis. These structures of linkage criteria are called algorithms. Many algorithms have been written for individual historical research projects and some form the basis of software packages which have been designed to be sold or disseminated for specific historical applications. The family reconstitution software developed by the Cambridge Group is one such example, as is the software developed by Mark Overton, at the University of Exeter, to store and analyse early modern probate inventories.[7]

With a **relational database** it is very important to specify fields of information (e.g. surname, forename, date, place) in the same way in all tables, and each case in each table must have a unique reference number. Field lengths for the same variables must be the same across all tables and there must be consistency in the use of characters or integers (letters or numbers). This is because the computer is only able to make links by comparing like with like. Where spellings vary, for example with surnames or where there may be many descriptions for the same occupation, it will generally be necessary to add fields which group or code such variations (e.g. in surnames or occupations). The fuzzy searching required to make a link could be built into the algorithms, but this can make the algorithm too cumbersome and too slow to run. Table 9.2 gives a design for baptism entries for the seventeenth to the nineteenth centuries, and Figure 9.3 shows a page from the corresponding primary source, the parish register. The number of fields and field lengths are designed to cover all cases. There was, for example, no grandparent details in the source until the end of the eighteenth century, and few residence or forename fields actually needed more than 12 characters (30 was assigned as a comfortable maximum). Fields have been added to code surnames and occupations. In this case, too, fields have been added, where available, from other sources to assist in identifying correct links. The *T*-score fields indicate the probability that a correct link has been made between the baptism entry and the marriage entries for both the parents and for the baptised child. Linking baptisms in this way is part of the process of computer-aided family reconstitution widely used in historical demography.[8]

The most recent development in devising algorithms has been the development of expert systems (i.e. advanced software which uses artificial intelligence to solve specialised problems). This software stores rules such as linkage criteria and formulates new rules for linkage from the data as more

Table 9.2 Design for family reconstitution database file of eighteenth-century baptisms

Fields	Function	Length[a]
Refno	Unique identification number	6
Bd	Birth day	2
Bm	Birth month	2
Byear	Birth year	4
Sx	Sex	1
Fname	Forename	15
Sname	Surname	20
Status I	Birth date	10
Status II	Status	10
Residence	Residence	30
Ffname	Father's forename	15
Fsname	Father's surname	20
Focc	Father's occupation	20
Fstatus	Father's status	10
Fres	Father's residence	30
Mfname	Mother's forename	15
Msname	Mother's surname	20
Mocc	Mother's occupation	20
Mstatus	Mother's status	10
Gppat	Paternal grandparent	35
Gpmat	Maternal grandparent	35
Psnamecode	Surname code of child	4
Fsnamecode	Surname code of father	4
Msnamecode	Surname code of mother	4
Tscoremdb	Refno of parent's marriage	8
Tscoremds	Refno of own marriage(s)	8
Tscormdg	Refno of kinship-linkedmarriages	20
Wbfamily	Social status indicator	1
Mfamily	Landholding indicator	1
Tscore	Confidence flag	2

[a] Number of characters/integers allowed.
Source: P. Hudson and S. A. King, research project on two textile townships.

is inputted. The drawback of expert systems is that they depend upon the existence of stable knowledge systems and are governed by identifiable rules. Such characteristics are often lacking in historical research.[9]

There has been some debate amongst historians about the need to maintain the integrity of the original source when a database is created. Should information be coded before input (as with different descriptors of the same occupation) and should surname, forename and other spellings be standardised? These are important questions given that databases in the future are likely to have a number of users. Historians will probably use databases which have been created (often at some expense) by someone else and primarily for one particular purpose.[10] Once coding or standardising occurs

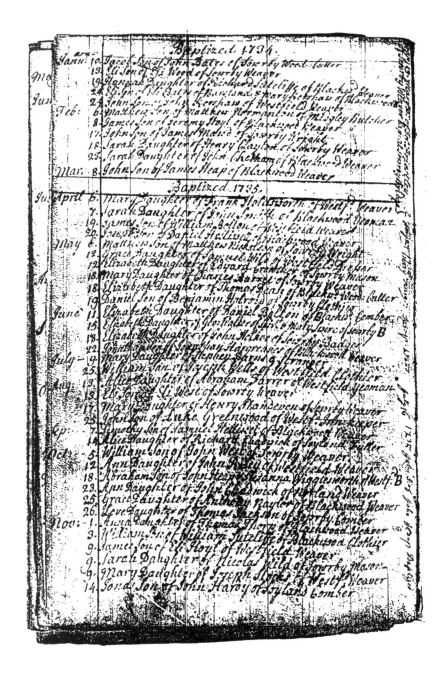

Fig. 9.3 Page from Sowerby Baptism Register, 1730s.
Source: West Yorkshire Archive Service, Halifax.

problems inevitably creep in. Information which might be useful or crucial to later users of the database is left out, and coding categories can sometimes force the data into misleading or unhelpful boxes. Standardisation of spellings can often eliminate fine differences which make it possible to distinguish between one case or another. The scope for error is legion when decisions about coding or standardisation have to be made 'on the hoof' during the process of inputting when unexpected information often fails to fit neatly into pre-given categories. Algorithms which look for similar as well as exact matches modify the problem a little but they by no means solve it. A dominant practice is to create the database with as little coding and standardising as possible. If it becomes necessary to code or standardise in order to speed processing or create algorithms, this is added (rather than substituted for column fields) at a later stage.[11]

The main problems of database use are that complex fields of information in the original documents have to be 'shoehorned' into regular matrix structures and that, although their handling of text has improved, most programmes lack sophisticated text-searching tools. DBMSs are thus mainly suited to structured sources and to cataloguing in particular. The full featured relational DBMSs are also very cumbersome, but there are some intermediate products such as Filemaker and Lotus Approach which are sufficiently sophisticated for smaller scale projects and which are a lot easier to use.

Software for textual processing and analysis: from number crunching to word crunching

The need for historians to deal with unstructured data and to use complementary sets of primary and secondary sources in a research project has led to increasing use of a range of software products which span the divide between DBMS systems and textual analysis software. These include text-oriented DBMSs which allow unstructured data to be entered into fields and then searched by using 'fuzzy matching' and proximity searches. In this way the user is able to create links between documents in a similar manner to links on a World Wide Web page.[12] At the other end of the spectrum are software packages which facilitate information management but avoid database structures. Instead they employ text-searching facilities which are used with indexed and tagged documents. Wordcruncher and Sonar are two such products. Both allow an array of search options with keywords, fuzzy matching, proximity searches and queries of the type: retrieve 'X' AND 'Y', 'X' OR 'Y', 'X' NOT 'Y'.[13] The main advantages of the index approach over DBMS text searching is speed of operation and the ability to accommodate much longer texts.

It is perhaps surprising that neither of the programmes mentioned above nor more fully developed textual analysis software, such as TACT (text-analysis computing tools) and the newer WordSmith Tools, have yet had much of an impact in historical research. Both of these can execute a variety of 'stylometric' analyses (word counts, word associations, collocations), as well as being capable of comparing many documents at once and identifying the hierarchical structure of the texts. The main problem is that historians are not primarily concerned with the use of words or strings of words in a document so much as with the ideas and concepts which lie behind them and which the computer is less able to handle. Such software is also most useful for projects where a distinct body of writings are being analysed rather than the mass of multisource evidence with which historians most often deal.

Software for qualitative data analysis

To facilitate the computer-aided analysis of qualitative data in the humanities and social sciences, and especially in ethnography and sociology, specialist software is evolving which can undertake some of the same 'stylometric' analysis done by textual analysis programmes but which can also do much more, with more varied documentary sources, using a rather different approach. Whereas textual analysis software looks for 'strings of characters' in a collection of documents, programmes for qualitative data analysis use a 'code-and-retrieve' system. Codes or tags are added to the documents to denote all sorts of networks, relationships, synonyms and hierarchies which the researcher sees fit. Searches can then be made on the codes and the mark-up as well as on the text of the document itself. Not only can one search for passages where the word 'male' precedes 'authority' it is also possible to find passages where a discussion of the concept of authority follows a section on males, men or boys, even when the keywords do not appear. Thus, rather than identifying patterns of words, this software allows the user to search for concepts, categories and ideas that have been identified by the researcher.

This type of 'code-and-retrieve' programme fits with the sort of iterative process which lies at the heart of conventional historical research: reading, querying and hypothesising. Despite this, there has been very little use of such software in historical research to date. The major drawback is the amount of time and effort required for the mark-up of the text and the fact that it can be justified only for certain projects where the source is not too extensive and where the text promises to yield 'webs' of coding. Given the drift of post-structuralist arguments about the importance of language in primary sources and in the writings of historians, it is likely that qualitative data analysis and textual analysis software will be more widely applied in history, and especially in historiographical analysis, in the coming years.

9.4 Getting started with computer use in historical research

Sources and computing

In embarking upon historical research the question of whether or not to use computers will usually arise. The answer to this question will depend upon the type of source material and the amount of source material. Computers can be a boon if there is a relatively large amount of easily classifiable data which need neatly summarising and/or analysing statistically. Yearly Land Tax returns from the eighteenth century are a good example of a semistructured source which is relatively easily adapted for computer-aided descriptive statistics: the information is already in columns giving owner, occupier and amount of tax paid. If several Land Tax returns are to be compared, the distribution of landed wealth (as reflected in tax paid) can be assessed and studied for different areas or over time. As is always the case, a close knowledge of the nature of the source is required alongside the ability to manipulate it. In the case of the Land Tax, particularly if one is interested in changes in the distribution of wealth over time, one must be aware of the fact that the schedules often went unrevised from one year to the next, and that a study of landholding and landownership would really need to be supported by other sources such as estate records, surveys or tithe returns. One could nevertheless make some tentative additions to knowledge by constructing frequency distributions and pie charts reflecting the distribution of tax paid as we did in the case of some of the Sowerby figures (as an example) in Chapter 3. One could use a spreadsheet or database here or move the data from one to the other. If one wanted to look for the same names appearing in different tax returns, one could either create a table for each return and use the relational database linkage or one could input all the returns required into the same database (making sure that unique identifiers and year fields are present for each case). Either method would enable one to test whether the tax paid by particular individuals had grown or declined over time, and one could probably imply from this some constants and some changes in the distribution of holdings.[14]

   Another source which one could use to create a spreadsheet and undertake some interesting statistical work would be parish registers. One could use aggregate figures, monthly or yearly, from the three classes of so-called 'vital events' (baptisms, marriages and burials), forming a matrix from these in a spreadsheet programme. These could then be used to test for similar movements over time through the construction of simple graphs, histograms or scatter graphs. More involved inferential statistics may also be appropriately applied: particularly time-series, growth-rate estimates and projections, and correlation and regression analysis. The data displayed in Table 5.8 and Figure 5.2 (pages 123 and 121) involves baptism and burial figures for St Martin in the Fields, London. Plague deaths, which were noted in the source, have also been recorded. Descriptive summary statistics could be applied to such data with benefit, the relationship between baptism and burial trends could be investigated, the growth rates of each could be calculated and the periodicity of any cycles of fertility or mortality (perhaps associated with plague) might be identified, especially if we had the much longer run of the data from which Table 5.8 has been extracted.

Alternatively, detailed data from each entry could be tabulated in a database containing three tables, one for each set of vital events. We have already seen how this can be done in comparing Figure 9.3 with Table 9.2. For a very small parish, or chapelry, it might be possible in a dissertation to input all events over a sufficient period of time to undertake some elementary family reconstitution. One would not need a semi-automated programme or advanced algorithms for this (such as used by the Cambridge Group). The ability of a database programme to sort and retrieve would enable some computer-assisted, manual reconstitution of families to be done along with associated calculations about age of marriage, death and family size.[15] The occupational information contained in many parish registers, together with details of illegitimacy, enables further interesting questions to be addressed. (The capital Bs after entries in Figure 9.3 indicate illegitimate births; for example, see the entry for 15 June 1735.)

When contemplating analysis of a text or texts (e.g. speeches, folksongs, autobiographies), the question of whether to use software for textual or further qualitative analysis arises. The important thing here is how much text would need inputting (and with what level of mark-up) because this is what will take the most time. Equally important is the question of whether the documents are appropriate for the application of such analysis. Speeches, political tracts and novels have proved most adaptable to 'stylometric' analysis. Autobiographies and diaries are likely to be other appropriate sources, though little of this sort of work has been done on them to date. Much good further advice on this can be found in the dedicated textbooks.[16]

Student projects often use existing machine-readable files instead of creating new ones. Much data are available, for example, on-line from the Economic and Social Research Council (ESRC) data archive at the University of Essex and from similar databanks, in the United States and Scandinavia in particular (see page 238). A ready-made spreadsheet of information, a database or a machine-readable set of texts both circumvent and create problems for the new researcher. There is the advantage of saving time and effort in inputting, and difficult decisions about the structure of the tables and matrices, categories and codes have generally already been made. However, this brings problems, as someone else's choices and decisions may distort the application of the data for new research purposes. This is an old problem, as the same difficulty applies to all information which has been collected and tabulated for purposes other than those of the researcher. The additional problem in this case is that the data may have been processed several times by the time they are preserved in a machine-readable data archive. It is always a good idea to ask the following questions and to discuss their implications in the introduction to the research.

- What do we know about the nature of the original documents and the ways in which elements of evidence, layout, style, form, as well as content, might have been obscured by the 'translation' to machine-readable form?
- What other sources might one have consulted had they been as easily available as the machine-readable data?

Things to look out for

- Always select a research or dissertation topic of manageable size given the time available and the amount of primary source material which you intend to analyse. Draw up a schedule allowing time for emergencies and delays. Carefully assess the time it will take to input data into the computer (time how long it takes you to enter each row of a database, for example, or each page of a text, and multiply this by the number of cases or pages you will be including). Never underestimate how long the dissertation will take to write up. Whatever your casual estimate for writing time, you would be wise to double it.
- Your choice of software will usually be a compromise between what would be ideal for your purpose and what is available on the server at your institution or on your PC. You will usually have some simple spreadsheet applications, database programmes, text analysis software, whilst more sophisticated software for qualitative data analysis is becoming increasingly widespread. The first problem with all of these is that none will have been designed specifically for your project and most will not even have been designed with history of any sort in mind. Some of the most difficult decisions you may have to make concern which package to use. You need to decide whether to use a spreadsheet or a database, for example, and whether you will need an additional graphics and statistical interface. There are books to guide you in this. Of these, the most up-to-date and accessible with step-by-step instruction for different sorts of small research projects using Microsoft tools is M. J. Lewis and R. Lloyd-Jones, *Using computers in history*.[17] But software availability is changing all the time and institutions vary greatly in what they have to offer on mainframe servers. The advice of your technical staff or your supervisor is often going to be critical.
- If using a spreadsheet, think carefully about the structure of the matrix and the content of the rows and columns. If using a database, spend time perfecting the database design (especially the number, type and size of

fields) so that you will be able to include all the information which you need for your analysis and make sure that the characteristics of field size and form are the same across any tables which you intend to use in a relational structure.

- If a field of information needs to be coded for analysis think hard about doing this and, if possible, leave it until after the inputting stage, adding an additional database field for the codes. You can then always go back to the 'original' entry. When coding nominal files, such as occupational ascriptions, be sure to use appropriate guides to nomenclature. Standard occupational classifications are often appropriate but can be misleading if applied to very different time periods or cultures than those for which the classification was established. In the same way it is always best to input all the variations of spellings which occur in the original document. Fuzzy searching minimises the problem of inaccurate searches or links which derive simply because of variations in spelling; you rarely know when a variation reflects a real difference until long after the inputting stage, by which time it may be too late to resurrect the original data with any ease. Always retain as much as possible of the richness of the original fields of information when forming a database.
- If inputting a text for textual or qualitative analysis make sure that the mark-up conventions and procedures are fully understood from the outset and are consistently applied.
- Finally, all pieces of research should include a historiographical context, a set of justifications for undertaking the research, discussion of the advantages and pitfalls of the chosen source material and some discussion of the strengths and weaknesses of the theoretical and methodological approach taken. Always remember that you are in charge, not the computer.

9.5 The impact of the computer on research and writing

The advent and increasing sophistication of computers in the past three decades has had several major influences upon historical research and writing. It is wise to bear these in mind when reading computer-aided research or when undertaking such research for yourself. Computing has:

- increased the efficiency of archive administration and of data storage and retrieval so that documents and data relevant to a particular research project can now be located and used more easily;
- simplified and speeded up many old established approaches and research methods and has allowed them to be applied more extensively;
- altered the way in which research is written up and presented;

- created the possibility of new sorts of historical research which, in practical terms, would be impossible without computers;
- encouraged the growth of particular types of historical research and particular languages of historical discussion which have probably been at the expense of others.

Let us consider each of these in turn.

Archive administration and data availability

The World Wide Web, the Internet and CD-ROMs have resulted in the easy availability of archive lists, bibliographies, press 'clippings', microfilmed materials and abstracts from repositories, libraries and other institutions, public and commercial, all over the world. The United States led the way in encouraging on-line availability of archive and library resource lists. Britain and other countries are catching up. British developments have been facilitated by standardised rules of archive description, including the *Manual of archival description* (MAD) and MODES, pioneered at the University of Liverpool.[18]

Apart from the new ease with which one can gain access to archive lists and bibliographies, documentary sources are often themselves transcribed, scanned or microfilmed into machine-readable form and their contents can be called up on-screen via the Internet or from CD-ROM. Sometimes this transcription or scanning is driven by conservation considerations, in other cases commercial publishers have engaged historians to advise on appropriate archive collections and selections (generally printed ones) which are then scanned for CD-ROM. Where a commercial selection is made, preference is often given to printed, rather than handwritten, sources because these are easier to scan. There is also the inevitable problem that all collections of archive material available on the Internet or CD-ROM are selective and partial. Commercial considerations come into play, but much influence is also exercised by those historians paid to advise upon which documents to include. Often this advice is based upon their personal research agenda and their future ambitions. Another pitfall of the spread of such easily available primary source material is the danger that researchers will take the easy course of prioritising research which uses these data, and the archives which are more difficult or slowest to be transcribed or scanned will be relatively neglected. In defence of these developments, the ease of availability of important research collections has 'democratised' many subjects of study. Many important collections available previously in only London or Oxford, for example, can now be researched easily by academics, and others, not only in the provinces but also in the United States, Japan and elsewhere and by disabled as well as able-bodied scholars. This broader catchment of researchers is likely to stimulate increased debate on a global scale, facilitated in turn by website networking and electronic bulletin boards.

Taking the availability of historical evidence a step further, material from original sources has also been processed by researchers to form databases, spreadsheets or marked-up text which are then deposited in databanks, and the files are made available to other historians. For example, the ESRC has a large computer data-storage facility at the University of Essex where researchers who have had ESRC grants (and others) are encouraged to store their data for Internet access so that others can use it.[19] The Inter-university Consortium for Political and Social Research (ICPSR) at the University of Michigan similarly holds machine-readable data archives for 350 member institutions. These are strongest on election and census data, which cover 130 countries (to varying degrees). Similar social science and history collections can be found in the Netherlands, Norway, Denmark, and Sweden, and large and growing text archives are located in Oxford, Rutgers University and in Washington, DC.[20]

There are, again, problems as well as advantages with these collections. First, the researcher will be relying on information extracted by someone else who had different interests or priorities. Any errors in the original transcriptions will be repeated and perhaps magnified in the course of further manipulation; information omitted from the original transcriptions or scanning may get forgotten, and there may develop a tendency for historians to analyse the same body of data again and again (with diminishing returns), rather than seeking new or revised evidence. It would certainly be a great mistake to carry out research entirely without contact with the original records and their wider context in other documents and sources not amenable to computer storage or analysis.

Speeding up old-established approaches and research methods

This is a particular advantage and feature where research involves cumbersome and time-consuming statistical applications, but it is also very apparent in any research involving the storage, retrieval and manipulation of large data sets. Projects are now undertaken which would have been simply too time-consuming and hence too costly to contemplate without computer use. This does have a downside, however. It is now so easy to run correlation and regression software that it has had the detrimental effect of blinding some historians to the shortcomings and inappropriate nature of the data for such purposes. The ease with which statistical analysis can be accomplished can also lead to very poor research practice. For example, the historian should always have a very good reason for posing the possibility of causal connections between variables before undertaking relevant statistical analysis. A hypothesis should be framed at the outset which is capable of being falsified. Poor practice creeps in where many regressions are run using different combinations of variables until a 'significant relationship' (statistically speaking) turns up. The historian then concentrates upon analysing the 'cause' of such a relationship, ignoring the fact that the correlation may be spurious or accidental.

Writing and presenting research

Word processing, and the interface between word processing and statistical and other software, has altered the way in which history is written up and presented. There is a greater tendency now to use graphical and other visual representations because they are so much easier to prepare and to incorporate than in the past and because they often look so much more impressive than previously generated material. There is little doubt that tables, figures and graphs provide the most concise way of conveying extensive or complex data and that they have the potential to clarify arguments. However, great care must be taken in using them appropriately, as the earlier chapters of this book have pointed out. Sometimes, the easy formation of figures, graphs, cartograms, etc., are made to substitute for careful thought about what is necessary or sufficient, most appropriate and least misleading.

The impact of word processing upon the nature of creative writing across a range of academic and artistic activities is thus far little understood, although it is likely to have been significant and will no doubt have its researchers in the future. The current emphasis upon language and vocabulary, narrative and rhetorical structures of academic works (as well as historical sources) which has been influenced by post-structuralism and by other linguistic theories, such as that attributed to Bakhtin, suggests that attention to the way in which things are written will only continue to grow.[21] Will the advent of word processing be seen as marking major changes in the content and structure of texts?

Do people write differently when they use a word processor? The ease with which paragraphs and pages, quotes, inserts can be moved around in a text must inevitably have had an impact on the way in which history (along with other subjects) is written. Word processing can be an uninhibiting release from the tension which used to surround 'putting pen to paper'. With handwriting or typing there was always the thought that a first or early draft must be near-final because of the time-consuming and costly problems of multiple redrafting. Computer use may encourage drafting and redrafting until better pieces of work are produced, or it may encourage laziness in transposing sentences and paragraphs from one draft or publication to another. The use of camera-ready copy and computer typesetting may also encourage both authors and publishers to publish prematurely and without the rigorous discipline of checking which the older system of typesetting and proof-reading required.

The fact that most writers now use word processing will at the very least mean that less evidence of the writing process is likely to survive. Marginal notes, improvements, alterations from one draft to the next are likely to be lost because only the discs containing the final versions will probably survive for the historians and literary theorists of the future.

New sorts of historical research

The biggest recent growth areas of computer use in new sorts of historical research have involved relational database software and, to a lesser extent, software for the analysis of texts and other 'qualitative' data. Relational database software enables multiple files of information to be built up and then linked together or cross-matched to create new features of historical evidence. This can be seen most clearly with the development of family reconstitution. Files of information are created from baptism, marriage and burial data from parish registers. Software is then developed to instruct the computer to match up these entries on the basis of carefully thought out linkage criteria (algorithms), so that families can be 'reconstituted'. Before computer use, although the technique had been developed it was possible to apply it to only very small communities because of the time taken to enter data on cards and to link records by hand rather than 'automatically' (the word *automatically* is placed in inverted commas because although linkage algorithms may be written and employed there will remain many cases where the linkage criteria either fail to secure a potentially correct link or where the criteria result in mistaken links, and only hand sorting at the margin and spot checks can go some way to counter these difficulties).

Reconstitution can be taken some steps further in a more fully developed community-reconstruction study which might involve data linkage across files of demographic evidence, tax records, wills, inventories, local government records, business and estate papers, etc. The same individuals often figure, momentarily at least, in different documentary sources. Through linking data by surname, forename and other identifiers (i.e. by nominal record linkage) new sorts of detailed research on the lives of ordinary people can be carried out. From the accumulation of many small shreds of evidence, a picture of the life course and lifestyles of ordinary people can be glimpsed. This new sort of 'history from below' would not be possible without computers because it would be impossible to both store and link shreds of evidence across such a large number of separate sets of information with use of index cards and by hand. One could argue that computer-aided research is rejuvenating local and microlevel history, freeing it from its antiquarian roots and providing useful alternative insights to those provided by macrolevel studies.[22] Similar projects to reconstruct information about local and non-local communities (such as professional communities) have been undertaken, for example the University of Glasgow study of the Scottish medical profession, various studies of the urban middle-class, undertaken at Edinburgh University in particular, and in the Westminster Historical Database project at Royal Holloway and Bedford College, London.[23]

Another area of research just about impossible without computers is research involving intensive textual analysis of large bodies of documentary sources. Examples can be found which use oral history transcripts where text encoding and keyword mark-up can be a boon in analysing a very large number of transcripts. Any other prose source such as speeches, biographies, diaries and novels can be analysed via similar textual analysis mark-up and software programmes to allow word frequency counts, word associations, common phraseology, etc., to be identified as well as to speed up analysis of content. These techniques have been used in verifying the authorship or authenticity of various documents as well as in analysing changes and constants in language and vocabulary use. As software for analysing such changes becomes increasingly sophisticated and as the current trend in history places more focus on the importance of language and discourse, the use of this type of computer analysis is likely to grow.

Perhaps the biggest future growth area for computers in history will be the use of software not just for the stylometric analysis of relatively homogeneous bodies of text but for the storage retrieval and analysis of heterogeneous documentary evidence derived from primary source transcripts or scans, information arranged in matrices and the content of tags and codes which incorporate the historian's own thoughts on the evidence. The use of computers for such qualitative data analysis, especially in history, is only in its infancy. A major disincentive to the spread of such techniques is the amount of time required at the outset for text mark-up, annotating and coding, classifying and categorising, but once these are done the potential of computer-aided analysis is great.[24]

Encouragement of particular types of research

It is certainly the case that early computer use in the discipline of history encouraged quantification and quantitative methods of all kinds, including econometric history. For a time, in some branches of history, computer-aided cliometrics was seen as the high-status edge of history whereas other approaches became less valued. One of the problems was that early software limited computer use to highly structured primary sources, such as censuses and tax returns, export and import figures, output statistics and population totals, and to a restricted range of largely quantitative research questions. Although software and hardware developments now mean that computers are no longer associated solely with a narrow range of sources, approaches or techniques, there is still the probability that computer use is leading history in certain directions and encouraging some approaches and methods and the study of certain time periods and topics at the expense of others.

It could certainly be argued that computers continue to encourage quantification and the study of historical topics and periods which lend themselves to quantification. The use of computers in all fields of quantification and statistical analysis is predictable not just because they facilitate and speed calculations and produce accurate and neat diagrams and figures but also because their use endorses the idea of scientific endeavour and objectivity. Freedom from subjectivity which is assumed to come from applying fixed rules and procedures to calculations lies at the heart of the idea of statistics as the language of science. Computers allow the application of the fixed rules of statistical analysis and inference with least danger of subjectivity and personal intervention. As we discussed in Chapter 2, this is simultaneously an advantage and a disadvantage in historical work.

As new software suitable for historical applications is developed research runs the danger of becoming biased in favour of the new techniques and approaches involved. The earliest products for textual analysis encouraged a focus upon relatively homogeneous bodies of text and overemphasised collocations and keywords at the expense of rhetorical and narrative structures and other aspects of text which were more difficult to identify and measure with use of computer-aided resources. The new qualitative data analysis tools of the past decade or so, although promising much for histories of the future, also run a risk of biasing research in favour of certain sorts of sources and issues which lend themselves best to the technique. More problematically, this approach foregrounds the iterative process whilst also reducing the separation of theory and data upon which it rests. If the historian's division of the data into overlapping 'data-bits', and her notes and codes all become part of the data set, merging with the primary evidence itself, iteration and especially the formation and testing of hypotheses may need to be replaced by something more akin to 'thick description'.[25]

Conclusion

In almost all branches of the profession computer use has begun to revolutionise the way in which history is researched and written. Computers have facilitated the location and the analysis of sources and have made many sorts of research projects viable or possible for the first time. There are, however, costs involved. The easy availability of machine-readable data may mean that the richness of original sources will be neglected. The ease of statistical manipulation may result in bad practice and in too little attention being paid to the reliability of the data or to historical context. By giving a tremendous impetus to quantitative work of all kinds computers have also been responsible for aggravating the division which already existed in the profession between supporters and critics of quantification. Interestingly, more recent software developments are now healing the rift by opening up the possibility of extensive computer use in text-based analysis, in the non-quantitative as well as in the quantitive study of communities and in research which utilises qualitative data. What must, however, be remembered is that all computing depends on numbers: the recognition by the computer of digits and characters, their manipulation, rearrangement and counting. Arranging, rearranging and categorising data, making connections between categories, forming matrices, adding and averaging, recognising and displaying frequencies, looking for and measuring associations, calculating probabilities: computers rely on all these basic tasks associated with statistical manipulation. Thus, computer-aided research, whether dealing with quantitative or qualitative evidence (or a mix of the two) is always an aspect of 'history by numbers'. As such it is subject to the same debates about the competing values of precision and ease of communication on the one hand and intuition and 'poetry' on the other. But there is no reason why we must take sides in this debate nor why historians cannot dwell upon concepts, subtleties, ambiguities and the detailed description of single events or individuals at the same time as they are cautiously guided by the 'science' of numbers.

Notes

1 Charles Tilly reminisces, in *As sociology meets history* (New York, 1981) p. 53.
2 R. Cobb, 'Historians in white coats', *Times Literary Supplement*, 3 December 1971, quoted in C. Tilly, *As sociology meets history* (New York, 1981), p. 72.
3 Tilly, *As sociology meets history* (1981), p. 82.
4 Tilly, *As sociology meets history* (1981), p. 82.
5 See E. Mawdsley and T. Munck, *Computing for historians: an introductory guide* (Manchester, 1993), chapter 12; D. I. Greenstein, *A historian's guide to computing* (Oxford, 1994), chapters 5 and 6; I. Dey, *Qualitative data analysis: a user-friendly guide for social scientists* (London, 1993); E. A. Weitzman and B. M. Matthew, *Computer programs for qualitative data analysis: a software sourcebook* (Thousand Oaks, CA, 1995). Growth of interest in Britain in the 1980s was manifested in the foundation in 1986 of the Association for History and Computing.
6 For an early introduction to the principles of GIS, many of which still apply, see D. J. Maguire, M. F. Goodchild and D. W. Rind (eds), *Geographical information systems: principles and applications*, 2 vols (1991).
7 For the nature of the family-reconstitution software, and research accomplished with use of that software, see E. A. Wrigley, R. S. Davies, J. E. Oeppen and R. S. Schofield, *English population history from family reconstitution, 1580–1837* (Cambridge, 1997); for information on the probate software, refer to the Department of History, University of Exeter, Exeter EX4 4QH.
8 For more on this, see articles in S. W. Baskerville, P. Hudson, R. J. Morris (eds), *History and Computing*, 4, (1992), a special issue on record linkage, especially S. A. King, 'Record linkage in a proto-industrial community'. See also P. Hudson, 'A new history from below: computers and the maturing of local and

regional history', *The Local Historian* 25, 4 (1995), pp. 209–22. On the process of computer-aided family reconstitution, see E. A. Wrigley and R. S. Schofield, 'Nominal record linkage by computer and the logic of family reconstitution', in E. A. Wrigley (ed.), *Identifying people in the past* (London, 1973); and, for recent results see E. A. Wrigley, R. S. Davies, J. E. Oeppen and R. S. Schofield, *English population history from family reconstitution 1580–1837* (Cambridge, 1997).

9 For earlier discussion of nominal record linkage, see S. W. Baskerville, P. Hudson and R. J. Morris (eds), *History and Computing*, 4, (1992), special issue on record linkage. On the shortcomings of expert systems and the alternative research into neuron networks, see Roger Penrose, *The emperor's new mind: concerning computers, minds and the laws of physics* (London, 1990).

10 An increasingly vast bank of social science data and databases which have been used in Economic and Social Research Council projects (and from other work) is located at the University of Essex, e-mail address: Archive@Essex.ac.uk

11 There are two excellent guides to database design and management: C. Harvey and J. Press, *Databases in historical research* (Basingstoke, 1996), and L. Weatherill and V. Hemingway, *Using and designing databases for academic work: a practical guide* (Newcastle, 1994). The problems of entry and coding and the need to work towards a standard to facilitate the comparability of data bases and research is discussed in D. I. Greenstein, *Modelling historical data: towards a standard for encoding and exchanging machine readable texts* (St Katharinen, 1991). See also Manfred Thaller 'Methods and techniques of historical computation', in P. Denley and D. Hopkin (eds), *History and Computing* (Manchester, 1987); K. Schurer 'The historical researcher and codes: master and slave or slave and master?', in E. Mawdsley, N. Morgan, L. Richmond and R. Trainor (eds), *Historians, computers and data: applications in research and teaching* (Manchester, 1990).

12 These applications are discussed by James E. Everett, in 'Annual Review of information technology developments for economic and social historians, 1997', in *Economic History Review*, 51, 2 (1998), pp. 382–97. He mentions askSam and IdeaList.

13 AND, OR and NOT as used here are called Boolean operators, after George Boole, who first distinguished them. See I. Dey, *Qualitative data analysis* (London, 1993), p. 174.

14 There are many pitfalls in using the Land Tax. These are explored in M. Turner and D. Mills (eds), *Land and property: the English Land Tax, 1692–1832* (Gloucester, 1986).

15 There are, of course, many pitfalls to this process, not least the fact that baptism dates are not an easy proxy for birth dates, that parish registers cover only a fraction of the population and that highly mobile populations make family reconstitution impossible. These and other problems are discussed in the classic 'handbook' for demographers: E. A. Wrigley (ed.), *Identifying people in the past* (London, 1973).

16 D. I. Greenstein, *A historian's guide to computing* (1994), E. Mawdsley and T. Munck, *Computing for historians* (Manchester, 1993), and I. Dey, *Qualitative data analysis* (1993).

17 Most useful are those by Greenstein, *A historians guide to computing* (Oxford, 1994); E. Mawdsley and T. Munck, *Computing for historians* (1993); L. Weatherill and V. Hemingway, *Using and designing databases for academic work* (Newcastle, 1994); and M. J. Lewis and R. Lloyd-Jones, *Using computers in history: a practical guide* (London, 1996).

18 Michael Cook was the leading figure. The international standard ISAD(G) is now adopted.

19 E-mail: Archive@Essex.ac.uk
20 ICPSR is at the web address ICPSR_Netmail@UM>CC>UMICH>EDU. Contact
   details of Scandinavian and other collections, including text collections can be
   found in D. I. Greenstein, *A historian's guide to computing* (Oxford, 1994),
   pp. 247–51.
21 For an introduction to current debates about the importance of language and
   discourse in determining the parameters of knowledge and communication, see
   Keith Jenkins, *The postmodern history reader* (London, 1997); M. Sarup, *An
   introductory guide to post-structuralism and postmodernism*, 2nd edn (Hemel
   Hempstead, 1993); A. Munslow, *Deconstructing history* (London, 1997). On
   Bakhtin, whose ideas are beginning to become very important in a range of
   historical work, see P. Morris (ed.), *The Bakhtin reader* (London, 1994).
22 For further discussion of the potentialities in this respect and a survey of the ways
   in which computer-aided research was contributing to change in regional and
   local history in the early 1990s, see P. Hudson, 'A new history from below:
   computers and the maturing of regional and local history', *The Local Historian*,
   25, 4 (1995). For more on nominal record linkage, see S. W. Baskerville, P.
   Hudson and R. J. Morris (eds), *History and computing*, 4 (1992), special issue
   on record linkage.
23 Stana Nenadic, 'Record linkage and the exploration of nineteenth-century social
   groups: a methodological perspective on the Glasgow middle class in 1861',
   Urban History Yearbook (1987); Stana Nenadic, 'Identifying social networks
   with computer aided analysis of personal diaries', and Marguerite Dupree, 'The
   medical profession in Scotland, 1911: the creation of a machine readable database', both in E. Mawdsley, N. Morgan, L. Richmond and R. Trainor (eds),
   Historians, computers and data: applications in research and training
   (Manchester, 1990). C. Harvey and J. Press, *Databases in historical research*
   (Basingstoke, 1996), has a section devoted to the Westminster Historical
   Database algorithms. This database is also available on CD-ROM.
24 For a useful account of procedures in qualitative data analysis, though not
   related to historical research, see Ian Dey, *Qualitative data analysis* (London,
   1993). Dey's software development Hypersoft looked very promising in the early
   1990s but this and similar products do not appear to have been adopted by historians to any notable degree.
25 'Thick description' is a term coined by Clifford Geertz to denote a form of enquiry
   dependent upon minute observation of traces and manifestations of local culture
   which reflect wider aspects of society. This was a counterpoise to a positivism
   dependent upon exhaustive 'scientific' enquiry, often at the level of nations or
   larger units, and using scientific methodologies of cause and effect such as the hypothesis testing. Geertz's discussion of the methodological issues involved in the growing emphasis upon linking action to its sense, rather than phenomena to their
   cause, is brilliantly described in his *The interpretation of cultures* (New York,
   1973) and in *Local knowledge: further essays in interpretive anthropology* (New
   York, 1983).

Further reading

A. Coffey and P. Atkinson *Making sense of qualitative data: complementary
research strategies* (Thousand Oaks, CA, 1996)
Ian Dey, *Qualitative data analysis: a user friendly guide for social scientists*
(London, 1993)

D. I. Greenstein, *A historian's guide to computing* (Oxford, 1994)

C. Harvey and J. Press, *Databases in historical research* (Basingstoke, 1996)

P. Hudson, 'Computers and the maturing of regional and local history', *The Local Historian* 25, 4 (1995), pp. 209–22

U. Kelle (ed.), *Computer-aided qualitative data analysis: theory, methods and practice* (Thousand Oaks, CA, 1995)

I. Lancashire, J. Bradley, W. McCarty and M. Stairs, *Using TACT with electronic texts: a guide to text-analysis computer tools: Version 21 for MS-DOS and PC DOS* (New York, 1996)

M. J. Lewis and R. Lloyd-Jones, *Using computers in history: a practical guide* (London, 1996)

E. Mawdsley and T. Munck, *Computing for historians: an introductory guide* (Manchester, 1993)

R. Middleton and P. Wardley, 'Information technology in economic and social history: the computer as philosopher's stone or Pandora's box?', *Economic History Review*, 43, 4 (1990), pp. 667–96

R. Solomon and C. Winch, *Calculating and computing for social science and arts students* (Buckingham, 1994), pp. 99–185

L. Weatherill and V. Hemingway, *Using and designing databases for academic work. A practical guide* (Newcastle, 1994)

E. A. Weitzman and B. M. Matthew, *Computing programs for qualitative data analysis: a software sourcebook* (Thousand Oaks, CA, 1995)

For surveys of software and other computer developments useful for economic and social historians in particular, see 'Annual review of information technology developments for economic and social historians', published yearly since 1991 in the May issue of *Economic History Review*.

For examples of current computer use in historical research, see issues of *History and Computing* and *Historical Methods*.

Appendix

This appendix contains questions about several research articles all of which employ quantitative methods of different kinds and in different ways. The questions are designed to assist discussion with students, aiming to improve their grasp of the application of quantitative techniques in history. The questions are framed not only to address the statistical techniques employed but also to dwell upon the choice of technique, upon the reliability of the data and upon the nature and purpose of the research.

Article 1

D. Vickers and V. Walsh, 'Young men and the sea: the sociology of sea faring in eighteenth century Salem, Massachusetts', *Social History,* **24, 1 (1999), pp. 17–38**
This article uses only simple descriptive statistics and is a rare application of quantitative information to life histories. This is a good exercise for those just starting to feel their way with quantitative reading.

1. What sorts of evidence and research techniques have been used in this piece of research?
2. Does nominal record linkage appear to have been undertaken?
3. Why did young Salem men go to sea?
4. How are the proportions of Salem men who were seafarers calculated (page 24)?
5. Would the random sample mentioned in footnote 22 guarantee an unbiased sample of Salem ship masters?
6. Comment on the use of deciles on page 25.
7. Would there be any better way of representing all of the information contained in figure 1?
8. Why has the median age of first recorded voyage been used in footnote 29 rather than the mean or the mode?

9. What advantage has the pie chart on page 27 got over alternative ways of presenting the data on the fate of young seafarers?
10. What variables appear to have been important in determining which seafarers were promoted to mate or master? How do the authors assess the relative importance of these variables?
11. What is meant by 'age specific mortality' and the 'population at risk' in footnote 30?
12. Why has the mean age of marriage been used in footnote 42?
13. For a small community, Salem appears to have received the attention of several researchers in the early twentieth century which these authors have been able to benefit from. What problems might attach to heavy reliance upon the works of Tapley, Perley, Crandall and Essex Institute?
14. Why have the contrasting median ages of Salem-born and other seamen been relegated to footnote 62 and why has the median been used here?

Article 2

S. Dobson and J. Goddard, 'Performance revenue and cross subsidisation in the football league, 1927–1994', *Economic History Review*, 51, 4 (1998), pp. 763–85
There is no complex quantification here, but it provides a good argument and some clumsy looking descriptive statistics which are essential to the case.

1. With what justification can the football league as a whole be regarded as a firm?
2. Why do sporting authorities commonly restrict player mobility, decide who plays whom, when and where and promote the sharing of gate receipts, commercial and media revenues?
3. In table 1 what is the coefficient of variation and why is it given here?
4. What are real gate revenues and why are they given (alongside real average admission prices) in index form?
5. Could the data in table 2 have been more attractively and convincingly displayed?
6. Are there any difficulties with the way in which the performance score has been derived and in comparing this score with attendance and gate revenues in table 3?
7. Could the data in table 4 have been more attractively and convincingly displayed?
8. What was the rationale and the effect of the maximum wage and the retain-and-transfer system which existed until the early 1960s?
9. Could the information in table 5 have been more effectively displayed for the purposes of the argument being made?
10. What has been the impact of the overhaul of the retain-and-transfer system in the 1960s and in 1977?

11. In what ways has the transfer system since the 1960s resulted in a redistribution of income between clubs?
12. Could the data in table 6 be more attractively and economically displayed?
13. What has been the impact of the erosion of explicit schemes for the redistribution of match receipts between clubs and how have cup competitions helped to compensate for this?
14. What has been the financial effect on the rest of league football of the creation of the premiership?
15. Why are the authors sanguine about the rise of increasingly individualistic, profit motivated attitudes amongst the major clubs in particular?

Article 3

P. H. Lindert and J. G. Williamson, 'English workers' living standards during the industrial revolution', *Economic History Review*, 36, 1 (1983), pp. 1–25
This is another good piece to start with, providing much opportunity to question sources and the formation of composite and real indices.
1. What are the aims of this study?
2. What is an index? Why are indices useful? What is a composite index and what is a real index?
3. What are the pitfalls in building up a wage series for the mass of the population in this period?
4. In what way does Lindert and Williamson's wage series claim to be better than earlier ones?
5. Are there any problems with the way in which wages in the service sector are calculated and included?
6. Does the new wage series determine the conclusions of the article?
7. What do Lindert and Williamson say is wrong with earlier price series?
8. How is the price series for cotton derived?
9. What other alterations are made in the price series compared with earlier price series?
10. Have you any comments about the incorporation of rents?
11. Why are weights so important and yet so problematic in constructing price series?
12. What do Lindert and Williamson say about unemployment and how do they allow for it? Is this satisfactory?
13. How do they allow for family earnings?
14. Is family size important?
15. What other forms of income should one include in ascertaining well being?
16. Should life-time income be considered?

17. What are benchmark years?
18. What are disamenities and how are they measured?
19. What is the importance of considering push factors in migration in relation to the disamenities argument?

This article should be compared with the much more recent work of Feinstein: C. H. Feinstein, 'Pessimism perpetuated: real wages and the standard of living in Britain during and after the industrial revolution', *Journal of Economic History*, 58, 3 (1998), 625–58. Here Feinstein addresses some of the weaknesses of the earlier estimates such as that of Lindert and Williamson. A good exercise, having read both pieces, would be to list the questions regarding sources and statistics which still attach to our knowledge on this subject.

Article 4

E. A. Wrigley, 'Family limitation in pre-industrial England', *Economic History Review*, 19, 1 (1966), pp. 82–109

A famous article, one of the first to be published based upon family reconstitution of an English parish, this gives an insight into the potentialities and the pitfalls of family reconstitution. Statistical techniques employed vary from measures of central tendency and interesting use of histograms to correlation, and the chi-squared (χ^2) test.

1. What is the aim of the article and why is family reconstitution necessary?
2. Exactly what is family reconstitution and what are the pitfalls of undertaking this with English parish registers?
3. Why is a nine-year moving average used in figure 1?
4. What is meant by a 'marked inverse correlation', page 85?
5. Why does Wrigley give the mean, the median and the modal age of marriage in table 1? (see Floud, *An introduction to quantitative methods for historians*, second edition (London, 1979), pp. 83–5, or this volume, pp. 91–2).
6. What is age-specific marital fertility?
7. Why does the concavity of the some of the curves in figure 2 on the upper side possibly indicate family limitation?
8. What statistical procedure is used to consider whether there is a significant difference in age-specific marital fertility in the upper age-groups between the early and later seventeenth century?
9. What is the point and what are the pitfalls of studying birth spacing?
10. What considerations should one bear in mind when assessing the validity of findings in figure 4?
11. What makes Wrigley so sure that he has found evidence of family limitation (see page 95 especially)?

12. What is the significance of figure 5 (i.e. what does it purport to show)?
13. Why has a χ^2 test been carried out?
14. What other explanations might there be for the statistical results?
15. What wider implications does Wrigley suggest that his findings for Colyton might have for English demographic history?

Article 5

J. M. Beattie, 'Patterns of prosecution and the character of property crime', from *Crime and the courts in England, 1660–1800* (Princeton, 1986), chapter 5

Crime statistics are notoriously problematic, not least for the eighteenth century. This piece uses time-series analysis to look at the determinants of property crime.

1. What factors might influence the pattern of indictments for crimes against property? Is Beattie sufficiently sceptical about the extent to which indictments can 'provide clues' to the nature of property crime in the period?
2. Why might the late eighteenth-century increases shown in the graphs on pages 203–4 be a misleading indication of increases in indictment rates?
3. How does Beattie test his hypothesis that there is a relationship between the movement of property crime indictments and the price level?
4. Why was the median used in table 1 rather than the mean or mode?
5. Why did wartime see fewer indictments and why was the coming of peace often accompanied by a surge of crime? What evidence does Beattie use to explain this?
6. What role did moral panics play?
7. Why did the 1780s see more crime, more panic, fuller prisons and increases in the numbers being hanged?
8. Why are de-trended figures used on page 235?
9. How might the lower levels of female indictments be explained?
10. 'All historical statistics have their pitfalls but statistics reporting crime or indictments for crime are amongst the hardest to interpret': do you agree?
11. How else might the data in table 5 (page 245) have been presented?

Article 6

P. Hudson, 'Ploughed-back profits', from *The genesis of industrial capital* (Cambridge, 1986), chapter 10

This is a really poor piece of regression analysis but it does serve to clarify ideas about the various forces which may have been operating upon plough-back.

1. What does the chapter set out to do and what statistical methods does it use?
2. Have you any comments to make about the robustness of worsted and woollen profit rates as shown in graphs 10.1 and 10.2?
3. Do the worsted and woollen profit rates themselves appear to be determined by a common set of factors?
4. Have you any comments on the various export series used in table 10.1?
5. How important were export levels in determining profitability in woollen and worsted manufacturing?
6. 'Translate' the following: 'data runs are too short to show significance at the 5% level' (page 242).
7. Why are there minus signs in column 4 of table 10.2?
8. Why are lagged profit rates used in table 10.3 and what determines the length of the lag?
9. Why are both money wage and real wage indices used in table 10.3?
10. Examine the reliability of the wage indices for the purpose of the correlations undertaken in table 10.3.
11. What figures and what sorts of statistical exercises would help in making firm statements about the role of ploughed-back profits in industrial expansion?
12. What are the main problems in performing correlations with time-series data?

Article 7

C. H. Lee, 'The service sector, regional specialisation and economic growth in the Victorian economy', *Journal of Historical Geography*, **10, 2 (1984), pp. 139–55**
This is a good example of cross-sectional correlation, with many opportunities to criticise the formation of variables in the model and the sources upon which they are based.

1. What is the proposition Lee is testing?
2. What are the possible sources of error in the employment data?
3. What is the nature of the data set and what does it contain?
4. How does Lee test the proposition that service provision is simply proportional to population?
5. Tables 3 and 4 test two alternative hypotheses. What are they?
6. What are the proxies for income? What dangers are there in using proxy figures?
7. Note the use of dummy variables. What are they and why are they used?
8. How does Lee justify the low R value for distribution in 1861 and 1881?

9. Translate: 'Indeed this dummy variable showed a high level of correlation with the uninhabited house duty variable . . . so that much of its explanatory power was lost in the income variable with which it was multicolinear' (page 147–148).
10. What effect does the development of suburbs have on the model?

Article 8

P. K. O'Brien, 'Agriculture and the home market for English industry, 1660–1820', *English Historical Review*, 344, 4 (1985), pp. 773–800
This is a good article to examine for debating the creation of composite indices and the use of time series.
1. On what new data is the argument in this article based?
2. What are the advantages of indices rather than retaining data in its original form in this instance?
3. What are log scale graphs (page 775)?
4. What assumptions lie behind reliance on the fact that relative prices of agricultural and industrial commodities will reflect the real terms of trade?
5. What is a moving average and why is it used in the graphs on page 776?
6. How were the two indices constructed and what are their likely weaknesses?
7. What assumptions does O'Brien employ to enable him to calculate the impact of agricultural changes on the demand for British manufactures?

Article 9

S. Nicholas and D. Oxley, 'The living standards of women during the industrial revolution', *Economic History Review*, 46, 4 (1993), 723–49
This is an anthropometric study using convict data to consider gender differences in living standards and differences between urban and rural women. It is thought-provoking social history but easy to criticise.
1. What does the article set out to do?
2. What problems occur with using military recruitment data for heights which do not occur with using the convict data?
3. What is the normal distribution referred to on page 725, and what is seen as responsible for the heaping in the distributions of height for English and rural Irish females?
4. How was the representativeness of female convicts, in terms of occupations and skills, compared with the female population of England and Ireland as a whole? What difficulties arose with this?

5. Is it a problem for this analysis that the age structure of the convicts was concentrated in the 21–31 years range?
6. What weaknesses do you think there may be in the literacy data?
7. What are the three components of height-for-age? What evidence suggests that height-for-age is a good indication of nutritional and environmental impacts during the growing years?
8. Explain what is meant by the statement that urban–rural terminal height differentials were statistically significant at the 0.05 level (page 733).
9. Why was the urban–rural height differential less important in Ireland?
10. What is a moving average and why has one been used in figure 2?
11. What interesting thesis about the Irish potato famine do the data on male and female convict heights support (page 735)?
12. What reasons do the authors give for the probable deterioration of English diets for women, especially in the towns, from the end of the eighteenth century?
13. What might account for the greater decline in female than in male heights over time?
14. Explain the purpose of the regression model for the composition effects by occupation (pages 742–3).
15. From the regional regression models on pages 743–6, what is suggested:
    (a) about the differences in living standards between regions in England?
    (b) about the differences between the Irish and the English economies and their deployment of household and family labour?
16. How convinced are you about the conclusions of this article given the sources and methods used?

Article 10

Daniel Benjamin and Levis A. Kochin, 'Unemployment in interwar Britain', *Journal of Political Economy*, 87 (1979), 441–78
This was a controversial article when it first appeared as it was used to bolster Thatcherite policy with respect to unemployment benefit. It contains a rather crude economic model and time-series analysis.

1. What does the article set out to do and what are the 'three solid strands of evidence' upon which the argument is based?
2. What is time-series evidence (page 442)?
3. Describe the graph which is figure 1 and explain what it shows.
4. What three aspects of the benefits system contributed, in the view of the authors, to easy movement from employment to unemployment?
5. What sort of unemployment are Benjamin and Kochin seeking to explain and why have they little interest in unemployment which might arise from deficient demand?

6. What ratio is the basis of their time-series analysis?
7. From what sources do Benjamin *et al.* draw for their calculations? Are you satisfied with the reliability of the sources **for these purposes?** If not why not?
8. What is reverse causation and how do the authors cover themselves against this being the reason for their time-series findings (page 455)?
9. How does the behaviour of juvenile unemployment appear to add weight to their argument?
10. What other reasons might there be for such movements in the rates of juvenile unemployment?
11. What weaknesses are there in the aspect of their argument that relies on the movement of unemployment rates of married women?
12. Especially in view of the calculations attempted in the final section, what is your view of the relationship between the sources and data and the quantitative methods attempted in this research?

Article 11

Martha J. Olney, 'When your word is not enough: race, collateral and household credit', *Journal of Economic History*, 58, 2 (1998), pp. 408–31
This is a more complicated article but is very clearly expressed and has a good blend of social as well as economic history, the application of some modern economic theory as well as multiple regression.

1. Discuss the potential pitfalls of using the 1918–19 Consumer Purchases Survey to consider credit and race, given the way in which it was organised and executed (pages 409–10).
2. List all of the reasons (in theory) why black families may have:
   (a) used less shop or merchant credit than whites;
   (b) used more instalment credit than whites;
   (c) had higher rates of savings than whites on similar incomes.
3. Are there any ways of summarising and simplifying the data contained in table 1 which would strengthen the case being made in the text?
4. Do you have any further comments to make about the variations of instalment credit related to different items in table 3?
5. Discuss the impact of chain stores upon grocery credit.
6. Why are small sample sizes a consideration on page 418?
7. Have the problems which you identified in relation to question 1 been addressed on pages 417–18? List those problems which you feel still remain.
8. List the independent variables in the logit analysis on the supply side and on the demand side and check whether you can identify these in column 1 of table 7.

9. Rehearse the aims and potential pitfalls of multiple regression analysis.
10. What are the 90 and 99 per cent confidence indicators mentioned in the notes to table 7?
11. What are the *t* statistics referred to in the notes to table 7?
12. Do you see any problems in the proxy for wealth described in the notes to table 7.
13. Define 'asymmetric information' and discuss the use of this concept in the argument on pages 424–7.
14. Do you find the argument about poor black families substituting savings for merchant credit convincing (page 428)?
15. Explain in simple terminology 'The creditor remedy . . . offset the risks of adverse selection and moral hazard'.

Article 12

M. Botticini, 'A loveless economy? Intergenerational altruism and the marriage market in a Tuscan town', *Journal of Economic History*, **59, 1 (1999), pp. 104–21**
This is an application of models of economic and social relationships to the marriage market in early fifteenth-century Tuscany.

1. What is a dowry?
2. List the potential implications of dowry payments as
   (a) a marriage payment;
   (b) an intergenerational transfer.
3. What sorts of other things may need to be held constant by applying the *ceteris paribus* notion on page 106?
4. Do you have any comments about the size or nature of the sample of marriage contracts?
5. What sort of information can be derived just from table 1, assuming the marriage sample was representative of Tuscany as a whole? Look at the differences between medians and means here and at the measures of dispersion.
6. What relationship appears to be present between the male–female age gap in marriage and the prevalence of women 'marrying down'?.
7. What is the 'present net value hypothesis' (pages 106 and 109–11)? With what justification is this tested by running a correlation test upon dowry size and bride's age?
8. What is meant by the altruism model and how is it proposed that it should be tested?
9. What is the purpose of table 4 and does it succeed?
10. Has the problem of measuring the wealth of groom and bride households been satisfactorily solved for cases where the *Castato* evidence post dates the marriage contract?
11. What are dummy variables? Comment on their use here.

12. In table 5 what is meant by:
    (a) the t statistic;
    (b) R squared (R^2);
    (c) the levels of significance indicated by the asterisks?
13. Is the finding that dowry size and fertility were correlated of any causal significance (page 117)?
14. To what extent are the present net value and altruism models supported by this research? What other unrelated explanations could help to account for these findings?
15. Given the sex ratios of table 1 in the appendix, what is wrong with calling Cortona a 'Tuscan town' in the title of the article? How would factors peculiar to Cortona work to reduce confidence in the applicability of these research findings to the rest of Tuscany?

Article 13

G. E. Boyar and T. J. Hatton, 'Migration and labour market integration in late nineteenth-century England and Wales', *Economic History Review*, 50, 4 (1997), pp. 697–734
This provides an example of multiple regression analysis using economic models.

1. What is meant by 'labour market integration'?
2. What model of migration is depicted in figure 1 and what assumptions lie behind it?
3. What factors prevent all dwellers in lower-wage areas from having the same reaction to wage differentials?
4. Why might examining the level of migration be a poor guide to labour mobility (pages 698–9)?
5. What factors would cause the migration function to shift downwards?
6. What is the purpose of the simultaneous equations on pages 700–2?
7. From surveys of the existing literature on pages 702–10, what appear to be the major characteristics of migration flows in England and Wales in the later nineteenth century?
8. How and why did the migration flows of females and males differ and why is it so much more difficult to test models of female migration streams and female labour market integration?
9. What are the major variables in the regression exercises in table 3?
10. What dummy variables have been used?
11. What is expected income and why is it seen as potentially important?
12. In what ways is the migrant stock variable likely to have influenced migration? How important has the regression analysis shown this to be?
13. How important are rural wages and employment in determining the agricultural wage (table 5)?

14. What is the *t* statistic in tables 3 and 5?
15. Why has the Durbin–Watson statistic been calculated in table 5?
16. To what extent has this article proved that labour markets were integrated in the second half of the nineteenth century?
17. What further research is needed on this subject?

Article 14

Ken Bartley, 'Classifying the past: discriminant analysis and its application to medieval farming systems', *History and Computing*, 8, 1 (1996), pp. 1–10

1. What is cluster analysis and in what circumstances might it be used?
2. What are the drawbacks of cluster analysis and how does the computer help?
3. What problems might arise in using feed requirements as a common measure for livestock?
4. What are the advantages and the disadvantages of using ratios of the variables for the cluster analysis?
5. Why are logarithms (logs) used in table 2?
6. What are principal components?
7. Why are three different techniques of cluster analysis used?
8. What are the advantages and the disadvantages of each technique?
9. What is discriminant analysis and how may the accuracy of the discriminant functions be analysed?
10. Would this type of analysis have been possible without the computer?
11. What future benefits accrue to having set up a database in this form?

Article 15

Roger Miller and Gunnar Thorvaldsen, 'Beyond record linkage: longitudinal analysis of turn of the century inter-urban Swedish migrants', *History and Computing*, 9, 2 (1997), pp. 106–21.

1. What is meant by longitudinal analysis in this context?
2. Why are demographic sources often inimical to longitudinal analysis?
3. What does the demographic data base at Umeå contain and what pitfalls face the user?
4. Why was the special registration system in Stockholm established in 1878 and what did it record?
5. Why is it difficult to link individuals across the Umeå and Stockholm databases?
6. What advantages and what drawbacks does the Stockholm database base have compared with Umea in terms of its use by historians?

7. State the differences, the advantages and the disadvantages between a relational and a flatfile database.
8. Why are unique identifiers used in relational databases?
9. What is SQL and what does it enable one to do?
10. What are the main research questions posed?
11. A new database was created for this project; how?
12. What is the ODBC and what does it do?
13. What is dichotomous analysis and is its use clearly explained here in relation to the cross-sectional analysis?
14. Is the information in figures 4a and 4b displayed as efficiently as possible?
15. Why is observation time important?
16. Do the inconsistencies of civil status give grounds for concern about the general accuracy of the sources?
17. What does figure 5 show?
18. Why were occupation and economic sector variables recorded?
19. Why is little intragenerational or intergenerational social mobility found amongst migrants in this sample?

Glossary

age pyramid Figure which represents the age structure in a population, usually of males and females, by placing histograms of each back to back, thus allowing immediate visual comparison.

aggregate data Information about a group which produces, or is in the form of, a total.

anthropometric studies Studies which rely on measurements of human characteristics, such as heights and weights, as a proxy for other more important variables (e.g. the use of time-series of heights to consider changes in nutrition and living standards).

arithmetic mean See **mean**.

autocorrelation A distortion introduced into regression and correlation results with time-series data because of the impact of non-random errors

average A measure of the central tendency of a distribution, usually calculated as the arithmetic mean, the median or the mode.

back projection A technique used to infer or estimate figures for periods where data are unavailable on the basis of later periods where the figures do exist.

bar chart A diagrammatic method for displaying frequency distributions in which bars of equal width are drawn to represent each category, with the length of each bar being proportional to the number, or frequency of occurrence, of each category.

base period (usually **base year**) The case in a time-series used as the point of view in looking at other cases and the yard stick against which all other cases in an index are measured.

basket of goods A list of the components of expediture of an average individual or family, used to form a measure of the cost of living and changes in that cost.

bias Any situation in which the accuracy, reliability and validity of historical data or research results are distorted by the limitations of a research method or by a researcher's predispositions. In a narrower statistical sense bias is the difference between a hypothetical 'true' value of a variable in a population and that obtained from studying a sample.

biometrics The statistical study of biological phenomena

Bipolar variable See **variable**

Boolean operators Computer retrievals based on the instruction retrieve all 'X' AND 'Y' or retrieve all 'X' NOT 'Y', named after the nineteenth-century logician George Boole.

cartogram A map on which piecharts, graphs or other symbols are superimposed to represent quantities or variables.

categorical data Gives qualitative information only, though this may be ranked in some kind of hierarchy (e.g. status or value). See **data**.

case A unit of study around which information is gathered and arranged.

cell A box containing numbers or text in a data matrix or table: the intersection of a row and a column.

ceteris paribus A term meaning 'other things being equal'. It is much used by economists and econometric historians interested in examining the importance of one amongst several independent variables which are acting simultaneously in a model. Statistical techniques enable one to simulate the impact of just one independent variable by filtering out the effect of the other variables.

chart A common word for graph (see **graph**).

class interval The range of values of a category of information in a grouped frequency distribution.

cliometrics The quantitative study of history, usually used synonymously with econometric history.

cluster sample Sample formed in a non-random manner on the basis of ease of access to a particular group within the population.

cluster techniques Methods for grouping cases in a large data set in accordance with their common characterisitcs.

coding A standardised abbreviation assigned to a piece of information (e.g. F for Female, M for Male).

coefficient of determination represents the degree to which the movement of one variable is associated with variation in another.

coefficient of variation A measure of the extent to which a variable differs from its mean. It is the standard deviation of the distribution expressed as a percentage of the mean.

composite index a series formed by blending several component series together in a weighted combination. See also **index, weights**.

constant prices A valuation time-series which has been adjusted to allow for the effects of inflation or deflation. Usually this is done by using the prices. obtaining in a given base year rather than those current for each time period.

contingency coefficient A measure of the relationship between two variables which have been tabulated in a **contingency table**.

contingency table A table in which two variables are plotted against one another or are cross-tabulated.

continuous data Interval data, such as heights, weights or wages, measured on a scale which includes fractions or decimals as well as whole numbers. See **data**.

continuous variable See **variable**.

correlation The association between two variables such that when one changes in magnitude, the other does so also: there is a concomitant variation.

correlation coefficient A measure of the association between two variables. The nearer the correlation coefficient is to ±1, the greater the strength of the relationship between the two variables.

cost–benefit analysis A comparison of all the important costs and benefits (including social costs and benefits expressed in monetary valuations) of the innovation of a particular institution, innovation or technology over a stated time period or at a certain date.

cost-of-living index A measure of the movement of prices of a collection of consumer goods regarded as typically demanded by households.

counterfactual A hypothetical event or state of being which is measured or described for the purposes of evaluating the costs or benefits of what really happened against what might have happened in the 'second-best' scenario.

counterfactual history The calculation of costs and benefits of a particular innovation or institution in the past compared with the costs and benefits that would have obtained in the absence of the innovation or institution, using a 'second best' alternative.

covariance A measure of how closely two variables move together, with no necessary implication that the two may be related.

cross-sectional data Information on cases which are not in a time-series but which refer to a measure at a particular point in time (e.g. Land Tax details of a township's inhabitants in 1782).

cycle A boom and slump (growth followed by decline) in a time-series. Cycles, often with an identifiable periodicity, are often repeated many times throughout a time-series.

cyclical Exhibiting a regular movement.

data Information relating to cases.

database A collection of related data, organised in a predetermined manner, according to a set of logical rules. Usually the data are arranged in tabular form, which contains discrete categories of information called **fields** for a number of distinct and unique cases. A database can contain one or more tables and is usually stored in a computer.

database management system (DBMS) A computer application which allows the user to create, manage and analyse electronic tables in a database.

data matrix A way of organising a data set in the form of a table with rows and columns.

data processing The production of results using a computer.

data set Information relating to cases which the researcher selects in order to address a particular question.

decile A tenth of a distribution when the observations are ranked in rising size order. Thus the upper decile is the top 10 per cent, the lowest decile is the bottom 10 per cent of observations.

deduction The process of building up knowledge by testing theories or ideas against the facts. Compare with **induction**.

denominator The lower element in a fraction. Compare with **numerator**.

dependent variable A variable the measure of which is determined by the movement of another variable or other variables under consideration.

descriptive statistics Statistics concerned with summarising or describing a distribution or a sample. They consist of methods of statistical display and rearrangement which contribute to clarity of information and often provide a basis for initial analysis of the figures.

de-trended series A time-series which has been modified to eliminate long-term growth or decline.

dichotomous variable A variable which can only take two values e.g. sex, which takes either male or female.

discrete data Interval data which can be expressed only in whole numbers e.g. numbers of people. See **data**.

distribution A range of values observed for any one variable.

dummy variables These are used to recode some sorts of categorical data (most commonly dichotomous variables) in numerical form.

econometrics The application of mathematical statistics to economics.

econometric history Application of economic theory and the methods of mathematical statistics in economic history.

endogenous An endogenous factor or variable is one which is generated and acts from within the system or model under investigation (e.g. population growth or levels of literacy within an economy, or the impact of real wage levels or levels of trade union organisation upon the size of public demonstrations).

European Economic Community (EEC) A free-trade area with a common external tariff. There were six original member states, enlarged to nine (including the UK) in 1973, to 12 in the 1980s, and to 15 in the 1990s, to become the EC (European Community).

exogenous An exogenous factor or variable is one which acts from outside of the particular system or model being examined (e.g. the impact of external trade on an economy or the impact of weather upon the size and nature of public demonstrations or soccer crowds).

exponential scale A vertical scale on a graph where units are successively the square roots of the previous unit.

externality An economic or social cost or benefit which is not generally included in the market or price costs of an innovation or process (e.g. the increased disease and death rates experienced by migrants to towns and cities in the process of industrialisation; or the noise, traffic and environmental pollution resulting from the building of additional airport runways); the private pleasure gained by using a public park.

extrapolation The estimation of values of a variable beyond the range of the given values, based on the trend apparent in the given values (e.g. on a regression line).

field Information contained in one column of a database table.

filter The application of a set of criteria to show a subset of the records in a database or to sort the records. Filters are also applied to time series to remove seasonal or cyclical features (as explained on p. 164).

fluctuation A marked, often cyclical, movement of a variable in a time-series.

frequency The number of times which a particular value of a variable appears.

frequency distribution Distribution of the number of times each value of a variable occurs in a set of observations. Often the observations are arranged in groups and the frequency distribution is displayed in a table.

fuzzy searching 'Fuzzy' is a technical term used to indicate a computer software search command which allows results of specified 'near matches' as well as those of exact matches.

Gini coefficient A summary measure of distributional inequality.

graph A figure which relates the movement of one variable to another or which charts the movement of one or more variables over time.

growth rate Measure of the speed of growth in a variable, e.g. output, crime figures. The measure may be negative, indicating decline, as well as positive.

histogram A diagrammatic representation of a frequency distribution consisting of a series of rectangles or bars with a width proportional to the class interval concerned and an area proportional to the frequency.

Human Development Index (HDI) Index by means of which to measure and compare, chronologically and/or internationally, standards of living or economic 'well being'. It incorporates such elements as literacy levels and life expectancy as well as real incomes.

hypothesis A working theory relating to cause, effect or change.

hypothetical Made-up, unreal but useful as a reflection of reality.

independent random sample A sample selected in such a way that each case has an equal change of being chosen.

independent variable A variable the value of which is not determined by the movement of another variable, or other variables, under consideration.

index, pl. indices A way of recording variation in a time-series by converting all values to a percentage of the value in a certain base year, day or month. This is especially useful in highlighting movements in one or more time-series when the original units were complex or different from one another. See also **composite index, real index**.

index number problem The problems of selecting the elements in a compositie index and of assigning accurate weights to each variable.

induction The process of building up knowledge by generalising on the basis of facts or data which have been assembled. Compare with **deduction**.

inferential statistics Statistics concerned with generalising from a sample, to make estimates, inferences or predictions about a wider population.

inflation Price increases which reduce the purchasing power of money wages and especially of fixed incomes such as pensions and which make it difficult to sell goods competitively in external markets.

instrumentalism Judging theories on the basis of their predictive ability rather than their relationship to reality in other respects.

interpolation The estimation of missing values in a data set based on the data given.

interquartile range A measure of dispersion around the median: the range of the middle 50 per cent of values of a data set which is arranged in rank order.

Laspeyres index A composite index which throughout the series uses weights based on estimated weights at the outset.

life tables Tables which present estimates of longevity (under various conditions, occupations, etc.), based upon probabilities of death rates calculated from experience.

line of best fit A line on a graph (often the linear trend in a time series or a regression line in a scatter graph) which is drawn in such a way that all the distances of observations above the line equal all those below.

log-linear analysis A technique of statistical analysis which transforms non-linear models into linear models by the use of logarithms. This is necessary because social data are often nominal or ordinal and therefore do not meet the assumptions needed for many statistical techniques. It is a causal modelling device involving setting up models to test against the data, successively adjusting the model until the best fit is found.

logarithms Representations of numbers expressed as a power or exponent of 10. Their use facilitates multiplication and division calculations for large or complex numbers but they have now been superseded for this purpose by calculators and computers.

logarithmic scale Scale, normally on the vertical axis of a graph, where successive calibrations get proportionally smaller in tenths.

logistic growth curve A pattern of growth common in studies of social phenomena where growth begins slowly, increases rapidly and finally stabilises.

logit analysis A form of regression in time-series analysis which assists in avoiding the assumption of uniform linear change which lies behind normal time-series regression.

Lorenz curve A cumulative percentage curve (usually of the income of a nation). The shape of the curve (its deviation away from a straight line) is a visual indication of income inequality.

macroeconomic Refers to a whole economic system which is the aggregate of the behaviour of individual economic agents and which generally exhibits regularities of character and behaviour different from those identifiable at the individual level.

matrix In statistics, an arrangement of data where the variables relating to cases are arranged in columns and the cases arranged in rows to provide cells of information.

mean, or arithmetic mean A measure of average which is found by adding all the values and dividing by the number of cases.

mechanical objectivity See **objectivity**.

median A measure of average formed by ranking all observations in size order and taking the middle reading (or the mean of the two middle readings in the case of an even number of observations).

microeconomic Refers to the actions of individual economic agents and their choices as producers and consumers.

modal class The class containing the most observations (or the highest frequency of observations).

mode A measure of average: the most frequently occurring observation in a data set.

monotonic association An association between two variables which takes a curvilinear rather than a linear form.

moving average An average for the movement of a variable over several years (or other time periods). It is called moving because as the time periods pass the earlier ones are dropped from the average and the mid point of the averages moves.

multicollinearity A distortion introduced into regression and correlation results with time-series because of common trend or cyclical elements in the movment of the variables.

multivariate analysis Statistical procedures involving more than one dependent variable.

negatively skewed Description of a distribution where most observations lie above the mean.

neoclassical economics The dominant form of theorising in Western economics since the late nineteenth century. Based upon logical analysis of the rational profit-seeking behaviour of large numbers of well-informed individuals active in markets governed by legal systems which enforce property rights and contracts.

nominal data Categorical, qualitative information where the order in which it appears is not important. See **data**.

non-parametric statistics Statistical methods for the analysis of ordinal and categorical sample data which do not require assumptions about the shape of the distribution from which the samples have been drawn.

normal distribution or error curve A continuous distribution of a random variable. The normal curve is bell-shaped and the mean, median and mode are equal.

normative theory Any theory which seeks to establish the values or norms which best fit the perceived overall needs or requirements of society.

null hypothesis Used in calculations of the degree to which two variables may be related to one another: this hypothesis relates to the distribution of the variables as they would be if there were no relationship at all.

numerator The upper element in a fraction. Compare with **denominator.**

numeric data Data expressed in numbers. See **data.**

objectivity Accounts of the external world held to represent the world as it exists independently of our conceptions. A more frequent usage is knowledge claimed to meet criteria of validity and reliability and held to be free from bias: avoiding subjectivity by following impartial rules of measurement, observation and experiment (in the process ignoring what experience, intuition and moral inclination suggest to be correct). This **mechanical objectivity** involves personal restraint and following the rules. To some extent this describes quantification and the language and discipline of quantification.

ordinal data Categorical, qualitative data where the order in which it appears is of some importance. See **data.**

outliers Atypical cases at the extremes of a distribution.

Paasche index A composite index which uses the current year or series-end weights through the series (i.e. based on estimates of weights at the end of the time period).

parametric statistics A sample of figures where we assume that the parent population has a normal distribution (in reality a normal distribution is only approximated but this is regarded as acceptable to fulfil the criteria for parametric analysis).

percentile Used with rank order distributions, this is the range of values which is included in any 1 per cent of the distribution.

pie chart A way of displaying the distribution of nominal, ordinal or interval data by drawing a circle divided into sectors of the appropriate size to represent each class of data.

political arithmetic A way of viewing society and of analysing social and political issues associated first with William Petty, from the late seventeenth century. The foundation of political arithmetic was the idea that the prosperity and strength of the state rested on the number and condition of its subjects.

population The entire group of subjects to which a researcher intends the results of a study to apply; the larger group to which inferences are made on the basis of the particular set of people studied.

positively skewed Description of a distribution where most observations lie below the mean.

positivism A doctrine formulated by Auguste Comte which asserts that the only true knowledge is scientific knowledge: the study and explanation of observable phenomena whether natural or social. Positive knowledge of social phenomena was expected to encourage scientifically grounded intervention in social and economic affairs which would transform social life.

probability A number ranging from 0 (impossible) to 1 (certain) that indicates how likely it is that a specific outcome will occur in the long run.

probability theory A list of rules for calculating the probabilities of complex events. It predicts how variables are likely to behave and provides a numerical estimate of that prediction. In history and social science, probability theory is important in relation to sampling.

proportional sample See systematic sample.

proxy A 'stand-in': in statistics this refers to a figure which we must use (because it is available) instead of the figure which we would ideally like to use for the analysis at hand but which is not available.

pyramid chart A triangular chart used to illustrate the distribution of a small number of variables in a population where categories have a clear hierarchy and where the proportion of the population in each category varies inversely with rank.

quartile The points at which a rank ordered series divides into four equal parts.

quintile The points at which a rank ordered series divides into into five equal parts.

random sample See **independent random sample.**

rank order The distribution of a variable ranked in size order from the smallest to the largest.

rationality A culturally constructed set of concepts and ideas about moral behaviour. In neoclassical economic theory the rationality postulate states that if an individual is presented with a situation of choice in an economic setting he or she will act to optimise his or her economic position.

real index An index which has been adjusted (deflated or inflated) to allow for the movement of another series, most often prices.

real movements A money value adjusted for changes in prices. Used commonly in economics where a variable (e.g. real wages) has been adjusted for inflation or deflation of prices (so that the purchasing power of money wages is, in this case, being expressed). To convert money values to real values requires the use of an appropriate deflator (e.g. the Retail Price Index, which is the official index of change in consumer prices in Britain).

regression Technique for analysing the relationship between two or more interval level variables in order to predict the value of one from the other(s).

regression coefficient (also known as the **slope coefficient**). The slope of the regression line. It is the coefficient by which the dependent variable moves in response to the independent variable.

regression line A line which represents the closeness and pattern of movement between two variables. It can be drawn as the least squares line of best fit through a scatter graph. It represents the best estimate of the relationship between the variables based upon the available evidence.

relational database A database containing two or more database tables with overlapping cases or fields. These can be interrogated to extract information in common fields or for specific cases and for cross-referencing across the data set.

relational database management system (RDBMS) A programme which allows one to associate data in two or more tables on the basis of common fields or cases.

sample A selection of data from the whole population.

sampling The procedures used to extract a number of cases for analysis from a larger population. The general aim is to generate a sample which is representative of the population as a whole.

sampling error The difference between the 'true' value of a characteristic within a population and the value estimated from a sample of that population.

sampling theory Statistical theory which enables estimation of the degree to which sample results reflect or vary from results which would obtain had the whole population been examined.

scatter graph A graph in which pairs of variables are plotted as an initial indication of the extent to which there is a relationship between the two. Also called a scatter diagram or scatter plot.

seasonal Description of variations in data which occur because of changing climatic or other factors which regularly change over the course of a year.

seasonality A regular seasonal pattern of fluctuations which may be present in a time-series.

serial history History, often regional history, based upon the study of long-term movements in vital variables such as agricultural output, population indices, prices, wages.

series A run of data relating to one variable.

significance A much-debated and highly problematic term in statistics which derives from the degree of probability or chance associated with a result and which can be expressed at various levels. The real significance of statistical occurrences, particularly relationships between variables, can, however, only be assessed by experts for whom statistics is a tool or guide rather than an answer in itself.

significance test A test of the probability of an observed result in sample data occurring by chance. The result of the test is expressed as a statistics (e.g. *t* ratio, *f* ratio) which can be assessed against different levels of probability.

skewed distribution A distribution where observations are distributed very unevenly around the mean.

slope coefficient See **regression coefficient**.

social savings The benefit from a project which accrues to society as a whole.

spreadsheet Software for organising and processing numerical information, arranged in a matrix table of rows and columns.

SQL Structured query language: the most common query language encountered in a **database management system (DBMS)**. Developed by IBM, it consists of basic commands such as INSERT, SELECT, UPDATE and DELETE, which can be enhanced by using an array of supplementary commands.

standard deviation A measure of dispersion of a distribution around the mean, normally represented by the letter *s* or *SD*.

statistics Before the mid-nineteenth century statistics was an ill-defined 'science' of states and conditions: data (numerical and other) relating to the wealth and power of the state. Standard usage by the 1830s and 1840s was that statistics referred to numbers of things and it came gradually to represent an empirical, usually quantitative, science. The term came to be applied to a field of applied mathematics only in the twentieth century. Today it is concerned with scientific methods for collecting, organising, summarising and presenting data.

stratified sample A sample which is deliberately selected proportionally to represent the different classes or categories of the wider population.

structured data A source of historical information which is organised into clearly defined categories.

substantivism A set of ideas, associated originally with Karl Polanyi, which places stress upon the need to understand economies and economic exchanges in their own terms and not through the lens of our own time and culture.

survey Information collected by interviews or questionnaires with respondents chosen in a variety of possible ways but subject to the constraints (in terms of their typicality) formed by willingness to participate and availability.

surviving sample Data which are chosen for analysis because the records have survived but not because they necessarily reflect the experience of the whole population of cases.

systematic sample A selected proportion of the population, chosen in such a way as to avoid bias as much as is possible.

textual data Information in non-numeric form (i.e. letters, words, prose).

time-series A dataset which contains the movement of a variable or variables over time.

trend A straight line which best expresses the direction of movement of a time-series over the longer term.

trend line A line of best fit through a time-series positioned in such a way that all the distances of observations above the line equal all those below.

***t* test** A hypothesis-testing procedure in which the population variance is unknown; it compares *t* scores from a sample to a comparison distribution called a *t* distribution to give levels of statistical significance for sample results.

variable A characteristic which can be measured. It may vary along a continuum (**continuous variable**), as with heights or weights; be discrete, i.e. measured only in single units (**discrete variable**), as with household size; or be **bipolar**, as with sex (male or female)

variance A measure of the dispersal of a distribution which is formed from the average of the squares of the deviations of observations from the mean.

vector A column (or row) of numerical information, usually expressing the movement of a variable relating to a number of different cases.

views Screens of information which can be called up from a database.

virtual history Hypothetical history derived from assessing and imagining what might have been the result if particular historical events, crises or conjunctures had had an outcome very different from that which obtained in reality.

weights Measures reflecting the relative importance of an element in a composite index.

***x* axis** The horizontal axis on a graph [which usually takes the independent variable (e.g. time), which is not affected by other variables].

***y* axis** The vertical axis on a graph (which usually takes the dependent variable(s), that is those which may be affected by other variables, in some cases appearing to be causally dependent upon them).

Z score The number of standard deviations an observation is above (or below, if it is negative) the mean in its distribution.

Index